THE SMELL OF
FOOTBALL

MICK 'BAZ' RATHBONE

VSP

Published by Vision Sports Publishing in 2011

Vision Sports Publishing
19-23 High Street
Kingston upon Thames
Surrey
KT1 1LL

www.visionsp.co.uk

ISBN: 978-1-907637-14-8

Editor: Jim Drewett
Copy editing: John Murray and Alex Morton
Cover design: Doug Cheeseman
Cover photography: 3Objective

Typeset by Palimpsest Book Production Limited, Falkirk, Stirlingshire

Printed in the UK by CPI Mackays, Chatham, ME5 8TD

A CIP Catalogue record for this book is available from the British Library

CONTENTS

ACKNOWLEDGEMENTS I

FOREWORD by Phil Neville 3

PROLOGUE 7

Part One **PLAYER (1975-91)**

Chapter One **INNOCENCE** II

Chapter Two **INNOCENCE LOST** 26

Chapter Three **FEAR**. 42

Chapter Four **RESCUE** 63

Chapter Five **THE GOLDEN YEARS** 76

Chapter Six **REALITY BITES** 94

Part Two **MANAGER (1992-95)**

Chapter Seven **HISTORY BECKONS**. 119

Chapter Eight **MY PLACE IN HISTORY** 139

Chapter Nine **THE FINAL RECKONING** . . . 157

Chapter Ten **AFTERMATH**. 166

Part Three **PHYSIO (1995-2010)**

Chapter Eleven **THE ROAD TO GLORY** 177

Chapter Twelve **DESTINY CALLS**. 191

Chapter Thirteen **BACK TO THE TOP** 199

Chapter Fourteen **LIFE AT THE TOP** 231

EPILOGUE 249

Postscript **FINAL THOUGHTS** 255

ACKNOWLEDGEMENTS

I would like to thank everybody who contributed in any way to the publication of this book – every player I played with or against and every manager who had the dubious honour of managing me. To all the coaches who encouraged me and equally all the coaches who did not encourage me, ironically it is that second group of people who are most responsible for this book. To all the fans who paid to watch me and all the fans who paid to boo me you are equally respected.

Some people have had a profound effect on my career: David Moyes, Howard Kendall, Jim Smith, John McGrath, Bob Saxton – how lucky I am to count such people amongst my mentors.

Thanks to all those players who were brave enough to let me loose on their valuable bodies and all the brilliant physios and doctors I have worked with. To everyone. In 35 years in the game I only met three guys I never liked, which tells you all the need to know about this marvellous brotherood that is football.

Thanks to Jim Drewett and Toby Trotman at Vision Sports Publishing who believed in the book and worked so hard in its formation. My gut instincts on our first meeting in Starbucks in Trafalgar Square have proven to be right.

Thank you to all the people who wrote such nice things about me at the end of the book – that was a truly humbling experience. And thank you Phil for writing the foreword. That somebody of your standing in the game would go to such trouble really means the world to me.

Finally, and in an uncharacteristic moment of self-indulgence, I would like to pay tribute to my family: Julie, Charlotte, Lucy and Oliver, without whose support and encouragement this book would still be a collection of folded up paper in the bedside cabinet.

Mick 'Baz' Rathbone, July 2011

The publishers would also like to thank John Murray and Justyn Barnes for their editing work and Doug Cheeseman for his brilliant cover design. Also Andrew Cowie and all at Colorsport for their meticulous picture research, Andy Betteridge and Dave Fletcher at the *Halifax Courier* for helping us to track down the fantastic photograph of Baz in the dressing room at the Shay and Paul Downes at 3Objectives for photographing the Deep Heat tube. Thanks to Giles Ivey for his idea of putting the thoughts of Baz's former colleagues and friends at the back of the book, and to Darren Griffiths at Everton FC and Ken Beamish at Blackburn Rovers FC for all their help.

FOREWORD

by Phil Neville

When I signed for Everton in 2005, Baz was the first person at the club I met. I arrived at the training ground and the manager wasn't there, so I went for my medical and it must have been the quickest in the history of football. Baz looked at my medical records, lay me down and did a few stretches and then he just said, "You've had one injury in 11 years and you never miss a game. I think you'll be OK won't you!"

So that was that. I signed, of course, but the rest of the players weren't in the next day so he said I should come in for some light training. He said, "We'll just do about 20-30 minutes, you won't even get a sweat on." So I turn up the next day expecting an easy workout, and I'm not joking me and Baz ended up doing the toughest session I'd ever done in 15 years at United!

Apart from being just about the fittest man at the club, he had this incredible enthusiasm and energy for the job. When a player was coming back from injury and needed to get fit again, Baz would be out there on the training pitch doing it with them – the running, the weights, the bleep tests. And because he had been a player himself and had had most of the injuries himself, he understood the psychological side of injuries.

I think that side of things was his real strength. He understood what a massive part the mind plays in recovering from injuries. He'd just be so positive. I remember one week I was playing for England and I pulled my hamstring in the warm-up. I pulled out of the game but stayed and watched. When I switched on my phone later there was a message from Baz which just said: "Phil Neville does not get hamstring injuries. You'll be fit in two days!"

I was thinking 'Baz, you're mad,' but he had realised that as my game is not based on speed and I had no history of problems in that area it was most likely to be a fatigue injury and, sure enough, after a couple of days rest I played against Middlesbrough the following Saturday with no problems.

He just had this incredible energy and enthusiasm for the job which made an impact on me straight away. And I soon learnt that although he was the physio, or head of medicine which I think was his correct title, in fact he was so much more than that. He was David Moyes's first lieutenant, really, almost like an assistant manager.

On match days he really came alive. He'd be in the dressing room cracking jokes and telling funny stories about his time at Birmingham and Blackburn. He knew which players to leave alone and which players to put his arm round. We knew from his stories that he'd not reached the level of football that perhaps he should have, but you could see on a matchday his eyes would light up and he was revelling in being in the Premier League environment and taking on the likes of Manchester United and Liverpool every week. He was like a kid, it was as if he was saying to himself that he was going to enjoy every minute.

And because of this great attitude and his humour, not to mention being a great physio, the players leaned very heavily on him. I think that because he felt that the environment he'd experienced when he started in football had not been great, he made that special effort to be positive and encouraging all the time to create the kind of environment that maybe he didn't have as a player.

He joked about his time at Birmingham when he had confidence issues, about the fear he had when he had to cross balls to Trevor Francis, and how on the bus to games he'd be praying there would be an earthquake so the match would have to be called off. It was very funny, but there was also a message to us that we were very lucky to have made it to the top level and that we should enjoy every second. That made him a great guy to have around the place and a key reason why we had such a good team spirit.

But, perhaps because of his insecurities, I'm not sure that Baz realised his standing at the club and how everyone felt about him. I used to joke that he was running the club. He could never take a day off, I mean even in the summer, and it was almost as if he came to work every day feeling that he had to prove himself all over again, like it was a trial.

I used to say to him: "Baz, relax, take a break." But I think that perhaps even though he was head of medicine at one of the biggest football clubs in the world and was loved and respected by everybody, he still had a daily battle to fully believe in himself. But he did belong there and he was there because he was good, no brilliant, at what he did. And we all miss him...

I'm sure you will enjoy Baz's book because it's a great read, and anybody who loves the game will get a real insight into football and one of its true great characters.

Phil Neville, Everton FC, July 2011

PROLOGUE

The condemned man sits quietly in the small Spartan room. Bare walls and uncarpeted floors making it feel appropriately cold and austere.

The only sound is the relentless, remorseless ticking of the clock – tirelessly and inexorably counting down to his date with destiny.

How has it come to this?

What decisions, random choices and quirks of fate have culminated in him sitting in this sparse room, watching these final precious seconds slip away?

Is he scared? Yes, of course he is. Who wouldn't be scared in the face of such a horrific situation?

Try to black out the terror, try to be philosophical, try to accept your fate with dignity.

Still the clock ticks – time and tide wait for no man. Then the footsteps approaching. Nearly time now.

He gets to his feet under his own efforts – too proud, even now, to ask for help.

The footsteps get closer and then stop outside the door.

A simple light knock and the door opens.

There in the doorway stands the man in black – the man who has come for him.

The man in black approaches him and asks him to turn around

with a politeness that is at complete odds with the gravity of the situation.

Now the fear, now the realisation it is about to happen.

There is no escape now.

He is asked to lift his feet – first the left one and then the right one – and show the soles of his shoes to the man in black.

"OK, that's fine, son, your studs are fine. Remember, no jewellery to be worn, no bad language and no arguing with the officials."

He blows his whistle and off they go.

PART ONE

PLAYER

(1975-91)

Chapter One

INNOCENCE

Some things stay with you for life. Events so momentous that time can neither diminish nor distort them.

They remain burnt into the psyche, available for precise instant recall, no matter where, no matter when. So vivid are these memories that 35 years can melt away in a split-second. One such experience is indelibly etched into my memory and survives as an instant focal point to summarise a particularly significant period of my life in a brief moment.

This earth-shattering event happened on my first day as a professional footballer. I will say it again – my first day as a professional footballer. July 31, 1975.

Can you imagine what it felt like to sign for the club you supported? Think about it for a while. People talk, superficially, about "dreams coming true", a convenient and well-used phrase but seldom with any substance. But not in this case. I had truly stepped off the terrace and into the dressing room at Birmingham City.

I was, as the Americans would say, "living the dream". Look, the facts don't lie. Virtually every kid on the planet has played football, but only the best of the best of the very best can ever be good enough to earn a living from it.

The incident in question happened early in the morning of that very first day. Standing at the edge of the training ground, I became aware of a presence next to me. I don't know whether I had actually half-looked across or it was a psychic moment, but I just knew it was him – the man from my bedroom wall.

To people who didn't frequent St Andrew's during that period, it is so difficult to convey the demi-god-like status this man enjoyed. He was Rooney, Gerrard and Lampard all rolled into one. His cult status was probably even greater than those players because, while they were superstars in teams of superstars, Trevor Francis was a superstar in a team of relatively ordinary British First Division players.

Every morning, when I opened my eyes, I saw Trevor staring down from my bedroom wall. Trevor scoring, Trevor shooting, Trevor gliding, Trevor flowing, Trevor magnificent in the blue-and-white penguin kit Birmingham City wore during that period (there were also a few pictures of Linda Lovelace, Deep Purple, Charlie's Angels and those two blokes from *Easy Rider* riding Harley Davidsons).

It had become a lifetime quest just to get the autograph of my hero, let alone play in the same team as him. How many times had my brother and I waited, to no avail, outside the players' entrance at St Andrew's after matches? And now? Well, I could actually have reached out and touched him. Talk about surreal. It is almost impossible to put into words what that experience was like to someone such as me – the fan from the Tilton Road End.

In some ways, what happened next would play a major part in the formation of the rest of my life. Sometimes small, seemingly unimportant events set in train a course of actions that ultimately shape and affect one's life. Incidents in some way trivial, yet with long-term ramifications. Now, as I sit back and reflect upon my life and the key points which shaped and altered it, this one, of all, is the most profound, although it wasn't until much later that I was truly aware of the significance of what was about to happen.

I was standing next to my hero and it seemed a conversation must ensue. It was a truly incredible and momentous experience. I was, however, becoming aware of a series of unpleasant physiological responses, presumably a result of being in the vicinity of this legend. I had butterflies in my stomach – well, more like a flock of seagulls picking at my insides. Nausea overwhelmed me. I felt that sudden release of sweat on my forehead and then, in quick succession, my armpits and finally the palms of my hands.

It was quite a warm day, but not hot enough to provoke such a severe reaction, and my mouth became much drier than it would be in two hours' time after we had completed the first cross country.

My heart was racing. My body was telling me to move away and seek respite from the emotion of the occasion, but my legs had become heavy and resistant to movement. Looking back now I suppose I was having some kind of panic attack – in fact, I may indeed have invented the panic attack as there was really no such thing in those days. I think the simplest thing is to refer to it as a Trevor attack!

It's quite easy to explain. Let's be honest, I have spent enough time reliving it over the past 35 years. I had elevated, in my mind, this man to such a level of adulation that now, as he stood next to me in flesh and blood, his metamorphosis from bedroom wall-occupying icon to potential team-mate who I might conceivably become friends with or, even more unbelievably, play in the same team as, was simply too much for my adolescent mind to handle, hence the alarming reaction. Or to put it more simply and in layman's terms – he was God and I was an insignificant, incapable of being in his company, hence the collywobbles.

This uncomfortable impasse lasted for minutes (probably seconds). Fucking hell, if he speaks to me, I think I might possibly drop dead with shock, let alone engage him in small talk.

But he didn't speak; he just sort of drifted away – well, anyway, he wasn't there any more and my heart returned to normal and my legs regained the ability to move.

Sadly, that would not be my last Trevor attack. We were team-mates for four years, though I doubt if he even noticed. Every day when he did speak to me, even if it was just a brief "good morning", I would clam up and end up stuttering and stammering some unintelligible reply. And as for actually passing the ball to the guy, forget it, not a chance. I would look up, see it was him and, as if by magic, my leg would lose all its sensory input and he would curse me as the ball evaded his touch. I don't know what he really thought of me. Presumably that I must have been retarded mentally and physically. Of course, I was neither (I don't think); I just couldn't take him down from the bedroom wall.

We went our different ways – eventually. He became the first million-pound player and I slowly but surely drifted down the leagues. I am not blaming Trevor for that, of course, but in many ways he was unknowingly responsible, in small part, because our mismatched relationship highlighted the difficulties I encountered when trying to 'make it' at my local club.

The struggle to make it at your 'home' team, when all your family, friends and old schoolteachers are watching you, kicking every ball for you, praying you will play well – or, more pointedly, some of them praying you will not play well – can be a crushing experience.

An interesting footnote to the Trevor Francis experience happened about 20 years later when I next spoke to him.

I was the physiotherapist at Preston North End and we were about to play Arsenal in a live televised FA Cup tie at Deepdale on a Friday night. I had, on many occasions, told stories about my inability to pass or kick the ball to Trevor, taking advantage of my gift of accurately impersonating his distinctive Devonian accent when he would bollock me as my passes evaded him. My best friend, Brian Hickson (the Preston kit man), had enjoyed them many times over the years.

I was in the medical room at about 6.30pm with the door

slightly ajar and could hear Brian, who was outside in the corridor, saying, "Good evening Mr Francis, there is a bald-headed bloke behind that door who knows you very well and speaks very highly of you, and I am certain he would love to meet you again."

The penny dropped – Trevor was the Sky Sports commentator for the match and, more to the point, was about to walk into the room. It was surreal as the door slowly opened and once again I felt the sweat start to break out – even after all that time. It had been almost a quarter of a century since my last Trevor attack.

What happened? Well, surprisingly little. We chatted and reminisced and laughed and, more to the point, spoke (without the stammering) as old pals and ex-team-mates do. What a nice guy. I wish we could have had more time to talk. I could have explained I wasn't retarded and, what's more, was actually a very good player who simply could not cope with that extra pressure which playing for your hometown club brought, but still ended up having a decent career at a respectable level.

But I didn't explain any of that. How can you ever really relate to anybody the implications of that incident on that warm summer's day all those years ago – especially the man himself?

So began my career at Birmingham City. The Blues were in the First Division (in the days before the First Division became the Third Division). I really was the boy next door, and walked to training every day from the family home in Sheldon singing *Bohemian Rhapsody* and walking tall in my platform shoes. This was the era of the ground staff – the apprentice who spent as much time cleaning boots as actually wearing them. In what was probably the last vestige of the slave trade and in return for our £16 per week and cheese sandwiches at lunchtime, we were expected to clean the baths, boots, training ground, manager's car, St Andrew's, coach's car, etc. I had six pairs of boots to clean every day – 14, 16, 29, 32, 39 and 42 (we had more than 50 professionals at the time). Later, I retained those 'lucky' numbers as my lottery numbers and, surprise surprise, over the last 15 years have never won so much as a sodding tenner. Maybe that was a portent of what was to come.

The environment the young apprentices operated in then was totally different to that which today's 'academy students' enjoy. Notwithstanding the fact today's hopefuls don't do any jobs while we spent at least 50 per cent of our apprenticeship performing – let's say – off-field duties, there was also a vast difference in the senior players' perception of the role of the young players and, more importantly, their perceived status at the club.

Back in the mid-'70s things were very different. (There was no naughty step at home – if you misbehaved you got a bloody clip around the ear.) Discipline in the workplace, schools and football clubs was much tougher than in today's liberal environment; the young players just did not go into the senior players' dressing room uninvited and did not initiate conversation with them. They were generally treated with disdain by the senior players. Similarly, some of the coaches seemed to enjoy exerting their authority over the young boys. I will stop short of using the word bullying – but only just. I think some of the treatment we were on the receiving end of might be described in those terms by some of today's more liberal thinkers.

It was tough. The club seemed to purposely create an unnecessarily harsh environment. Maybe their theory was that one day you would be going out into the hostile atmosphere of a first-team game where the criticism could be vocal and fierce, and perhaps they thought in treating us that way it would toughen us up and prepare us for that day. Perhaps they were right. Survival of the fittest, natural selection and all that. But I didn't like it, didn't thrive on it and it didn't make me a better player.

Let me try and be a little bit more specific about the social dynamics in place at a soccer club in those days. If you had the wrong type of jeans, the wrong width of tie, a lisp or a big nose (which I did), then it was open season on you from the other players – and that included the coaches and other staff. However, it was done not with good humour but with malice, and every comment was designed to cause maximum hurt. And God forbid if you gave anybody a bad pass. Things like that were seized upon voraciously by the pack and the fragile self-confidence of the young players was ripped to shreds.

There was a really dark side to the whole proceedings and I admit I was terrified of going into the first-team dressing room. I remember in my first pre-season one of my fellow newcomers had started a week after us because of a family holiday, presumably booked before he was offered an apprenticeship at Birmingham. When he reported for his first day, the second-team coach started screaming at him for not being in the previous week. Really aggressive and unpleasant, and to what purpose? Well, I don't know – maybe he could tell us – but that just seemed to be the norm at the club then with a permanent open season on the young lads.

One thing, though, that was better back then was that the clubs didn't start getting interested in talent-spotting young players until they were 14 or 15 years old. Unlike today where we have the crazy system of scouting four and five-year-olds. For Christ's sake. When I was four years old, I was more concerned about getting my first cubs uniform and saving up my 10p-a-week pocket money for the latest Action Man than being invited to join a football academy. Back then, everything went through the schoolboy football system; the best players got picked for the school team, and then the best players in the school team got sent for trials for the Birmingham schools team, and then the best players in that team got selected for the county team (Warwickshire, not the West Midlands, in those days). And that was it, nice and simple. No pressure stuff but, more importantly, absolutely no thought or suggestion of becoming professional footballers. It was just about the honour of representing your school, city or county and designed solely for physical recreation.

If you didn't get picked, it was no big deal, or if you got into the county team, it was pats on the back and well dones all round, but no feeling you were anything special or destined for stardom.

I went through all those trials and ended up captain of both Birmingham and Warwickshire schools – I was very proud and pleased of this, but didn't have any grandiose ideas about the future. The point is this: I was allowed to play all my junior football up until the age of 15 or 16 with no pressure at all. At the excellent school I went to, Sir Wilfrid Martineau, you were expected to partake equally in all the sporting activities, so I played a lot of rugby and did a lot of cricket and cross country and athletics and enjoyed all these sports.

Naturally, we all loved soccer the most and dreamed of being professional footballers, but without any of the associated pressures that, dare I say, are heaped on to today's talented younger generation. It was only in the final years of school that a few scouts from the local clubs dropped by at the county games and started to express an interest in the better players, and this is how it was – almost perfunctory.

I was invited to sign apprentice forms for a host of local clubs but opted for the Blues because I supported them and it also meant I could continue to live at home. It was only really at that stage that the excitement and realisation that I was on the verge of a career in professional football grabbed me. The beauty of that system – although it wasn't really a system as such – was when you got to the club on your first day it was all new, exciting and even a bit daunting because you hadn't had the exposure to this environment since you were four. Nowadays you could get a testimonial on your 14th birthday.

At 4pm every afternoon, the young apprentices would congregate in the boot room at St Andrew's, waiting for the ritual inspection of the jobs we had done by one of the senior coaches. If I close my eyes, I can still remember all the smells from that little room – polish, leather from the room itself intermingled with the Deep

Heat and Vicks Vapour Rub from the physio room and the smell of drying kit from the laundry. Throw in the stench – and I use that word advisedly – of the lads' aftershaves of that era (Blue Stratos, Brut and Old Spice) and you had a heady mix. Those smells are implanted in my memory.

However, there was a degree of tension to proceedings as the jobs were thoroughly scrutinised in a sort of parody of the national service era – you know, fingers running along edges, skirting boards, studs of boots, rim of toilets (my job), before inevitably finding fault with some small aspect of the work to justify making us all get changed into our kits again to redo everything. That guy, who we all hated, would then walk away muttering the immortal words, "Sloppy off the pitch, sloppy on the pitch."

As I said before, it was probably not overtly bullying, but more just a case of him being a twat, and for no other reason than to make everybody miserable for an hour or so and to show us what a big man (wanker) he was.

Despite all the child labour, my first season in a football life of more than 35 years was the one I enjoyed the most – not because it was the first and not because I was a Birmingham City player (or cleaner). No, it was a time of intense happiness and genuine joy to get up and walk to our Elmdon training ground with the same thoughts going through my head constantly: "You are being paid to play football, you are being paid to play football, you are being paid to play football", or to paraphrase good old Freddie Mercury: "Is this the real life, or is this just fantasy?" It took me about six months to come to terms with this marvellous situation I was in.

I grew up in a typical working-class, close, happy family. Dad had a shit day job in a factory and Mom worked a shit night job in a factory. They were the best parents ever and my greatest sorrow is that my dad died at 47 and never saw me play (for Blackburn Rovers, not Birmingham City, as you'll quickly realise), especially when I consider my joy at watching my own son play.

My childhood, my life, was football. Every opportunity to kick a ball was eagerly accepted. Before school, morning break, lunch-time, afternoon break, after school, evening practice, Saturday morning match, a break to watch Blues in the afternoon, and two games on a Sunday. And guess what (and this goes to all the fitness gurus)? Nobody got injured and nobody got burnt out. Why? Because we were left alone to enjoy it, that's why. Not a coach in sight; just the teacher picking the teams. Of course, I wanted to be a footballer from the day I first walked and so did all the kids I grew up with. Is it still the case today? I doubt it. I think the PlayStation has prevailed.

But now I was truly living the dream. Pinch yourself, you are being paid to play football with Trevor Francis, Kenny Burns and Howard Kendall – OK, fair enough, they didn't really know I existed. We were training at the opposite end of the training ground, we weren't allowed into their changing room (except to clean it), we weren't allowed to talk to them and were only getting £16 per week, and there was this unpleasant atmosphere of intimidation that pervaded the place, but so what? I was technically a Birmingham City player and nobody could take that away from me.

I was one of 16 or so other apprentices – half of them my age, half a year older. Those second-years were greatly experienced in giving all the shit jobs to the new crop. It always surprised me that the majority of the lads came from all over the UK and few from Birmingham itself.

We reported to the training ground at 9am to start getting the kits and boots ready for the senior players who would arrive at 10am. We had a big drying room to hang the wet kit in overnight as, in those far-off days, the keepers wore woollen gloves and the players wore big woollen jumpers over their training kit on cold days. Sometimes, wet boots were left in there with newspaper inside them, and I used to love that smell – the smell of damp leather, damp wool and damp paper. I can still recall those smells even today.

After the pros' needs were met and if we had any energy left, then it was time for our own training. Training which can only be described as fantastic. Ken Oliver, the youth-team coach, took us every day – warm-up, crossing and shooting, and five-a-side. Perfection. They were halcyon days. We played matches on a Wednesday afternoon and on a Saturday morning. We had a mediocre team but Ken never bollocked us. He cared for us, looked after us and provided a tranquil nurturing environment well away from the angry 'others'. Thanks for everything, Ken. I will never forget your kindness.

In that wonderfully sheltered and protected environment, it was almost an age of innocence – free kit, free boots on demand, free cheese sandwiches in the afternoons and, most importantly, free entry to the home games (to do the jobs). We were young, fit and happy – baggy pants, platform shoes, kipper ties, Slade, Gary Glitter (I told you it was an age of innocence!), Babychams, Cherry Bs, Ford Anglias, Capris and Cortinas, *Steptoe and Son*, *Till Death us do Part, Parkinson* and *Crossroads*, Watergate and the Ali/Frazier trilogy, Black Power and troops out of Vietnam. A historic period worldwide and a historic period for me. The world was our proverbial oyster and we thought the sun was going to shine all day.

I vividly remember my second day at the club when Ray, the kit man, took me down to St Andrew's and unlocked the door to a hidden room. I gasped in amazement and my eyes lit up like a child's on Christmas morning. This room was filled from floor to ceiling with hundreds of blue Adidas football boot boxes emblazoned with those legendary names – Santiago, 2000, Penarol, World Cup. Every model in every size.

We are talking about the mid-'70s here and I, like the majority of kids my age, came from a working-class background. We couldn't afford boots like that. You wore what you could afford, often the ones your older brother wore last season. Talk about an

Aladdin's Cave – and that deep, rich, almost intoxicating smell of brand new leather.

"OK," Ray said. "You are getting three pairs. What size are you?"

"Right, thanks, two eights and a nine please."

"Yeah and how does that work?"

"Well, just in case my feet grow."

"Here," he said. "Here's three eights and tell your brother to fucking well buy his own."

But that's what it was like in those days; most kids went to school in jumpers knitted by their moms. Can you imagine that happening today? In fact, do people even still knit today now that Primark has landed?

But, as I was to discover the next season, the real reason why we were so ridiculously happy was we had not tasted any real pressure – the pressure to win. In fact, the pressure to win at all costs, any cost, or otherwise feel the wrath of the manager, fans, other players or press.

Sadly, over the next couple of years, I would come to realise how the whole thing worked – we weren't really being paid to enjoy playing football at all; we were being paid to win games, and I came to realise, with dismay, just how diametrically opposed these two things could be.

But, at that time, in the 1975/76 season, life was achingly good. Magic moments like cleaning the away team dressing room after a match at St Andrew's when stars of the likes of Lou Macari, Malcolm Macdonald and Kevin Keegan spoke to me. Mind you, they were usually in a good mood as they were frequent winners – the Blues were crap that season (and the next and the next... in fact, pretty much every season until a couple of years ago). Often the away teams would allow us to start our cleaning jobs while they were still getting changed.

Oh, to be invited into that most sacred of places – the dressing room, the footballers' inner sanctum. Steam from the bath, the noise of the players and, above all, those marvellous smells

– leather, Vicks, Deep Heat, shampoo and soap. I would go into so many dressing rooms over the next 35 years at every level of the game and in every role in the game, and one thing always remained reassuringly the same – those smells. But back then, rubbing shoulders with those legends (when I was mopping) was truly miraculous. Once Steve Kindon of Wolves was drying himself and asked me to pick up his flip-flops. As I bent down, he farted in my face and everybody laughed. What joy. What an honour to be included in one of Big Stevie's jokes.

One thing I did notice at this time was I seemed to be progressing a lot better than the rest of the other lads of my age and the word from above was that I was destined for the first team at an early age. Wow, that actually scared me to death – all the piss-taking from the senior players and stick from the fans – which on reflection probably wasn't the correct reaction from a supposedly aspiring young player.

A couple of things stick in my mind from those days. We were each given a bottle of full-fat milk after every training session. Some of the modern nutritionists might be surprised to discover not only did nobody drop dead, but we could still manage to run around for 90 minutes without obvious harm or hardship. Nothing tasted as good as ice-cold, full-fat milk taken from the crates at the side of the training pitch as soon as training was over.

Sometimes though (probably because of the milk), you did get injured and then you were well and truly fucked. Being injured was probably a bit like the classic analogy of war – 99 per cent boredom and one per cent terror. You hung around all day while the senior players got their treatment and then had short periods of intense discomfort as they stuck needles containing this new wonder drug Cortisone into you. I had a couple into my groin and it bloody hurt.

Did it cure me? Yes it did, because there was no fucking way I was going back for another. If you weren't getting jabbed, you received a deep massage to the area, which was all the rage at the time (in fact, it's probably been in and out of vogue four or five times since, which tells you a lot about sports medicine). Basically, it consisted of the physio sticking his thumbs, with all his body-weight, into your most tender area until you thought you would pass out with pain.

Before I got the injection, I had undergone this brutality on my poor adolescent groin. I had been trying to play through the injury for ages because I knew exactly what the treatment consisted of, but it hadn't worked and I was booked in for the torture.

One afternoon, late obviously because all the senior players had to get looked after first, I was given the dreaded friction massage. I screamed so loudly that Lionel, the groundsman, came rushing into the medical room brandishing his scythe, fearing, in his words, "somebody was getting fucking murdered!"

In a strange way, that extremely painful ordeal stood me in good stead for the future and taught me a valuable lesson for when I became a physio myself. That was to ensure all the players under my care, whether the most famous international or the humblest junior, were treated identically in terms of respect and consideration, and were treated in the most professional way possible by the best people available, notwithstanding their value to the club. Most importantly, I can categorically state, in all the years I was a physio at a professional club, I never urged any player to take a steroid injection, and I certainly didn't friction-massage the players until they were passing out with pain. (I've always been far too lazy for that.)

And so that magical first season slipped away in a blur, but a blur of pure joy. Unfortunately, virtually all the second-year appren-tices were released and I remember looking at their tear-stained faces as they emerged from the coach's office one by one with the realisation they would never fulfil their dreams of becoming professional footballers. So near yet, at the same time, so far. It might sound cruel and heartless, but I don't even remember feeling too sorry for those lads – when you are young and insensitive it doesn't really register too much. It was nearly 20 years later

– when I would be that man, breaking the same bad news to a different generation – that I was at last able to understand the pain of the occasion.

But now, to more important things – holidays. I had just spent ten months getting paid for playing for the Blues; now I was going to be paid for going on holiday for two months. Surely it couldn't get any better than this? Sadly, it couldn't.

Chapter Two

INNOCENCE LOST

Pre-season training – just three simple words, but words to strike fear into even the most hardened pro. That six-week period dreaded by all when the players are dragged, pushed, kicked and tortured back into shape. In the 1970s, the close season was much longer than in today's football and I remember we seldom reported back before mid-July. Add to that the fact the season used to finish a week or so earlier back then, and you ended up with a good couple of months off.

Over the years, the close season has been gradually eroded down to about six weeks (even less if some players have been involved in international football). The fitness coaches, sports scientists and nutritionists are arguing, and winning the case, for a shorter break based entirely on physiological grounds (maybe they are right), citing the dangers of de-conditioning if the players are given too much time off. The result, these days, is that most players go off for the summer break armed with sets of exercises and drills to perform to maintain their fitness. Then, before they know it, they are brought back to the club after an ever-decreasing break from the mental pressures which so sap the modern player.

From my point of view, I always felt it was important to have as long a break as possible to recharge the psychological batteries.

Forget the body-fat tests, the blood tests and the bleep tests; give the players extra time off and you will probably get much more from them. Drag them back too soon and they won't be as fresh and eager to start anew.

When you've played 50 or 60 games in a season, trained every day and been under huge pressure to perform day in and day out, trust me, by the end of the season you never want to see another ball as long as you live. But then, as June slips by, you slowly feel that old hunger returning, all the aches and pains have gone, you find yourself going for a couple of runs, or a game of tennis, maybe a kick-around on the beach, and slowly but surely the freshness, hunger and enthusiasm start to return. Eventually, you can't wait to play football again.

Back in the '70s, though, players certainly did relax and take a breather. There were two things synonymous with the first day of pre-season – it was always the hottest day of the year and everybody gathered around the scales for the annual pre-season weigh-in. Quite frankly, some of the players were fat when they came back. Not slightly overweight or slightly above their ideal playing weight – no, they were fat. Some had gained so much weight that they looked completely different from when we last saw them back in May and everybody, from coaches to groundstaff, congregated around the scales to witness the ritual humiliation of these porkers. Nowadays, all any player would expect to gain would be a couple of pounds maximum.

When all the laughing had died down and the new training gear had been issued, it was time to commence pre-season training and that meant just one thing – cross country. All Blues players, including apprentices, had to walk the short distance from our training ground to Elmdon Park, the big adjacent country park. On the walk, the young players were told by a cartel of the most senior players that any young player showing up a senior player on the run, i.e. going past them in the race, "will get their fucking bollocks chopped off!" So, a bizarre sight gradually unfolded over the three-mile race. All the fatties were comfortably holding their own mid-pack, running surprisingly well for their new-found girths, and amazingly keeping up with the younger, lighter and fitter apprentices.

If the manner of the pre-season training came as a surprise to me (a lad who had won numerous school cross countries and athletics medals), then what came next would be an almighty shock. I had been selected, as the most promising apprentice, to accompany the senior squad on their pre-season tour of Holland and Belgium in August 1976. Fuck me, what an awful thought – me, all alone with them.

I should point out it did disturb me greatly that this was my reaction to what was a great honour and privilege, but that was the truth of it – a combination of the vicious piss-taking, the aloofness of the coaches and players, and my complete inability to perform even the simplest motor function in the presence of Trevor Francis reduced me to a trembling wreck. I know it was a million miles from any kind of normal reaction but that was just how I felt. This wasn't the way it should have been.

There were two stand-out incidents from that trip which would have long-term ramifications. The first happened after the opening friendly match, back at the hotel in the room of a player called Tony Want. As the debutant, I was invited to Tony's room for a nice friendly game of cards. Well, a game of cards, but with a drinking game thrown in.

Tony had the pack of cards and on the table there was a bottle of vodka, a bottle of whisky and a bottle of Coca-Cola. The game went like this: Tony dealt one card at a time to the eight or so players sat around the table. The first player to receive an ace had to name the drink (not too difficult given the paucity of choice), the second ace poured the drink – hey, steady with the coke, don't drown it. You can just imagine it, can't you? Third ace sipped the drink and finally the last person to receive an ace from the deck had to drink the whole fucking lot down in one go. "Oh no, Mickey Rath again, third time on the trot. What are the odds of that?"

Up until then, I had never drunk more than a single pint of

Ansells Bitter; now I had just drunk more than a pint of spirits. Suffice to say, by the time the penny had dropped, so had the contents of my stomach, and I finally passed out and spent the next three days in bed.

During that era, the post-match refuelling was very different, but nobody seemed to mind when the players had a few drinks. In fact, you could get pissed and drive home and nobody seemed to mind about that either. The upshot of my rather harsh initiation ceremony was that, to this day, I still can't stand the smell of whisky.

The other life-affecting experience was a good deal more sinister. When I finally emerged from my alcoholic coma, I had to train, of course, and for the first time it was just me alone with all the senior players and senior coaching staff, and I was really, really nervous. One bad pass with these twats and you would get it. I just about got through the first session without making myself look too bad – mainly because my many bad passes were not put down to me being a shit player, but more to the fact I had been at death's door after the whisky incident.

I thought I had got away with it until the boss, Willie Bell, decided we would have a game of tunnel ball to finish. You know the game – two teams compete against each other, first man runs out from the back of the line ball in hand, around the cone, before volleying it to the next man who passes it back through the team's legs, and then the next man goes until everybody has done it. Simple game, easy skill, difficult to mess up.

But then it was announced the losing team would have to do 50 press-ups so, all of a sudden, there was a bit of pressure on and I felt the familiar feeling of muscle turning to jelly. Even worse, I was the last man – the key role.

What happened next was the absolute confirmation of all my worst fears and a marvellous example of the power of catastrophic thinking. We were winning by miles when the ball was tunnelled back to me. As last man and with a huge lead, I just had the simple task of picking up the ball and racing out and around the cone before completing a simple volley back to our team leader, saluting victory and going back to bed because I still felt ill from the drink.

The only problem, though, was my colossal fear of ballsing up the whole task, so I took my time, concentrating fully on the admittedly simple job in hand. Yes! The ball was through the tunnel and safely in my sweaty hands. I ran out to the cone on unsteady legs but still got there OK. Phew, so far so good, I believed I could do this – I could make it. Just one simple little volley and I would have survived the day. But, oh my God, no, it couldn't be. Oh please God no. To my absolute horror, I realised that the man who I had to volley the ball to a mere six feet away and thus win the race, save my team from the press-ups and be greeted as the hero and saviour, was none other than my arch-nemesis, my very own *bête noir* – Trevor Francis. And he was yelling at me in that West Country accent to hurry up because the other team were catching up. Fuck, what a dire situation.

The rest is now enshrined in football folklore.

Due to the pressure of having to pass to 'TF', my leg suddenly ceased to function and I was unable even to make the slightest gesture of kicking the ball.

Everybody was screaming at me to just kick the fucking thing. Finally, by recruiting the muscles of my hip (a trick that is used by lower limb amputees, for fuck's sake), I made some vain attempt to propel the bloody ball to Trev, but it just bounced on the grass in front of me. The game was lost, to the fury of my team-mates and great amusement of everybody else.

Sadly, that incident would have great significance regarding the future of my career.

I will never know how on earth I got through that bloody week – drinking a full bottle of scotch, the tunnel ball debacle and the general difficulties I had establishing myself as a player or just a functioning human being among those former heroes of mine.

Even such simple things as meal times were an ordeal. Basically, everybody waited with bated breath for my next faux-pas. We had just finished our main course and I remember somebody took the piss out of the way I chewed. Well, the laughter had only just died down from that latest "harmless bit of banter" when the sweet trolley arrived and halted next to me. My turn to order first. All went quiet, everybody in the room straining their ears to catch the latest hilarious uttering from the village idiot, and I didn't disappoint – I never did. I looked at the variety of delightful desserts and fixed my desires on the brown blancmange-like substance. I cleared my throat to order as people leaned forward to enjoy the latest offering from Birmingham's new idiot-savant.

"I would like some of that brown trifle please." Well, the whole room erupted into hysterics which seemed to go on for ages. How was I to know it was mousse? I had never even heard of fucking mousse. We used to have bananas and custard where I came from. But that's how it was back then and it was slowly but surely destroying me.

Two days later, I returned to the Blues' training ground and back into the bosom of Ken and those great five-a-sides and cleaning boots and cheese sandwiches, pool comps in the afternoon, and happiness and confidence. Away from the senior players and my nemesis Trev. The only problem, though, was it wasn't the same; it could never be the same again. The age of innocence was over. This was the new order. Now I had one foot in the youth team camp, where I was the star player, and the other foot in the first-team squad desperately trying to get the ball to within ten feet of Trevor.

Every morning, depending on the numbers of players fit and available to train with the first team, I was just a short shout from Willie Bell away from being pulled in with the seniors to make up the numbers and cruelly taken away from my mates and the good life with Ken. To my undying embarrassment, I had designed a strategy to overcome this problem. As soon as the senior players trooped out on to the training pitch and just as Willie, having counted the numbers and realised they were in need of a make-weight from the apprentices, started to seek me out, I would blast a ball over the perimeter hedge into the farmer's field next door, so I was forced to go and retrieve it. Thus I disappeared from the manager's view and avoided being recruited into 'the killing fields' of the professional squad.

Over the last 35 years, I have made it my business to ask dozens of other players and former players what they were like for them and if, in similar circumstances, they reacted the same as me. And guess what? Many admitted to similar problems and similar feelings. Let's face it, many people are sensitive and don't thrive on being shouted at and bollocked every time a pass goes astray.

At that time, I was greatly troubled by my mindset. Of course, I had mouthed all the usual words about being "desperate to get my chance" but, to be brutally honest, I didn't want a chance. Certainly not at that stage, at just 17 years of age; I just wanted to stay with my mates in the youth team and enjoy my football. Don't forget, I had stood on those terraces on a Saturday when the team were struggling and the abuse was raining down on them. Notwithstanding the fact that among that baying crowd would be all my own family and friends – I couldn't subject my mom to that.

From a purely footballing point of view, things were going really well. It was autumn and I was a regular in the reserves – quite a feat with such a big squad at such a big club. I had been made to play left back because I could use both feet equally well. This was to become my biggest regret professionally as I was to spend the next 20 years at full back. I didn't think that position was ideal for nervous types like me, with its close proximity to the touchline and the boo boys. But, to be fair, I was playing extremely well in the reserves and enjoying the games on all those famous grounds – just don't put me in the first team yet.

A few months later, I played for the reserves down in London – at Crystal Palace, I think. It was definitely somewhere in London because we went to the Hendon Hall Hotel for our pre-match meal. We had huge fillet steaks at about noon, three hours before kick-off – the real highlight of the whole day. Coming from a working-class family during that era, you just did not have food like that at home – no way. The steaks were delicious and washed down with pints of full-fat milk; we were led to believe it gave you strength for the game.

Over the next couple of decades, though, once the nutritionists had appeared and got their teeth into the menus (no pun intended), and managed somehow to convince everybody if you didn't eat the right kind of food you couldn't play football properly (which was odd really because, during that period on that diet, English clubs were dominating European football), everything changed. A magic food was invented with magic powers – pasta. That was it. Pasta was the word and pasta was the future. It could transform you from a non-league player to a full international with just a couple of helpings. Not potatoes, not rice, not bread, even though they are virtually the same foods – no, pasta ruled, pasta was the word.

Having said that, I recently read they have discovered a new food called steak. Yes, steak is back – it contains creatine, you see. Move over pasta, steak is back in town.

And the moral of the story? There isn't one.

Clearly, the steak didn't have an adverse effect on me as I was having another good game in that reserve match in London and enjoying it. I loved the reserve games with my fellow apprentices. I loved having the ball. I was confident on the ball. Everything was going really well until I committed the ultimate footballer's crime – a crime so heinous to be deemed unforgivable. I gave a bad backpass. Yes, just that. I underhit the ball, that was all. The grass was quite thick on the flanks and it slowed the ball down quicker than I had anticipated. I knew it was a bad pass because they nearly scored. I was determined not to do it again. Next time I would put a little bit more weight on the pass and avoid making the same mistake twice. OK?

No, not OK. Not in a million years OK. The coach went mad at me at half time. Up close and personal, in my face, calling me a fucker and a cunt. I was totally shocked and, to be honest, scared. Nobody had talked to me like that before. Not the schoolteachers with their Corinthian attitudes, not the Birmingham or Warwickshire schools team managers, certainly not our beloved father figure Ken Oliver. I went out for the second half terrified of making a mistake, not wanting the ball and praying for the end of the game. And why? Because I underhit a backpass on the thick grass.

How could that man in such a position of trust and responsibility working with young and impressionable teenagers in his wildest dreams imagine anybody could ever respond favourably to that kind of abuse? Sadly, though, this guy wasn't unique. There were other coaches like him, and many of the players too, and the saddest thing of all is it is still going on to this day.

What's that saying? Give a small man some power and he will show you just how small he is. In all the games I played, I never bollocked or shouted any kind of derogatory stuff at any player (well, maybe the ref a couple of times) and, odd though it might seem to some, I am very proud of that. At the end of the day we were all supposed to be in the same team, weren't we?

Looking back I must have been an extremely talented player because – despite my severe neurological condition which manifested itself around TF, the disastrous performances when I trained with the senior players and the latest realisation that if anybody shouted at me at half time I would completely crack up – at the tender age of 17 I was called into the first-team squad for a mid-week League Cup game at Second Division side Blackpool.

How did I feel when I walked past the noticeboard that Monday morning and saw my name in the squad to travel to Blackpool? Let's put it like this: I went straight to the toilets. We had a few suspensions for the game so I tried to reassure myself this was probably just a one-off and by the weekend, with any luck, I could be back scoffing fillet steaks with the lads. Yes, I know, an unbelievable, shocking and pathetic attitude – guilty as charged – but that's how I felt. Believe me, I didn't feel good about any of it.

Blackpool were an average side, struggling in the division below, and it should have been an easy night for us but, as you are quickly coming to learn, nothing was straightforward for me as a player.

Here goes. We lost and I played crap – I was at fault for both the goals and, as such, found myself on the receiving end of several tongue-lashings. The only saving grace was, as a young debutant playing in a not very important game, I just about got away with it, just about escaped all the usual vitriol reserved for such disappointing results.

As I was only 17, I managed to avoid any real censure for that night and was still very much considered an outstanding prospect for the future. But let's not kid anybody; I was a million miles away from being anything like a good prospect for the future. The only good thing to emerge from that night was I was quickly dropped back to the reserves – what a relief.

When I look back, I shouldn't have been so hard on myself. I had been considered good enough to make my first-team debut at age 17, been a regular in the reserves and played for the England youth team. That was missing the point entirely, however. The fact was I had problems, real problems, and I didn't imagine them going away any time soon. The stark reality was I had absolutely no confidence at all. End of story.

Still though, I had to endure the morning ordeal of Willie Bell looking across for me and calling me away from my pals and an environment where I was king, to an environment where I just couldn't do it, just couldn't perform at any level due to lack of confidence. People talk about pace, skill, touch and technique, and debate which is the most important. Well, the answer is none of them, trust me. It is confidence because, without it, you will never be able to perform any of the others to your maximum ability.

I can't begin to tell the frustration and really deep unhappiness I felt at not being able to produce a fraction of what I was capable of due to nervousness. One afternoon I was told to cross balls for Trevor Francis and Kenny Burns.

No chance.

Forget it.

I couldn't get a single solitary fucking cross off the deck. What an embarrassment. What a humiliation. What a shame. They just stood there glaring at me and the real tragedy was that in fact nobody at that club could cross the ball as well as me – and with either foot. I think that was what hurt the most. Fair enough, if you are not good enough, you are not good enough, you can accept it and move on. Give it your best shot and all that. But to be rendered physically incapable due to lack of confidence, lack of moral courage – whatever you want to call it – that was the real heartbreaker.

Amazingly, nobody seemed to notice I was a nervous wreck and they still had high hopes for me. It was mid-autumn when the inevitable happened.

We had loads of injuries as usual and I knew it would only be a matter of time before Willie Bell's eyes would seek me out again (there was only so much time you could spend hiding in the farmer's field). We had a first-team match at White Hart Lane. It was a midweek game and I was in the squad. Even worse, I was selected to be on the bench.

I think it was the Spurs debut of a player called Peter Taylor. He was a flying winger and an England Under-23 international – one of the most feared attacking players in the land. He was on fire that night. I sat in the dugout with Willie Bell and Jim the physio praying I wouldn't have to go on.

In those days, whenever I was sub I used to close my eyes and count backwards from 5400, and then open my eyes and the game would be over.

Pathetic – yes, I know. Well, I was doing well and had got down to about 600 seconds left when our left back, Archie Styles, hobbled over to the dugout and launched my league career with the immortal words: "My groin's gone, get that cunt on." I looked around in vain but, sadly, because this was the '70s, there was only one sub, so if somebody got injured – too bad, pal, you were on.

I climbed out of the dugout with legs like jelly (it was like the scene from *Bambi* when the new-born fawn was trying to get to its feet) and entered the fray.

And to my surprise, I played OK – actually quite well. I don't know why or how. Was it because we were already beaten? Was it because I had only gone on as sub? Probably a combination of the two. In fact – whisper it – I quite enjoyed it and some of the players said, "Well played" after the game.

So without Archie injured, I stayed in the team for the weekend game at Newcastle. But I felt OK. I surprised myself. We lost 3-2 but I played well again. It was quite easy, just like being with the apprentices. What was happening to me? Was I becoming a player? I was picked for the next game too – Bristol City away on a Tuesday night. This time I played very well and we won 1-0. Christ, I was in danger of becoming a regular.

Now let's just take a second to quantify the situation concerning my fragile mind. I was still terrified of playing, could hardly sleep the night before a game and would have welcomed a serious injury to get me out of the firing line but, at the same time, I was able to play reasonably well and justify my inclusion in the team.

I was just turning 18 and it was time to find out if I was going to be offered a professional contract, so I had to go and see the boss in his office.

Of course, I was sure I was going to be offered one as I had already made my first-team debut at 17 and had represented England's youth team; it was more a case of what wages I would be paid. The first-year wage for a young pro was normally £45 per week, but I felt I deserved more because I had played in the first team while some of the other young lads being offered the same contracts had hardly played in the reserves. I had consulted some of the senior players (not TF as I still couldn't speak to him) and their consensus, given the fact I was a first-team squad member, was the princely sum of £100 per week was not unreasonable. Wow. That was big money, especially where I came from – the average wage in the Sheldon area, where I was born, was about half of that.

Having said that, I was only being realistic. I was a professional footballer at the end of the day. I wasn't asking for anything I didn't deserve.

I was shaking when I went into Willie Bell's office.

"Congratulations Mick," he said. "We are going to offer you a professional contract on £45 per week."

"Thank you," I stammered and turned to go out. No, that was just not fair. I turned around.

"Excuse me, Mr Bell, I just thought as I had been playing in the first team and for the England youth team I should get more than the minimum wage."

"OK," he said. "Good point, you will get £50 per week, but don't tell the rest of the lads."

"Thank you," I said and just walked out. When I look back it was a joke and a total injustice, but equally I melted as soon as the pressure was on. That became the story of my life in football. If you don't ask, you don't get. I never asked and I never got. That followed me all through my career and, slightly ironically, it was only when I became a physiotherapist that I thought I got paid anything near my worth.

Even so, I was now a first-team regular, youth international and professional. That period represented a little golden era for me at Birmingham (my only one, sadly) as I played well enough to stay in the squad. Next came my home debut, against West Ham, and then the thrill of playing in the FA Cup match against Portsmouth just after Christmas 1976.

I played really well in both games and the fans were right behind me. There was even talk of me being awarded the man-of-the-match trophy, but Trevor got it – on both occasions. After the second game I went into the city centre to a nightclub called Snobs (amazingly, it's still there). I had my best flares on and boogied away to all the latest disco hits of the time while swigging back numerous rum and blacks. Later, TF himself made an appearance and we stood boozing together with the fans flocking around us – two Birmingham legends!

How had this happened? It was most likely the result of a couple pints of Double Diamond in the players' bar after the match than any illusions Trevor and I deserved to share the same oxygen. It would prove to be a one-night stand.

I didn't even feel that nervous in those games for some reason; it was as if I had accepted my fate. They were almost like out-of-body experiences. I made some good passes and good tackles, and every time I did something good the applause was deafening for the local lad. I didn't know it at the time, but it would be downhill all the way from here.

This all too short 'golden period' of a few games represented the high point of my professional career at my beloved Birmingham City – first-team regular, England youth international, local lad made good. OK, there was the slight problem that I was terrified of actually crossing the white line but, for this short, glorious period, nothing could touch me.

Invited back to my old school to say a few words, presenting the prizes at all the Christmas dos for the local teams, my mom getting her shopping specially packed at Waitrose in Sheldon – I was living the dream. And oh, the money. In addition to the £50 per week I had courageously negotiated during that epic man-to-man confrontation with the manager, more importantly I was now on the first-team win bonus, draw bonus and appearance money.

It was great – lose and you still got £25 appearance money just for turning out (fancy that, you could lose and get 50 per cent of your wages). If you could scrape a draw, you got an additional £60, and if you could actually perform a miracle and win a game, then the princely sum of £120 was on its way. Sometimes it was so much money it was difficult to blow it all but, by changing my car every couple of weeks and buying lots of clothes, I just about managed it. (Where were the financial advisers?)

I think there were even times during that golden period when

I dared to think I could actually do it – put all the terrors behind me and be a success at Blues – but this was usually only after a couple of pints of Worthington E. I knew I had the natural ability, but did I have the mental toughness to face up to that baying crowd when things weren't going well? (I believe that is what is known as a rhetorical question.) Unfortunately, you can have all the natural ability in the world, but if you don't have the confidence to express it then you may as well have no ability at all.

So, during that 1976/77 season, I embarked on a long period of either being in the squad or on the bench, and even started the odd game. We won some, drew some and lost most. I was just about holding my own now. The euphoria of those first couple of home games had well and truly worn off and the shortest honeymoon on record was officially over. I was starting to struggle now.

We played at Anfield and lost 4-1. There are two things I will always remember from that game. Firstly, it was on *Match of the Day*, I was marking Steve Heighway and he scored a hat-trick; secondly, Kevin Keegan spoke some really nice words of encouragement to me during the game. I really appreciated that kindness and, funnily enough, reminded Kevin of it and thanked him when I saw him not that long ago when Everton played Man City – it meant an awful lot to me.

Now some people might say, "Yes, you got a roasting and yes it was on *Match of the Day*, but how many youngsters would give their right arms just to be on that pitch?" Well, to all those people, I would have gladly handed my shirt to any of you as Stevie repeatedly skipped by.

Suffice to say, it was an almighty relief when I was eventually dropped back down to the reserves and my mates. Fortunately, due to my age again, I guess, and a few half-decent performances earlier on, I escaped the usual vitriol reserved for the off-form players.

Hallelujah. Back to the ressies and a chance to catch up on three months' sleep.

In summary then, in the 1976/77 season, the records will show I played about a dozen times for Birmingham City FC and got capped for my country at youth level. Not bad for an 18-year-old and I should have been mightily proud of what I had achieved and enjoyed the rest of the season back in the bosom of Ken Oliver and the young lads.

But deep down I knew it wasn't right; it wasn't how it should have been. Instead of celebrating a positive start to my career, I was breathing a huge sigh of relief that I was out of the firing line. I had been on those terraces – the Tilton Road and the Kop – and I knew what that crowd was capable of when a player was playing badly. In all honesty, was I made of the right stuff to repeatedly go out in front of those people week in, week out?

Sadly, I knew the answer to that particular question.

Chapter Three

FEAR

Another long close-season break. But not a break like the previous year, not a period of happiness and relaxation, taking long walks in the park with the dogs and two carefree weeks' holiday in a caravan in Devon. This time the days skipped by at an alarming rate.

No, this was not so much a break – more a lull between the storms. Although the last season had been a qualified success, I had been given a brief taste of the pressure involved in playing professional football at the highest level. The previous summer, the days had passed slowly but happily as I impatiently counted down to the resumption of my footballing life. Now, though, the stakes had changed. No more Ken, training with my pals, five-a-sides, cheese sandwiches at St Andrew's in the afternoon, pool competitions and cleaning out the bath after home games. No, it was back to my new life – nerves, uncertainty and pressure.

That carefree period of my life had gone forever and I think towards the end of the previous season, when I had been briefly 'rested' from the first-team pressure cooker and sent back to train with the apprentices, I did detect even there, in that once cosseted and sheltered environment, that things had changed. I don't know whether it was their attitude towards me or mine to them – I wasn't sure. Perhaps it was a touch of jealousy from them towards me because I had progressed much more quickly than them, or more likely envy from me that they had never been touched by the harsh reality that is life as a first-team footballer. The truth is it was probably nobody's attitude to anybody; the status quo had changed and things could never be the same again.

I can't remember the exact sequence of events at St Andrew's regarding managerial change, but suffice to say, Birmingham, although in the top division, were struggling and underachieving, and the next season brought about several big changes at the club that were to have a profound effect on my career.

So, after a summer break that flew by in the blink of an eye, it was back to pre-season, the weigh-in and the cross countries. We had a new intake of young players – Pat Van Den Hauwe, Mark Dennis and Kevin Dillon were good players and went on to break into the first team and be successful at Birmingham. They were all from out of town and I am sure it was no coincidence that it was this bunch of players who did the best while all the local lads, despite being equally as good, seemed to suffer the same problems (although to a much lesser extent than me) of trying to establish themselves at their hometown club with all the additional pressures it apparently brought.

These out-of-towners would all make it at Birmingham – unlike me. They had the confidence, you see. From day one, while I would struggle to cope with the banter and the piss-taking from the senior pros, they would give back as good as they got. While I still could not physically pass the ball to Trev and one withering look from the fearsome Kenny Burns would reduce me to a shivering wreck, they thrived on the cut and thrust. When Kenny glared, they just glared back.

Things were not going well. As usual with the rest of the young lads, I was the best but, in with all my nemeses, I was hopeless, a bag of nerves.

Over the next few months, Birmingham struggled even more than usual (hardly surprising if they had to rely on players with my mentality), and Willie Bell was sacked.

I was on the periphery of things; with the first team half the time and with the reserves the other half. I had played the odd game in the first team and, to be honest, much of it was just a blur – just hoping and praying to get through the games without making too much of a mess of things.

In September 1977 Sir Alf Ramsey took over as manager. He was a director of the club and, when Willie Bell left, became caretaker on the understanding he would, under no circumstances, be persuaded to do the job for anything other than a few weeks.

Wow, Sir Alf Ramsey was my boss. It was sensational stuff. The great man himself, winner of the World Cup with England no less. A man used to winning, a man used to being around winners. What the fuck would he make of me? The names just seem to roll off the tongue: Charlton, Moore, Stiles, Hurst, Peters... Rathbone.

I can remember his first team meeting. Even the 'big hitters' were in awe as this legend addressed us. Oh, those classic, clipped tones. The quintessential English gentleman. Somehow, even now, I can remember that opening address.

First, he introduced himself (I knew I had seen him somewhere before) and then instructed us how we should address him.

"I don't like the words boss or gaffer – it smacks of the factory floor – and Alf is far too familiar. If you call me Sir Alf, then I think we should get on famously."

Initially, things went well and, as is often the case when a new manager takes over, the Blues rallied and won a few games. The pressure on Sir Alf to take over full time was irresistible and he reluctantly became permanent manager. Then, crucially, he made his first big mistake – he put me in the team. I just couldn't get my head around that one. Surely somebody who had won the fucking World Cup should have known better?

The previous season, although I had been lacking in confidence, I had still been just about holding my own. This time, however, my bottle had completely gone and the power of negative thinking had completely overwhelmed my psyche. I am not proud to admit this, but it is the naked truth and I wonder, if they are honest, how many players and ex-players could identify with my plight.

Two things stick in my mind from that torturous period. Number one – we used to wait for the teams for Saturday to be pinned up on the notice board after training on Friday. In those days, the reserves played on Saturdays in what was usually the opposite fixture to the first team so, for example, if the first team were playing Arsenal at home, then the reserves would travel down to London to play at Highbury.

I used to wait in a state of terror for the teams to be announced. You were either in the first-team squad and en route to a sleepless night, or in the reserves with a nice trip to London with your pals, playing cards on the bus, fillet steaks and an enjoyable game with no pressure.

I remember in my first season at the club a player called John Roberts, a fine centre half and a Welsh international, found he had been demoted to the reserves. In his fury and disgust, he spat on the team sheet and walked out. The spittle made the names run and all the other players were looking at the sheet trying to work out if their names were actually on it.

That walk up to the team sheet was probably the biggest ordeal of the whole week. I would close my eyes, count to ten and then just open one of them. Did I really think that would make any difference? Three... two... one... open one eye. I was out. What a relief, what a fucking relief. It would be another year or so before this ordeal would be over for me when, at last, I too would become a proper player. And then, thankfully, I would completely understand where big John was coming from.

Number two – when I was picked for the first team and we were playing at home, we would get changed in the dressing rooms that were in the corner of the stadium, and as kick-off approached you could start to hear the noise of the crowd as the ground filled up. Thirty thousand or so, many with a couple of pints in them, all there to cheer a win or, more worryingly, jeer a defeat. To get onto the pitch, we had to walk in procession, side by side with the opposition, from the corner of the ground all along the tunnel under the main stand to emerge from the halfway line.

God, that walk. It was torturous, agonisingly slow, especially when your legs had turned to jelly. I remember studying Charles I in history at school, how he lost the throne and finally ended up getting beheaded. Apparently he refused a blindfold and insisted on walking to the scaffold unaided. I wondered how in such dire circumstances you could still walk and, as I edged my way down that dark tunnel, I realised how he must have felt. It was all right for Charles, though, he only had to go through the ordeal once; I had to do it every bloody Saturday.

Once the tunnel of death had been negotiated, that wait, that long, long wait as the teams were announced. We knew when it was time to sprint out into the light and receive the indifference of the crowd because they would always play the same tune and then it was no turning back. That tune, that fucking tune which took the last vestiges of energy from my legs, was called *Mr Blue Sky* by local superstar pop group ELO. It had distinctive opening bars and, as soon as we heard those, it was time to go. Even now, nearly 35 years later, when I hear those distinctive opening lines of that damned song, my legs still turn to jelly. What would Pavlov and his dogs have made of that?

It's good I can laugh about it now but, back then, I can hardly find words to describe how scared I was (I nearly wrote nervous, but it wasn't nervousness; it was bloody fear). I didn't know it at the time but one day it would be very different and, in a couple of years, it would be a completely different Mick Rathbone who would walk the tunnel and stand on the halfway line waiting for that music before sprinting out onto the pitch – confident, determined and with nerves of steel.

Sir Alf was OK. I really liked and respected him, but he kept putting me in the bloody squad. I had to get away – I felt perhaps if I went to another club far away (preferably somewhere in the Outer Hebrides), I would be all right. Finally, and to my undying gratitude, the penny dropped with Sir Alf. He realised I wasn't going to be the next Bobby Moore and dropped me from the squad. Phew, what a relief. Finally some respite, a chance to get some sleep but no, worse was to come.

In what I now realise was the greatest wind-up in the history of the game, some of the senior players accosted me and started to say it was a joke that I had been dropped. I shouldn't put up with it or otherwise I would get walked over all my career and the only solution in these circumstances was to go straight down to St Andrew's to confront Sir Alf and ask for – no, *demand* – a transfer. I tried to argue that I didn't really think that was neces-sary and I thought I had been treated fairly, but they were adamant. "Trust us," they said.

What happens when a naive, inexperienced 18-year-old locks horns with one of the greatest figures in British footballing history and a man known not to suffer fools?

I drove from the training ground to his office at St Andrew's in my Daf Variomatic and knocked on his door. He said, "Come." Not "Come in", just "Come" – in that classic tone. He was reading a newspaper much larger than my daily *Sun*.

He looked up. "Yes?"

"Look," I stammered. "I want a transfer. I've had enough of being messed around and not given a fair chance, my mind's made up, don't try and talk me out of it, I want to go."

He folded his newspaper and looked at me. His judgement, when delivered, went through me like a matador's sword through a bull. In a totally matter-of-fact, sangfroid way and with those classic clipped tones, he destroyed me in a couple of sentences. "OK," he said. "You can go by all means, but who's going to sign you? You are fucking crap!"

I can laugh now and I have entertained my friends for 35 years with that one. But it was no joke at the time, just another footstep on my personal road to hell. Talk about in like a lion, out like a lamb. The only good thing was I was definitely not going to have to worry about getting a game in the team in the foreseeable future.

Sadly, Sir Alf didn't last much longer and left the club mid-season. Then the 'Bald Eagle' landed.

Jim Smith was to save my career and my life – but not for another year or so.

Known as the Bald Eagle for obvious reasons, he used to shout and scream so much that his whole head went red or even purple on a particularly bad day. He was a good manager, though, and, when the purple had subsided, a nice bloke. I have seen him many times over the years, and we always talk fondly of those times (talk about a selective memory). Jim gave me another chance – thanks for nothing, mate. I was still only 19 and had a good pedigree. The club knew what I could do (unfortunately only in the reserves, though) and, notwithstanding my seriously fucked-up mental state, they could see I was immensely gifted – even if I say so myself – so they tried to persevere with me.

We used to have practice matches all the time and this next incident beautifully demonstrates the effect that confidence – or lack of it – can have and, more to the point, that I was not the only one suffering from a complete absence of it.

In this particular match, I am playing left back for the first team and my best mate, Steve Fox, is playing right wing for the reserves. The game starts and I am directly up against my pal. For the first 45 minutes, Steve destroys me. He, full of tricks, vigour and confidence; me, leaden-legged, unable to turn, breathe or pass the ball to Trevor. Half time comes and Jim calls the teams in to the centre of the pitch – bollockings for some (me) and pats on the back for others (Steve).

"Right, I am going to make a few changes. Mick Rathbone, not good enough, son, you go over there and join the reserves for the second half. Stevie, well done, son, good half, you come and play in the first team now."

Into the second half and I am still playing against Steve, but now he's not getting a kick, he can't control the ball, his passes are going astray and he's lost that change of pace. And me? Now I am tackling and overlapping and crossing and smiling and enjoying the game and my legs are working properly – full of power.

If ever there was an anecdote to demonstrate the importance of confidence, then surely that is it.

I was still getting the odd appearance in the first team. I used to be terrified the games would be on *Match of the Day* and hence expose my shortcomings to the whole nation. Back in the '70s, there was no live football, except the FA Cup final, and the only televised soccer was the one game featured on *Match of the Day* on a Saturday night. I had already suffered one humiliation the season before when my frailties were so cruelly exposed to the watching nation by Steve Heighway at Anfield and I was fearful of the same thing happening again.

If the game was going to be televised, then the cameras would turn up at St Andrew's at about 3pm on the Friday afternoon. I would drive down there alone and with a knot in the pit of my stomach, just to see if the camera crews were setting up their equipment. What on earth was the point of that? OK, if the cameras weren't there, I could relax up to a point – just the 30,000 fans to appease. However, if to my shock and horror they were being set up, then my body would go into total meltdown.

In hindsight, I shouldn't have worried, as I was going to get a sleepless night anyway. By now, the fans had taken a definite dislike to me; my name was now greeted by a deep groan when the teams announced over the tannoy. That didn't exactly fill me with confidence. I can't really complain, though, because I was crap, absolutely crap. I had lost my way completely and, to be honest, I was just going through the motions. I had stopped wearing my shin pads in the faint hope of getting injured but even that stroke of luck evaded me. Would I really have preferred a fucking broken leg at that stage? Was it really that bad?

Yes.

I was still trying my best and still really loved the club but, to put it as succinctly as possible, I was fucked.

People can be so cruel. The neighbours and mom's 'friends' ensured she was informed every time I was awarded a meagre five out of ten in the newspaper for my performance. I went to the local pub, The Wheatsheaf, on a Sunday evening and some of my brother's friends would come in one by one and inform me (with relish) how much stick I had got on the local radio phone-in. Thanks.

Probably the worst aspect of the suffering I went through during that period was the effect it was having on my mother. She never said anything to me; she didn't have to. I knew she was hurting just as badly as I was. To see her little boy reduced to this shell must have been so hard for her. I had always been so happy. Full of confidence, optimistic, enthusiastic and always the best – at football, academically, athletics, everything. Just a young guy with the world at his feet.

We never spoke about it and haven't to this day, but when you are as close as my mom and I are, you just know. I could see it in her eyes every Sunday after reading the match reports or callously being reminded of my poor performances by 'well-wishers', but good days would come, days when she would again sit in the stand and glow with pride at her son's performances and all the good things people were saying about him.

It was during this awful period that I developed my deeply unhealthy obsession with my player rating mark, the merit mark given to every player by the *Sunday People*, based on the reporter's valuation of each player's performance. There was a table at the foot of the page that described what each mark meant. Ten was 'Out of this World', nine 'Excellent', eight 'Very Good', seven 'Good', six 'Average' and five (the lowest mark) meant 'Poor Performance'. During that period, I think I must have held the record for consecutive fives. What I wouldn't have given for the luxury of a six. There was no escaping that stigma of a five. It meant even people who never went to the game knew you were playing shit.

I used to lie awake at night following a match, waiting for the newspaper to arrive – the footsteps on the gravel, the bark of the dog and the thump of the letterbox. I would climb out of bed on unsteady legs and make my way down the stairs, clutching the banister for support with my heart racing. Please be a six. Just this once, I did two good passes. I would pick up the newspaper and nervously flick through the sports pages until I found our report and, sure enough, week in week out there it was, as expected – Rathbone: five. It became as big a Sunday morning tradition as the fried breakfast. At least once I had got my five, I could go back to bed and try and get a few hours' sleep.

Once I got up at about 3am and drove into the centre of Birmingham to New Street Station to meet the early morning express train up from London which, back in those days, delivered the papers from Fleet Street. I purchased my *Sunday People* from the railway platform and flicked through the pages in the murky pre-dawn light. Yes, there it was – sure as eggs and bacon – Rathbone: five. At least I got some extra sleep that night.

For a short period, I even stopped buying the wretched paper. Simple enough? Afraid not, some bastard would still go out of his way to let me know I got a five. Even later in my career when I was performing so well I still couldn't really unwind and enjoy Sundays until I had checked my mark in the *Sunday People*.

Of course, the whole thing was nonsense, and what does one man passing judgement from the stands really know? How can one person accurately mark the whole 22 players? The saving grace to the whole episode would come some years later when all the newspapers started using this marking system. As you could get five in one and eight in another for the same performance, it started to show the marks up for the nonsense they were. I'm glad to say that later in my career I got eights and nines sometimes, my name in bold type as owner of the best mark and thus man of the match – just not at Birmingham City.

My very worst experience with the marks, though, happened during this period. Again, the same ordeal – the paperboy's footsteps, the dog barking, the thud of the letterbox, the shuffle down the stairs on jelly-legs, the nervous seeking out of the match report for the final and inevitable acceptance of the 'five' before the dejected trek back up the stairs. But not on this occasion.

"Oh my fucking God no, please, please no. How can that be?" I sank to my knees, barely able to take in the absolute horror of what I had just seen. There it was in bold type, the absolute and undeniable low point of my life – Rathbone: four!

That just can't be, there is no such thing. But as I scanned the grid at the bottom I realised with total shock there had been a change – eight was 'Very Good', seven was 'Good', six 'Average', five 'Poor Performance', four 'Stinker'.

STINKER. Fucking stinker.

Jesus Christ, I had plunged to a new low. I quickly checked all the other reports – no fours, no fours. Oh my God, they had invented a special category just for me. Stood there that Sunday morning in the hallway, I think I truly hit rock bottom.

However, there was to be another gut-wrenching twist. It transpired that one of the other Sunday papers was considering marking the players from one to 22 depending on their performance. The player who was considered to be the best on the pitch would be awarded the mark of 22, while the player considered to have been the worst on the pitch (me) would be awarded a solitary one. That news really freaked me out. No way would my fragile mindset cope with the inevitability of that mark of one and the associated honour of being considered the very worst player on the pitch.

I think that rumour cost me about five nights' sleep until Ricky Sbragia, who became a great mate and went on to manage Sunderland, admitted he had made it up just to wind me up. Please excuse me if I didn't see the funny side of that one, Ricky.

And then there were the boos from the terraces. The fans would probably say, "Too bad, mate, that's life, you chose to be a footballer. It's not like you are in a war zone or living in abject poverty in the Third World. Don't be such a bloody wimp and pull yourself together. We pay our money and we have the right to boo who we want."

My answer to that would be that they are right and I am certainly not proud of myself, but I would also say this: "You try it. You try being on the end of all that stuff when you are only 19 and see how you cope. The next time you hurl abuse, ask yourself if you would like it. If any amount of money is worth it."

During the week, I tried to live as normal a life as possible, going out for a pint or playing snooker with Kevin Dillon, Mark Dennis and Pat Van Den Hauwe. These lads who were all a year younger than me had got in the team and done well. I really envied them.

Meanwhile, the nightmare was growing all the time. It had now reached the point where I would try to do anything to spare myself from the ongoing ordeal. At training we could either wear a light blue hooded top or a red tracksuit top depending on our own personal preference. The players wore a mixture of both. The teams for the five-a-side were chosen quickly at the end of the session based on the top you had on – light blues at one end, red tops at the other. I used to wait in the kit room until the very last minute to see what colour Trevor had put on, so I could quickly change into the other one and thus avoid being on his side in the little game.

Yes, I know – pathetic, weak and unprofessional. Guilty as charged and, actually, totally unfair on Trevor who was OK really, a good bloke. His only crime was he was too bloody good. Looking back now, I can hardly identify with the poor pathetic creature I had become.

Once, we were due to play West Bromwich Albion at their ground. It was a midweek match and, therefore, an evening kick-off. I was selected to play at right back. That in itself was bad enough but even more worryingly I would probably be up against their star player – the legendary Scottish left winger Willie Johnston. Fast, aggressive, cocky, skilful (him, not me). I was dreading it. I had been having nightmares about him all week. The team coach left St Andrew's for the short ride to the Hawthorns. I was close to being comatose with fear. It had been raining heavily all day. As the coach was about to pull into the ground, there was a steward in a fluorescent coat standing in the middle of the road with his arms outstretched. He was shaking his head and mouthing words; he was trying to tell us something. What was it? What was he trying to tell us?

"Match off," I lip-read. "Waterlogged pitch, match off."

I will never forget the kindness that stranger did me that night. Thanks mate, there is a God.

I was totally ashamed of what I had become, but I am only being honest and telling you what it was like. Praying for a game to be postponed was pathetic, especially when I used to be so gutted as a schoolboy player if I turned up for a match and the pitch was frozen that I ended up crying and begging the ref to play the game even on the ice.

I admit I was a coward – but a mightily relieved coward. It is hard to put into words just how terrified of playing I had become, but I will try. One Friday night, before an away game at Bolton early the following season, we were staying in a hotel in nearby Blackburn. By this time, I had taken to staying awake for as long as I could to make the game seem as far off as possible but, of course, eventually, no matter how you try to fight it, you are over-whelmed by sleep. Then, you know what it's like when you wake up in the morning all nice and warm and dreamy and, for a second or two, you aren't quite sure exactly where you are or what day it is. We've all had those little magic moments where you initially think it's a working day, then suddenly realise it's actually a lovely, leisurely Sunday lie-in and you roll over and happily drop off again. Well, in this case in Blackburn, the exact opposite happened. Match day. Oh God, no. It hit me like a ton of bricks.

On that particular morning – once I had managed to drag myself out of bed – all the squad went for a walk together before the pre-match meal, and I recall walking up a steep hill with really nice houses on it. To cut a long story short, the road we walked up at the back of the Saxon Hotel is the road I now live on. What a coincidence. Even now, 35 years on, I sometimes look out of my kitchen window and remember me in my Birmingham City tracksuit, walking past absolutely shitting myself.

How many more examples of my demise do you want? Don't worry, there are plenty and, to this day, every single one of them is burnt into my memory. Once, we played Arsenal at home and drew 3-3. It was a remarkable match in that Trevor scored a hat-trick for us and 'Supermac' Malcolm MacDonald scored one for them. Late in the game, when we were leading 3-2 I think (quite a novelty in those days), Arsenal were on the attack. I will never forget what happened next – the memory of slap when the ball thudded off Supermac's forehead as he out-jumped me at the far post and equalised with a bullet-header is as clear today as it was then.

I am not a biomechanist or a neurophysicist but, clearly when your legs are like jelly, it is very hard to jump. Apparently, giraffes can't jump at all, but they do have long necks so I suppose a giraffe might have got away with it against Supermac. Not me, though, at 5'10" and with a normal neck. The ball was crossed into the box, an all-white ball in those days. I remember watching it floating towards me, spinning tantalisingly, just waiting to be headed. Unfortunately, not by me. I felt Supermac's arm on my shoulder and his body pressed up against mine as we both prepared to leap. Prepared to leap just about sums up my effort as he climbed above me and powerfully headed the ball home.

To a man, my fellow defenders rounded on me and, to be fair, I didn't blame them because it was my fault. My fault they scored, my fault they equalised, my fault we didn't win. My fault.

Another time I was playing at left back at St Andrew's and Trevor was over on the right wing. It was a typical game – Trevor was having a blinder and I was playing like a blind man. He performed a magnificent piece of ball control, beating two men before hitting a majestic crossfield pass perfectly into my path.

It was brilliant, what a player. I felt like applauding, but thought better of it. I was running, in open field, towards the ball with the opportunity of advancing at speed up the left flank and delivering an accurate cross (well, accurate if you were sat in Row Z). There was no one within 20 yards of me. I focused on the ball rolling relentlessly towards me and became transfixed by it, almost mesmerised by it, hypnotised by it.

It was a bit like that BBC production of *War and Peace* which was serialised in the early '70s. There is one bit where the hero is stood on the edge of the battlefield. He is a Russian nobleman, fighting in the Battle of Borodino against Napoleon, when a cannonball lands about 20 yards away and starts rolling towards him. He is similarly transfixed – mesmerised just like me. He becomes unable to detach himself from this fixation, unable to move, unable to react to it. Eventually it blows up in his face.

That's pretty much what happened to me. Obviously, the ball didn't blow up in my face (unfortunately, our fans might have said), but such was my fixation with it that I was unable to react and thus unable to control it. It rolled past my foot and out for a throw-in.

There was hell to pay.

I watched it trickle over the line and heard the fury of the fans. I witnessed their hands being flung up in anger and despair. I stared into the mass of angry spectators, their faces contorted with rage at my latest aberration.

One thing I will definitely never forget is the fan who kindly took the considerable trouble to run all the way down the aisle – from the very back of the Kop to the edge of the pitch – to abuse me. I can still see that guy clearly today with his long hair, big sideburns, wide jeans, checked shirt and Birmingham City scarves tied around his wrists.

I am sure it was my old chemistry teacher.

The one thing, the only thing, I take any pride or comfort in from those days is for all the fear and hostility I never bottled it, never once faked injury or phoned in sick. I always somehow managed to dig deep and drag myself over that white line.

What a bloody hero.

In a futile attempt to avoid public ridicule, I tried to disguise myself with the trendy curly perm beloved of the '70s footballer. I went into Rackham's in the city centre and plucked up the courage. There was the standard £8 perm or the deluxe £10 one. I went for the cheap one and, ever since then, when I look in the mirror and lament the loss of my barnet, I always wonder if all that is the result of me trying to save two fucking quid.

It didn't work anyway – I was still shit, still lambasted in public, but now I had a shit hairstyle to complete the whole sorry picture.

When I look back on all those collective nightmares from my Birmingham days, the one that stands out and was probably the worst performance was against Derby County. In fact, it could possibly have been the worst ever performance any Blues player has given in the club's 136-year history.

I played right back at Derby County, up against their talented Welsh winger, Leighton James. He roasted me for the full 90 minutes. Mind you, given the mental state I was in, my granny could have roasted me. When the final whistle went, I was devastated, close to tears. Leighton came over to me and said in his Welsh accent, "Don't worry son, I have roasted better full backs than you will ever fucking be."

Thanks for those kind words, mate. We were to meet a few years later in the big East Lancashire derby when he was playing for Burnley and so much had changed for me as a player.

So, Leighton, I never forgot those kind 'words of

encouragement'. I wonder if he knew, or cared, how much those remarks, delivered in that callous manner, hurt all those years ago. I would love to take him for a pint and just ask him quite simply, "Why? Why say those things?" He would probably say it was "just harmless banter". Oh yes, that harmless banter again.

The Birmingham nightmare would soon be over for me, but its conclusion would be the result of a bizarre set of circumstances.

By March 1979 I had gone completely. I couldn't kick the ball straight to save my life. I was mentally shattered. If this had been a war, I would have been sent home with shellshock. I played another first-team game. I can't even remember who it was against. And guess what? I was shit – again.

The team were struggling. It was ugly. Jim Smith was purple all the time. He called a meeting on the Monday morning and tore a strip out of all of us. That was OK, I was expecting it anyway, and the thing about a bollocking is that after a certain number they lose their impact. However, after his tirade had ceased Joe Gallagher, one of the senior players and an excellent centre half, got up. This wasn't like Joe; he was one of the senior players we liked the best and one of those strong silent types. What happened next, although I was too stunned to realise at the time, was a series of totally unfair and unjustified personal attacks on the young players in the team. I can still remember it virtually word-perfect as every syllable was delivered like a knockout punch.

"Mark Dennis, you fucking, fucking big-headed bastard, you arrogant cunt, who do you think you are? Mickey Rath, you think you are fucking great, but you are shit. (That wasn't entirely true – I thought I was shit too.) And as for you, Kev, if my kid turns out like you, I will fucking well strangle it."

Looking back now, he might have been right – although I don't agree – but the manner in which he said it and to isolate the young players in such a way just seemed so unfair. That was the final straw. For the first time in three years, I felt some anger –

at last – after all that time of being a pathetic, passive excuse for a man.

Jim Smith concluded the meeting by thanking Joe for having the passion and balls to stand up and say what he had (fucking big deal, Joe, well done) and finished off proceedings with the time-honoured rhetoric: "Right, now that's it, we've got a big game Saturday and we need some fucking points, so if any of you fuckers don't want to play, then I suggest you stay behind after the meeting and fucking well tell me."

Of course, it was just rhetoric and was meant more as a warning to get your finger out than an invitation to chat, but fuck it, I had had enough of this shit, this moaning, pressure, constant criticising, this fucking unpleasantness. When the players filed out of the meeting for training, I remained in my seat.

I just sat there until the room emptied and there was only Jim and me in the room.

"What the fuck do you want?"

"You know you said anybody who doesn't want to play for you should stay behind and tell you – well, I don't want to play anymore."

"You fucking what?" He was going purple again.

"I've got a job lined up at Dyno Rod and I can start this week."

Even writing this now, some 30-odd years later, it seems shocking yet hilarious in equal measures. How could somebody who was so highly academic he could have pursued a career in medicine, who had captained Birmingham and Warwickshire schools, won numerous cross country races and played for the England youth team, be reduced to this pathetic figure, happy to get a job cleaning other people's drains for a living? That should give you some idea of the state of mind I had been reduced to.

Whose fault was it? Trevor who was aloof and intimidated me? The coaches who shouted and constantly bollocked us for every mistake? The players who moaned at us when we didn't meet their expectations? The fans who crucified us?

The answer is none of them; it wasn't any of their faults. This is professional sport and, just as it can be glamorous and uplifting it can also be ugly and cruel and only the mentally-strong can survive. Certainly, being the local lad and subjected to those additional pressures was a big factor for me, and trying to fit into a team of players you had previously worshipped as a boy proved especially difficult – for me, anyway.

I have thought about what happened many times over the years and I see things so differently now. The players were all OK really, decent guys who just moaned a bit. I was too sensitive. What to them was harmless fun and good-natured banter was perceived by me to be cruel mickey-taking and harsh criticism.

Interestingly, I met Joe Gallagher a couple of years ago – some 30 years after that ghastly incident. Everton were playing at West Bromwich Albion and I was on the pitch before the game handing some drinks out when I heard a voice shouting, "Mickey, Mickey."

I knew it had to be somebody from my distant past because everybody has been calling me 'Baz' for so long now. I looked across. Incredibly, it was Joe (he hadn't changed a bit). He was doing a bit of commentating for the local station at weekends and working for Land Rover during the week. He was so friendly and appeared genuinely pleased to see me. He informed me he had followed my career with interest over the years and used to tell all his mates at Land Rover, proudly, he had been a team-mate of mine. Such a lovely fellow.

But back to the fearsome Jim Smith – I sat there waiting for the explosion and screaming that was sure to follow. But nothing. He smiled and put his arm around my shoulder.

"OK," he said with genuine affection. "I understand what you have been going through – don't worry, take a few days off, don't do anything hasty, you are far too good a player. Let me get you on loan for a month or two away from here where you can relax and start enjoying your football again."

I will never forget what Jim did for me that day, and as I went from success to success and regained my love for football, he was always in my thoughts.

A few days later, I signed for Blackburn Rovers on a three-month loan deal and my football career belatedly started.

That all seems such a long time ago and I know now I am a completely different character – strong and confident – to the point I can hardly identify with that pathetic teenager. I have reflected on that unhappy period of my life and my extreme reactions to it many, many times over the years and still don't really know what conclusions to draw or who to blame. The hard facts don't lie – my career (if you can call that collection of disasters a career) never took off at Birmingham. I didn't have the bottle, right stuff, balls or moral fibre, the courage required to be a success at the club I loved and supported. In mitigation, I was young, over-sensitive, in awe of my team-mates, had just gone through the trauma of losing my father but, even so, other young local players can and do succeed at their home-town clubs, so it can't just be explained purely in those terms.

But why not me then? Well, after about 30 years of deliberation... I still don't know. Was it cowardly to say to the ferocious Jim Smith I wouldn't play again or was it an act of amazing courage? It's like the old adage of people who commit suicide – cowardly or heroic? I'd prefer to believe what I did took great courage, but I suspect deep down it was the act of a coward.

Along with all this brutal self-analysis, you start to ask yourself what kind of person you are. What makes you tick? What are your strengths and weaknesses? I was recently asked by the sports psychologist at Everton to fill in a form whereby you analysed yourself and basically described how you saw yourself as a person. You had to tick words you thought applied to your personality and finally write, in no more than 100 words, how you would describe yourself as a person.

This is what I wrote: I consider myself to be a gentleman. I only treat people as I would want to be treated myself. I am sensitive, kind and generous. I care about people. I never lose my temper. My glass is always half full. Some people would possibly accuse me of being too nice. I have an outgoing personality, even though intrinsically I am basically a bit shy. My motto for life is this: it's nice to be important but it's much more important to be nice.

Was it Freud who once said something about us being the sum total of our life experiences?

I very much like the person I turned out to be. If I had achieved all the success at Birmingham at the tender age I should have done, then I might now be writing words to the effect that I am a winner, confident, assured, talented, etc. Who knows?

I don't think I would have liked that person half as much.

Chapter Four
RESCUE

With my brand new, stack-heeled cowboy boots making me limp, I arrived at New Street Station to start my train journey to Blackburn. My only previous visit to this Lancashire mill town was that solitary overnight stay the previous season en route to yet another personal disaster at Bolton Wanderers; not exactly fond memories then, but what the hell? Anything was better than staying at St Andrew's. To a Brummie like me who had seldom ventured out of the great metropolis, it was simply 'up north'.

On my way up to Blackburn, I remember reflecting upon the bizarre set of circumstances that had culminated in this journey. I had failed at my hometown club – not through lack of ability but through lack of confidence or, more precisely, lack of moral courage. I felt somewhat bitter about the whole experience. I knew it was ultimately down to my own lack of personal confidence but, at that time, I also felt strongly that the coaches and players were partly responsible too.

I suppose I should have been grateful for the second chance, but I wasn't really under any great illusions that things would be different this time – it would only end up being a brief interlude before my destiny was fulfilled and I took my rightful place, sluicing out the toilets of the good people of Birmingham.

As we travelled north, the scenery started to change. It was an unusual landscape – hilly and full of chimneys – but strangely picturesque. Ironically, the song being repeatedly played on another passenger's transistor radio was the current No. 1 single, *I will Survive*, by Gloria Gaynor, and that just about summed up how I felt.

I was met at the station by John Pickering – caretaker manager of Rovers and a great guy. Sadly, he died in 2001, and is loved and missed by all those who knew him. He dropped me off at a hotel (let's be honest, bed and breakfast) called The Woodlands. John's parting words were, "'Bails' will come round later."

John Bailey did indeed come round later in his red Ford Capri – he was Blackburn's star player, as he explained to me. We became firm friends and I am eternally grateful to him as he was partly responsible for me meeting my wife.

I was just 20 then, Bails was 22. He informed me he would take me for a slurp with 'The Birch' – Alan Birchenall. We went to Angels nightclub in Burnley. I was really drunk after only three pints of lager – I hadn't really drunk that much since the incident in Holland three years previously. When I got back to my room I vomited into my suitcase, all over my clothes for the next day. I went to training for the very first time with my new club with a terrible hangover.

How ironic that I had somehow contrived to make the same mistake again – to turn up for an important 'first impressions' training session with a raging hangover. Who said lightning doesn't strike in the same place twice? It does with prats like me.

I walked into the dressing room and Birch introduced me: "This is Mick Rathbone, but we will call him Basil (after '30s actor Basil Rathbone)." That was in March 1979, and the name stuck. I am now known by everybody as Baz – my wife and mom call me Michael, but to everybody else I am Baz.

To my surprise and total delight, I was greeted by everybody at the club and in the town itself with something approaching reverence – a whole new sensation for me. Being from a First

Division club and an England youth international obviously counted for something up here. My God, I can't begin to tell you how good that felt after what I had been through. The lads and the staff were great. They were genuinely friendly, full of banter and mickey-taking as you would expect, but this time it was done good-naturedly and with affection and respect, which was a whole new ball game.

I tasted the 'Lancashire Life' – cobbled streets, gravy on chips, steak puddings and flat caps. What a great place. I still live there now and I consider myself a true Blackburn lad 30 years on. The people of Blackburn were and are the salt of the earth, so friendly and genuine. All of a sudden, everybody wanted to know me. I was instantly respected. I was almost a star player. There were no Villa fans to give me stick because I played for the Blues or, more importantly, no Blues fans to give me stick because I played for the Blues.

It all felt so very different. I felt wanted, important, but most of all I felt respected. My self-esteem was starting to return and – whisper it – I was really looking forward to playing. Yes, me. It had been such a long time since I had experienced that feeling.

Why did I feel so much better up here? Well, nobody knew me, nobody expected too much from me, so I felt the slate had been wiped clean and it was a fresh start. When I went into town, nobody shouted, "Wanker." In fact they came over and asked for my autograph or asked the classic question all fans ask and to which there is no answer: "Are we gonna win Saturday, Baz?" At night I walked up to the West View public house (without Bails), and people came over, sat, talked, bought me a pint and spoke to me with genuine affection. I felt so much at home. This was it. This was how it should have been at Birmingham – to be fair, if I had played a bit better it probably would have been.

Rovers were actually doomed to relegation that season, bottom of the old Second Division and needing snookers to survive. When I got there we had 16 games to go. I made my Rovers debut in March 1979 at the Racecourse Ground against Wrexham. We lost

2-1 but that didn't matter one iota because, for the first time in ages, I enjoyed the match. I played well. I actually wanted the ball to come to me. I didn't want the game to end. My legs weren't filled with lead. I had tons of speed and energy. I was shouting for the ball. I had lots of confidence – it had been so long that I'd played with any self-belief.

It just all seemed so easy, so effortless. Was it easier? Was the standard inferior? Well, up to a point, it had to be. I was playing in a lower division, but I prefer to think my improved performance was more down to the fact I had regained voluntary control of my fucking lower limbs. Was it a different style of play? It was for me, because now I wasn't bombarding the people in Row Z with my passes.

After the game I remember being very emotional – a mixture of joy, relief and almost bitterness at the terrible experiences of the last few years. But this was different now, this was how it was meant to be. I could do it. I could be a player.

The rest of that season was nothing short of brilliant. Although relegation was unavoidable, John Pickering rallied us and we had some great results – away at Stoke and Sunderland in particular, who were at the time first and second in the league. I was starting to get a good reputation. People were saying good things about me now on the radio, in the newspapers and on the phone-ins. People were saying I was a very talented player again and that felt so good – not out of vanity, but sheer relief that my career had not been completely destroyed at Birmingham.

I loved the players – John Bailey, Alan Birchenall, John Waddington, Noel Brotherston, Derek Fazackerley, Paul Round, Glen Keeley, Simon Garner and Joe Craig. Or as I knew them – Bails, Birch, Waddy, Noel, Faz, Roundy, Keels, Garns and Craigy.

The most important thing was that we were equals. Now, instead of lying awake all night terrified of hearing the crunch of the paperboy's feet on the gravel, I would race up to the local newsagents to read all the good things people were writing about me. It was footballing paradise, and the pride I would feel over the next eight years every time I pulled on that fantastic blue-and-white-halved shirt never diminished.

However, through all this rediscovery of me as a player, one thing had completely slipped my mind. I was technically only on loan and, therefore, still a Birmingham player and, horror of horrors, they insisted I returned to them at the end of the season. It was a real body blow when John Pickering told me Jim Smith had been on the phone and wouldn't let me move to Blackburn permanently. I was totally shattered. One thing was for sure, though – I couldn't and wouldn't go back. Back to the fear, the frustration of being crap through no other reason than nerves, back to being criticised, undervalued, back to the reserves. I decided extreme situations call for extreme measures, so I plucked up my courage and phoned the Bald Eagle.

Not to put too fine a point on it, I begged him to let me stay. I pleaded with him. I told him I could never do it at Birmingham. Again, he showed a side of him that few people knew. Understanding and compassionate, he relented – although the stingy sod insisted on a fee of £40,000 which was a fortune for a provincial club to pay for a 20-year-old, especially a provincial club that had just been relegated. But with the generous help of the club chairman, David Brown (co-founder of the Graham & Brown wallpaper company), the deal was done and I signed a three-year contract at Rovers on £120 per week.

As I had been away from Birmingham on loan for three months prior to my permanent signing, there was no real impact or reaction to my departure – except a huge sigh of relief from the fans! I did pop back one day to say goodbye and collect my spare boots, but all the players were off and my boots had disappeared. A fitting end, I suppose.

In those days, players received five per cent of any transfer fee, so I took my £2,000 and bought an Alfasud motor car. Things were finally looking up. Young, well-off (relatively), posh car (for the '70s), and much more importantly, respected as a footballer,

I went away for the summer break truly happy and at peace with myself – I had confronted and overcome all the demons that had threatened to shatter me. I felt I had been right to the edge of the precipice and stepped back at the last minute. I had no illusions I could ever be anything other than a decent reliable player – some of the damage done at Birmingham was permanent – but compared to the shell of a player I had become there, I was only too happy to settle for that.

That initial loan period and subsequent signing started an eight-year spell of great personal and professional happiness. I established a wonderful rapport with the Blackburn supporters, married a fantastic local girl and became part of this fine town. I was flattered and somewhat choked a couple of years ago when I ran on to Ewood Park to tend to a player and there was some sporadic applause and a few cries of "Go on Baz" from some of the Rovers fans – presumably the older ones.

But it would take time for me to earn that respect from the fans. It wasn't all plain sailing after I completed my transfer and, within a few months, I faced a completely new and unexpected set of problems.

That close season – the summer of 1979 – had been class. I think I was entitled to feel proud of myself, a commodity that had been in short supply for several years. Troy romped home in the Derby, Maggie romped home in the general election and the Alfasud quickly turned into a blue Ford Capri and then, in quick succession, a very fast Triumph Dolomite Sprint, my dream car – teal blue, OBN 894R, black roof with a sunroof, overdrive. Three cars in three months – a perfect way to get rid of any surplus cash.

The '70s were nearing an end now – lapels were coming in, ties getting thinner, trousers tapered at the bottoms, shoes with pointy toes, mullets and New Wave music was on the radio. I was so looking forward to going back to the chimneys, cobbled streets, gravy on chips and famous blue-and-white halves of Blackburn Rovers. It was with great excitement and anticipation that I packed my cases, slid them into the boot of the 'Dolly' and set off back to Blackburn – or home as I was already calling it.

What was it like to be young, free, single, somewhat famous (OK only in Blackburn), and reasonably well-off? I had a newfound confidence and new-found self-esteem. Mercifully, I had once again become the same outgoing, fun-loving guy I had been at school and in my first year at Birmingham City. Regrettably, though, I was about to fall into the same trap that even now, more than 30 years on, young players are still falling into.

You can't put an old head on young shoulders, they say, and within a few weeks I would be failing again as a footballer. However, this time it was not through lack of confidence or self-belief, but lack of maturity and discipline.

I had stayed in the Woodlands Hotel while on loan the previous season, but now I had to find some digs to live in. We had signed Russell Coughlin from Manchester City. He was 19 years old, from Swansea, a great little lad and a good player. He was stocky and compact (that's being kind) but immensely skilful, and we became good pals.

We decided we would share digs on our return to Blackburn, so in July 1979 little Russ and I moved into Trevor Close in Blackburn to share a bedroom in the house owned by the delightful Harry and Hilda Wilkinson – great people, sadly both now passed away. So there were me and little Russ – young, free and single, with disposable income, both discovering beer, nightclubs and girls at the same time.

You can probably guess what happened next. I think most nutritionists and sports scientists would agree that boozing seven days a week, regularly staying up until the early hours of the morning and living on crisps, steak puddings, chips and beer is likely to have a detrimental effect on one's physical condition, and slowly but surely, Russ and I drank and ate ourselves out of the game.

Looking back, it was a bloody disgrace the way we conducted ourselves and let down the club that had put so much faith in us, but it seemed fine at the time and when you are young, immature and stupid the penny doesn't really drop until you are a good way down that road to nowhere.

Even when I was in such poor physical condition that I had to walk in the pre-season cross countries – despite the fact I had been a champion 800-metre and cross country runner at school – it still didn't really register that I was on the verge of stealing defeat from the jaws of victory.

Why? Why did I act like such a total idiot to the point that, for the sake of a good night out, I would jeopardise this second chance? I suppose it was the thrill of being away from home, that little bit of ego creeping in now I was one of the 'star players', and certainly an element of not realising the damage I was doing to my body and career.

This is how Russ and I lived: we would get back from training at lunchtime and go straight out for a couple of pints, often down to the Orchard Working Men's Club where it was about five pence a pint. Then we would have a couple of games of pool and five or six pints of cheap beer before returning to the digs for a wash and change at which point our drinking could start in earnest.

We always started proceedings at the Farthings pub just by our digs. We developed a bizarre little ritual in that he would go straight to the bar while I went straight to the jukebox to put on *I will Survive* (ironic or what?). He would then bring the drinks over and I would say, "Bloody hell, Russ, why did you get four pints?"

"Well, you know the boss said to rest and save your legs for the weekend – that's what I am doing, saving my legs," he would reply in his strong South Wales accent.

We always used to laugh, even though we repeated the same jokes every night. Then we set off on our pub crawl, but always ended up back at the Farthings just on the stroke of last orders where we had another couple of pints each, courtesy of Russ's ingenious energy-saving strategy.

Next, it was time for the highlight of the whole evening. We

RESCUE

used to walk to a chippy and Spar shop just up the road. Bearing in mind little Russ had a slight weight problem – no, sorry, a big weight problem – to the extent that our new manager, Howard Kendall, was repeatedly telling him to go on a diet or face the consequences, what happened next was quite incredible.

Russ would go into the Spar and buy an uncut loaf of bread before heading into the chip shop to buy what he affectionately referred to as the "full mog" (that classic delicacy of the region – steak pudding, chips, peas and gravy in a tray). He would then, with an admirable degree of manual dexterity belying the fact he had just had 12 pints of Daniel Thwaites's finest, proceed to hollow out the middle of the uncut loaf before tipping the full mog into the middle of it.

Finally, just before consuming what must have been in the region of 5,000 calories' worth of food, Russ would issue these profound words: "Baz, phone Howard will you and tell him the diet starts tomorrow." We would then laugh hysterically at this well-used and rehearsed joke.

Yes, we had become complete pillocks. But my God, we were having a great time, courtesy of the Danile Thwaites brewery and Hollands Pies. The trouble was it was having a seriously damaging effect on my football.

I was, sadly, back on familiar ground – playing crap. The only difference this time was that it was totally self-induced. The reason my legs weren't functioning now was not down to lack of confidence, but the fact I was out on the piss every night of the week.

Incredibly, I made the starting line-up for the first game of the season at home to Millwall. It was a baking hot day and, not to put too fine a point on it, I was fucking knackered. I was playing like a zombie and had already been responsible for giving away their goal.

I got sent off just after half time for arguing with the referee – difficult to do in those days, but somehow I managed it (maybe he could smell my breath). As I walked along the touchline in

71

disgrace, somebody shouted, "Get him on a health farm, Kendall!" It was a small town and people knew what was going on.

After the game, Howard was going mad at me, saying I had let everybody down and was a fucking disgrace to the shirt. Which, looking back, of course, I was. He banned me for three months but, to be fair, I wasn't even bothered. I was on the slippery slope to Dyno Rod again and it would take something special – miraculous even – to get me out of this nosedive.

But guess what? A few days later, that much-needed miracle happened.

I was in the Beechwood Pub (surprise, surprise), enjoying my new-found freedom with Russ, who was doing nearly as well as me. He had scoffed and boozed his way on to the transfer list. Then I saw this gorgeous girl playing on the fruit machine. I staggered over and apparently made some crude remark about my plums or her melons – you can just imagine it, can't you? I actually half-knew her – she was the sister of John Bailey's girlfriend – and I asked her out on a date.

The rest is history. It was one of those instant attractions where I knew immediately this was the person who I wanted to spend the rest of my life with. Luckily, she felt the same (or so she said – maybe she just wanted to marry a famous footballer, in which case it turned out to be a bad night for her).

We knew then we were destined to be together. We were married within the year and have now been married for nearly 30 years. She saved my life, my career, my self-esteem. Without Julie, there would be no book because there would be no story. They say behind every great man there is a great woman. If I can reverse that theory, I must be an incredible guy.

Julie's parents allowed me to move into their spare room. I had some stability in my private life at last. No more boozing or late nights – just think football. Slowly but surely, and with their help, I rehabilitated myself. I hauled myself back from the brink, started playing well in the reserves, got back into the first team and enjoyed an unbroken seven-year period, when fit, as first-choice full back for Blackburn Rovers. I got my physical fitness back and transformed myself from the clown who had to walk in the cross countries to the guy who won them by a huge margin – all due to that chance meeting. I shudder to think what would have happened to me if Julie had stayed in to wash her hair that night.

I learned a lot from that brief but very traumatic period: how everybody, with a given set of circumstances, has the capacity to self-destruct. It's still happening today. Young players – rich, famous, away from home – history repeating itself. So when I read lurid tales of footballers in the Sunday papers, getting pissed and misbehaving, I think back to my 'off-the-rails' days and understand it's a simple trap to get into, but a bloody difficult one to get out of.

Oh, and if you are interested in what happened to little Russ… when I left the digs to move in with Julie and her family, he was upset because we had become as close as brothers. Not wanting to stay on in the digs on his own for the remainder of the season he moved into some fresh and novel accommodation – his car. Amazingly, he went to live in his little green Chrysler Sunbeam, which he parked in the car park next to Ewood Park. I can still see him now coming into training every day for a shower and a cuppa, toothbrush in mouth, wearing his slippers while whistling the tune to *Travelling Light*.

He signed for Carlisle the following season and went on to have a fine career, playing well into his mid-thirties at a good level of professional football.

"Some are born great, some achieve greatness and some have greatness thrust upon them."

I'm not sure which of these descriptions from Shakespeare's *Twelfth Night* best fits Howard Kendall, but take it from me, that man was great – and still is great. Look up the word 'charisma' in the dictionary and you should find the words 'Howard Kendall' alongside it.

I first met him back in the '70s in my first year as an apprentice at Birmingham. Of all the players who played for the Blues during that period, he was the only one who ever stopped his car on Damson Lane, the long, winding road down to the training ground, to give me a lift. All the rest just drove by; I think some of them even drove through the puddles purposely trying to splash me. Sometimes, during the school holidays, my sister Linda would come with me and he would give her a lift too.

A great player (one season he kept the Blues in the First Division virtually single-handedly) and a fantastic guy. I think he genuinely felt for me when I imploded at Birmingham. He would put his arm around me and try to encourage me which nobody else (especially the coaches) did when I was struggling so badly.

Howard replaced 'Pick' at Blackburn for the start of the 1979/80 season – his first managerial job. He had, and still has, the ability to light up a room when he walks in by his sheer presence and charisma. He knows how to make everybody he comes into contact with feel special – whether by making a cup of tea for the cleaner at Ewood Park or asking my mom for the first dance on the night of my wedding. Talk about having the common touch; he would have made a great Prime Minister.

When Simon Garner's wife gave birth to their first child, Howard made sure she received flowers and champagne. Those small, simple touches engendered a sense of loyalty and affection that all the players shared. He got the best out of everybody and – let's be honest – that was the crux of his job. By whatever means, a manager's job is to get the best out of the players at his disposal.

Howard came to Rovers as player-manager. We had just been relegated to the old Third Division. We started his first season badly and, after about 15 games, were at the wrong end of the table. The crowd were turning, the press were sharpening their pencils and, you know what, he never changed. He never stopped treating everybody, from chairman to cleaner, like they were important and mattered.

Courteous, immaculate and dignified but, in equal measure, shrewd, tough and nobody's fool, Howard then presided over a run that took Rovers to promotion to the Second Division clinched at Bury one balmy night the following spring – and still he never changed, giving out praise and thanks to all while refusing to accept much himself.

Training was simple. No tactics, no running, just light ballwork designed to keep the players sharp. No long tactical sessions like the ones that bore and frustrate the modern footballer. No long team meetings talking up the opposition until everybody is shitting themselves. No, everything was built on the strongest building block of all – team spirit. You see it wasn't about them; it was only ever about us and what we were going to do. In those days when you walked into Ewood Park, you felt *it*. You felt the electricity about the place. This was the place to be and it was Howard who generated that electricity.

In his second season, with virtually the same modest team, he took us to within goal difference of the top division. An incredible record. We were sad when the Ayatollah left (my nickname for him which he seemed to enjoy more than anyone else), but we knew he was destined for greatness, which he achieved at Everton.

Years later, when I was working at Everton myself, I saw a lot of Howard and he always had the same spring in his step and sparkle in his eye.

Just recently my wife and I were house-hunting in Formby in Merseyside and we bumped into Howard. He had not seen Julie since we all did the conga around the car park of the Trafalgar Hotel on our wedding night back in 1981.

"Hi Julie, you look great. How's your Lynn? Tell your mum and dad I was asking after them."

And that conversation more than any other sums up the man.

Chapter Five
THE GOLDEN YEARS

Out with the old, in with the new. Howard Kendall to Everton and
Bob Saxton – or 'Sacko' as he was universally known – to Rovers.

It is the summer of 1981. I am 22 years old, happily married,
now the owner of a black, three-litre Capri, and about to start
my assault on the property ladder. I am the proud father of Max,
the long-haired Alsatian. We are very happy – the perfect family
unit. I am now a battle-hardened veteran of 80 or 90 league
games. Even the Iraq-Iran war with its implications for world
peace or the Toxteth street riots can't diminish my contentment.

All those terrible memories of Birmingham City and the genuine
unhappiness I felt there are fading slowly but surely. The lessons
of my boozy period with Russ are well learned and will not be
repeated. I am proud to be able to call myself a professional
footballer at last. Giving value for money, playing well, week in
week out and, amazingly, enjoying it.

The next six or seven years under Sacko would be my truly
golden period, the time when I finally became the player I should
have been at Birmingham City. Playing with a great bunch of lads
in a good, strong solid team that did the club proud year in year
out under a very good manager.

However, while I was set to enter my finest era as a player, conversely football as a game and a spectator sport was about to go through a very difficult period. This next decade would be scarred by the tragedies at Heysel, Bradford and Hillsborough. On the pitch, defensive, unexciting football predominated, driving the fans away from the decaying old stadiums. Thankfully, by the end of the decade, the Taylor Report had helped to drag the game kicking and screaming into the modern era; all-seater grounds, catering and caring for the safety and comfort of the paying supporters, allied to some subtle rule changes, would eventually breathe fresh life into the declining industry and, gradually, the fans would start to drift back.

While English football in general suffered, Lancashire football, in particular, was the hardest hit. Preston, Burnley, and Bolton (all founder members of the Football League) started to decline. With dwindling crowds, decrepit stadia and failure on the pitch, one by one, they sank to the lowest tier of the professional game. Former greats of those clubs – Tom Finney, Jimmy McIlroy and Nat Lofthouse – witnessed the gradual decline of these once legendary football institutions. It is to the undying credit of their supporters and directors, who so loyally stuck with these fallen giants during that lean period, that today they have all sprung back with new or improved stadia and restored pride and status.

Blackburn Rovers, alone, of those historic Lancashire clubs maintained its standing, and my team-mates and I who played our hearts out at a difficult time for English football should take special credit for the part we played.

Incredibly, during the reign of 'King Sacko', we kept virtually the same team and I believe in particular the defence – TG (Terry Genoe), Bran (Jim Brannigan), Keels (Glen Keeley), Faz (Derek Fazackerley) and I – held some kind of record for playing so many consecutive games together.

In that difficult period we held our own – and then some – against the likes of Leeds, Chelsea, West Ham, Sunderland and Newcastle. Bill Fox, who replaced David Brown as chairman, frequently reminded us of our responsibilities. "This club cannot afford to be relegated. It will go out of business if it is relegated," he told us regularly – and we responded to a man.

With our tiny squad of 15 or 16 players, probably on the lowest wages in the division, we stood firm as friends, fellow professionals and Rovers players, proud to pull on and fight for that famous shirt. The team spirit we developed, I would dare to suggest, had never been seen before and never will be seen again – at Blackburn Rovers or any other club.

I remember on Sacko's first day at the club he called Noel 'Stan' Brotherston (sadly now deceased – a marvellous talent but, more importantly, a marvellous man) and me together before training. I was left back and Stan was left wing. In a strange parody of Jesus's sermon on the mount, he sat us down on the warm, dry grass and preached the sermon according to St Sacko. He instructed us: "Be good friends, care for each other, go out and socialise with your wives together. You will find you become so close on a Saturday that you will have formed a bond so strong that you will ensure you give everything for each other and the rest of the team. If one of you is struggling, then the other one will go that extra yard to help him, and vice versa."

Talk about Mourinho. This was Sacko back in the early '80s – a man ahead of his time.

That *esprit de corps* ran through the whole team, and the whole club and those years, somewhat belatedly, finally made a man out of me.

If I close my eyes now, I can still see all the lads' faces and smell the liniment, the Vicks Vapour Rub, the boot polish and, of course, those Hollands Pies. We trained in the big country park, whatever the weather, and met up every Wednesday night, whatever the weather, at the Hare and Hounds or The Knowles.

At the risk of sounding simplistic and making the nutritionists choke on their energy bars, a few pints never hurt anybody. The benefits of socialising and bonding over a pint and the camaraderie it produces are worth a million times more than the sterile and almost impersonal atmospheres that pervade some modern clubs.

You can't even get a pint in the players' bars any more. Before all the killjoys start digging out the research to try and prove that alcohol is the great Satan and should be completely avoided, they should first consider this: football is about people performing in the entertainment industry. Footballers are human beings, not lab rats. Getting all the players together on a Wednesday night for a couple of pints and a sing-song or a game of darts will not affect your result on a Saturday. Sorry, I am wrong. It may affect your results; it will make them better.

I played nearly 300 games for Rovers. We won some, lost some and drew some but, generally, for the size of the club and the assets we had at our disposal, we enjoyed great success and continually punched above our weight with several top-six finishes and some good cup runs.

The preparation for matches in those days was totally different to the modern game. For home games, I used to wake up fairly late. My wife brought toast, a cup of tea and the newspaper up to the bedroom. I would be nervous. Not scared any more – just nervous. I didn't really enjoy being nervous (who does?) but I knew myself by now and I realised this feeling was the norm on the morning of the game. To clarify, this was nothing like how I had felt when I woke up on the morning of Birmingham games – that was fucking terror. I also knew by now that when I got to Ewood Park the simple act of removing my tie would make all those nerves magically disappear.

After breakfast in bed I would get up and take Max to the park (I don't think he ever got nervous). When I got back, I would put on my suit and eat the biggest omelette you have ever seen (it would have made a great episode of the reality TV series, *Man v Food*). I used to consume this monster meal at noon, three hours prior to kick-off.

Now before the nutritionists gnash their teeth in disapproval, it was OK, no problem. I felt great. I felt great in the warm-up, great in the game. You can say whatever you like about nutrition, digestion and preparation, but I ain't listening because I felt great (and I'd had a few cans of lager the night before).

I would then drive the three miles to Ewood Park. In those days we all lived locally – probably because we couldn't afford to live anywhere more salubrious. That was another big reason why you felt a great affinity to the club you played for, and why you felt so close to the club and responsible to the town for the fate of that club.

My wife would come to every home game. She always told me I was man of the match, even when I knew I wasn't. We would park on the lunar landscape that was the 'Little Wembley' car park. Cries of "Go on Baz" as we walked the hundred yards to the players' entrance pursued by a couple of fans with autograph books. You could feel the atmosphere starting to build. This was my most nervous moment – that initial entering of the ground. Greetings from the doorman and the inevitable asking of the time-honoured question: "Are we gonna win today, Baz?" God knows. I hope so, otherwise the weekend will be a write-off, and I need the bonus.

Push open the home team dressing room door and the magic would begin – oh those smells. Those marvellous life-defining smells: the liniment, always the liniment mixed with leather and boot polish, Vicks Vapour Rub and Deep Heat. The lads all assembled, laughing, joking, shaking hands, keyed up with common purpose.

And then, there it was, looming ahead. The Holy Grail.

What is the Holy Grail? What does it signify? Some say it is the cup Christ drank from, some argue it is merely a metaphor that can mean different things to different people which doesn't need to be something tangible but more a focus of something special, even spiritual, in one's life.

In that case, I was now looking up at my Holy Grail – hung up, washed and ironed with its back to me. The Blackburn Rovers No. 3 shirt – correction, *my* Blackburn Rovers No. 3 shirt. As far as I was concerned, nobody else should be allowed to wear that shirt and, for the best part of eight years – injuries notwithstanding – nobody did.

The simple act of just taking the shirt from the hanger and putting it on was deeply symbolic to me. I had been through so much, so many bad times, that just to have that blue-and-white-halved shirt in my hands meant more than words could ever say.

Then off came the tie and I would be transformed, energised, slightly hyper, and ready to go. Everything else was out of my mind. I'd get changed and feel the hairs rise on the back of my neck as I slipped the shirt over my head – my shirt. Finally, I knew why John Roberts had spat on the team sheet at Birmingham, now I understood.

Quick team meeting – basic, short and to the point. Not too much information – let's face it, most of the lads had failed their 11-plus. Quick cup of tea, lots of sugar – the nutritionists are beside themselves by this point – I still felt great.

In came the referee to check the studs. Then the bell sounded. The bell that previously would have sucked the last vestiges of power from my legs now produced a rush of adrenalin-fuelled energy that could have powered the floodlights. Shouting and encouraging each other, Sacko's last words and then the final ritual – the team spirit was handed out. Keels was responsible for getting the bottle of whisky out of the physio's bag before screaming, "All the best" and having a good swig before passing it to the next man. To TG, then Faz, Bran and me (I only pretended to drink it as I never got over that attempt on my life in Holland), then one by one all the rest of the boys.

Out we rushed, the roar of the crowd, the adrenalin surging through my muscles. Exhilaration, warriors, them or us. The whistle to release us from any final knots of tension. Running, heading, tackling, overlapping, noise, ebb and flow, cut and thrust, the fans right behind us. Shouts of "Go on Baz" as I raced forward, deafening noise, fans chanting the players' names, then my name. For me, they used to chant, "Hello, hello, Rambo Rathbone, Rambo Rathbone, hello, hello" in tribute to my fearless buccaneering style (I hope).

Trevor Francis, Sir Alf Ramsey, Bald Eagle, Maggie Thatcher,

Winston Churchill, Horatio Nelson, are you watching? Watch me go.

Then that winning goal, and when the final whistle sounded and you'd played well and won, believe me when I tell you that nothing in the world compares to that feeling – nothing. People may say, "Oh come on, it's only a game. What about the birth of your kids? What about other important moments in your private life? Other success? No, sorry (Charlotte, Lucy and Oliver), there was nothing like that final whistle after a famous victory.

Did I still carry the scars of that experience at Birmingham to the extent that every subsequent success became part of an ongoing cathartic experience? Who knows?

Cheered off. Back to the dressing room, laughing, shouting, screaming, hugging, genuine affection for each other and a job well done. We'd grab a can on our way into the big bath and all sing our victory chant in the manner of Sid Waddell, the famous darts commentator. "One hundreeeeed annnnd eeeeeeighty" – to signify the bonus we had just won. And then sink back into the warm soapy water and become intoxicated on those smells – those smells of victory: shampoo and sandwiches and pies and beer.

In those days, the win bonus could double your wages. You couldn't afford to get injured and miss a game because the basic wages were so poor. Apart from one season I missed with a broken leg (I could have done with that at Birmingham), I did not allow myself to get injured. I once played 100 straight games. That was my shirt and nobody else was allowed to wear it.

The broken leg was a test of my new resolve. I underwent all the usual doubts about whether I would recover, be the same player again, be afraid to tackle etc. I spent a lot of time on my own, thinking negative thoughts, constantly touching and testing the fracture site. I felt isolated from my team-mates, denied the intimacy and camaraderie I had enjoyed before the injury. Yes, people felt sorry for me, but not as sorry as I felt for myself.

If there was ever an example of how much I had changed, how far I had come, how desperately I just wanted to play football again, then this was it. I did recover, I did fight back, I did play again and I did get that can of beer and jump in the bath again. Another battle fought – and another battle won.

It also stood me in good stead for when I became a physiotherapist – how to empathise, how to motivate, how to encourage. Those seven months on the sidelines taught me more about sports injuries than a four-year physiotherapy degree ever could.

I suffered another injury which was not so serious, just very painful and very embarrassing. On the weekend before my wife and I got married, I broke a rib playing down at Watford. However, I managed to train every day the following week and was able to play the next Saturday, which was the day before our wedding.

We only booked a two-day honeymoon in the Lake District because of the time of the year (November). In training, the day after I returned, somebody blasted a ball which hit me in the back and must have opened up the original fracture site. The pain was unbearable and I missed six weeks.

My wife never lived it down as everyone was telling her it must have been one hell of a honeymoon for me to come back with a crushed rib.

Stories like that were all part of the banter we'd have at the club, be it during training, in the dressing room or in the bath after a game. After the bath, we'd get changed and Bill Fox would come in. "Well done, the sponsor's man of the match is Baz."

It did not get any better than that, take it from me.

Go and collect the sponsor's trophy or, better still, a tray of beer or bottle of wine. Into the '100 Club' bar to meet the fans. Everybody loves you. All the players and wives together – that was the key, *together*. Five or six pints in there. Garns and I and our wives out for the night. Big piss-up, home, bed.

The best day ever.

Of course, we didn't always win and I didn't always win man of the match, but we always went into the 100 Club to mix with the fans, whatever the result. We won together as a playing staff, backroom staff, set of fans and town, and we lost together. That was special – those days have gone forever.

Away games were just as fun, and a different kind of adventure. One highlight was each season's clash with Portsmouth, our big rivals at the time, at Fratton Park. There was lots of edge to this game due to the nature of previous encounters, our rivalry in the promotion race and plenty of bad feeling.

We used to depart for the south coast on a Friday afternoon. The trays of beers went on first, then the wine, then the 'team spirit' and finally the kit. There was much less traffic in those days, so the journey was comfortable.

Into the hotel, up to the room, raiding the minibar for snacks. I always roomed with my best mate, Garns. The hotels usually had a carvery restaurant and Garns and I used to have a competition to see who could eat the most (yes, we'd still feel great the next day). Then we'd head back to the room for the opening of the 'goodie bag' – crisps, chocolates and, last but not least, four cans of McEwan's Lager. Down the hatch. Garns finished off proceedings by chain-smoking 20 fags, while I passively chain-smoked 20 fags. Then Garns, with his now distended belly hanging over the top of his boxer shorts, would start to doze off – fag in hand. I always waited until he went to sleep before I put his fag out. There was no way I could ever go to sleep before him just in case he burnt the fucking place down.

We'd wake up the next morning, still feeling great, and get up for breakfast – let the eating competition commence. A full fry-up, then the pre-match meal – the ten-egg omelette (still felt great).

Then it was game time – always tough, had to battle, dig out a result, no faint hearts. Those games at Fratton Park got very personal. Portsmouth were the team with all the money (how times have changed) and paid big wages. Rumour had it that some of their players were on £800 per week, an extraordinary sum of money for that time and way beyond our comprehension.

They had a midfield player called Mick Kennedy. To be fair,

he was a very good player but very, very combative and aggressive, and he used to get involved verbally with our players during the match. He would run around the pitch shouting, "Fucking £250 a week players, that's all you fuckers are, £250 a week players." Well, Mick, I have got news for you: I was only on £220 but we did get a nice win bonus that day.

It's a shame that kind of stuff prevailed (and still does). It's a cheap shot really when somebody who is earning a great deal more than another fellow professional starts all that "What are you on? I can buy and sell you," nonsense.

In my first season at Blackburn we played, and beat, Coventry City in the FA Cup. They were in the top division at the time and I was up against their famous Scottish international Tommy Hutchison, one of the best left wingers around. He would probably agree he could be somewhat arrogant on the pitch. Anyway, I tackled Tommy very hard – but fairly. He got up and, with a look of absolute and utter contempt on his face, pushed me and said: "Hey son, I give my fucking kids more pocket money than you are on a week."

I was so taken aback and genuinely offended that I asked if he would be at all interested in adopting me.

That cruel exchange always stuck in my mind. I hope you are OK, Tommy, you probably don't even remember the incident but I never forgot it. Maybe you could join Leighton James and me for that pint and chat.

The old Mick Rathbone would have folded, but not any more. Those days had gone, all that shit was behind me now and would never return. We dug deep and got the result. It was another great win, another great day, another great experience.

When the away games ended, it was back into the dressing room. If we had won, it was time to bring out the old Sid Waddell banter again. A quick change and then we prepared ourselves for the biggest piss-up in the history of big piss-ups.

We'd head into the players' bar for a few pints just to loosen up for the long journey home (let's call it an old-fashioned cooldown). Onto the bus and into the cans, singing and dancing for the duration of the trip home before staggering off the coach at Ewood Park in the early hours of the morning. Well and truly cooled down.

I suppose in hindsight that behaviour – let's use modern-day sports science speak and refer to it as our 'refuelling strategy' – was a little extreme and probably not great for professional sportsmen. But so what? Those trips back were some of the most memorable experiences of my life. And guess what? On Monday morning I still felt great.

Although, like most players I assume, I preferred home games, I enjoyed those away days, in particular visiting the bigger clubs like Chelsea, Leeds, Manchester City and West Ham, who all had spells in the second tier in the early '80s. The bigger and noisier the crowd, the better. So different to my Birmingham City days when the prospect of a visit to Old Trafford or Anfield would fill me with dread.

Blackburn had a very good, loyal fan base and we always had fantastic away support. To run out at such far-flung places as Roker Park, Home Park and Carrow Road, and see your fans cheering for you, was heart-warming and, believe me, all of us were grateful to our travelling supporters. As we were living in the same world as our fans, we could more readily understand the cost and effort it took those guys to support us and, when we did lose, our first thoughts were always for the fans. That might sound like a load of bullshit, but I can assure you it wasn't – Sacko would always be the first to point it out.

After an away defeat, the journey home would be quiet and subdued – well, at least the first bit was. It hurt us to lose. We needed the fucking bonus, for a start. We also needed the points, needed our next contract and needed the fans to keep following us.

We would sit quietly on the bus, the 12 trays of Long Life beer sitting unmolested on the back seat, and the steam still coming out of Sacko's ears at the front. Then, after an hour or so, one of the directors would sidle up to Sacko with a can and a few words of encouragement. "Chin up" etc. Sacko would grunt, get up from his seat and walk to the back of the bus where we sat like scolded schoolchildren, before signalling the official mourning period was over with the same words: "Fuck it, another game next week. We'll fucking well beat the fuckers!" (He swore a lot.)

He'd then pass out the beers and sit among us and, together, we would all start the healing process. Just a few beers later and out would come the playing cards and the banter, and all would be forgiven. A family again.

I feel sorry for today's multi-millionaire players who disappear as soon as possible after that final whistle has gone, scribbling a couple of autographs, often with indecent haste, while some flunkey fetches their car. They don't know what they're missing.

Nothing lasts forever and that team grew old and faded. If you stand still, you go backwards. Rovers didn't have the finances to do anything other than stand still and, accordingly, after four or five good years a couple of lean ones followed. Sacko lived up to his name and got the sack. It wasn't his fault – for the money he had spent and the resources he had at his disposal he did a fantastic job. Those of us who played for him certainly felt we had been part of something special.

Big deal, you could argue, you won nothing. Average players, average team, average results. Yes, but certainly not average times. Great times, great experiences, a sense of purpose and belonging. Beauty is in the eye of the beholder and, for me, it was a truly beautiful period of my life.

I might be looking back through rose-tinted glasses because, to be frank, the wages were terrible and the facilities bordered on the non-existent. Every year we got a £20 per week pay rise – if we were lucky – and every day we got changed at Ewood Park before getting back into our cars and driving to the nearby 'training ground', otherwise known as 'dog shit' park. I couldn't really complain too much, though, as Max, who always came with me to training, had contributed his fair share.

But the team spirit and camaraderie shone through all of it – we were just happy, and maybe somewhat lucky, to be there. Although we certainly weren't rewarded financially, we felt valued, wanted and appreciated by the club and any students of psychology who have studied Maslow's *Hierarchy of Needs* theory will tell you it is this which is more satisfying and long-lasting.

So many good things happened to me during that period which shaped me as a man – memories that remain pin-sharp to this day. If Jim Smith hadn't been so considerate, I shudder to think what I might have ended up doing. I thank Jim every time I see him. I like to think, as a decent, hard-working guy, I would have been successful at anything I turned my hand to, but I certainly wouldn't have the memories of my time at Ewood Park. Even though I ended up with about £10 saved in my bank account, my soul and spirit were enriched beyond mere financial measure.

There are so many tales that illustrate the environment and conditions that '80s footballers performed in. It was an incredible achievement when we just missed out on promotion to the First Division on goal difference in the 1980/81 season, especially bearing in mind our scant resources. We were all expecting a decent pay rise – well, at least more than the usual paltry £20.

We arranged for a meeting with Bill Fox. Feelings were running high. We demanded he came down to Ewood Park for a confrontation. We all sat nervously in the home team dressing room, but we were united in our quest. This was player power 1980s style. Tick tock, tick tock, all sitting in silence, fidgeting, determined, looking at the door. Finally, it burst open and Blackburn's formidable chairman was standing there. Mohammed had come to our little mountain.

Bill was a ruddy-faced, gruff-talking man whose favourite phrase was, "I call a spade a fucking shovel."

"Right lads, job's fucked," he said. "There's no money in the piggy bank but I think I have come up with the perfect compromise."

He clapped his hands and in came one of his workers carrying several trays of beer. "Right lads, there's your pay rises, get stuck into those cans."

Two hours later we sat there pissed. The rebellion was over.

A similar incident happened when one of the players had the temerity to go and see Sacko in person about his contract and complain about his new offer. He told Sacko in no uncertain terms he wasn't happy and would not be signing under any circumstances. Final word – no argument.

It's worth noting, however, in this era you couldn't just leave a club or, equally, the club couldn't just get rid of you if you had been offered a new contract, so this bravery did contain a certain amount of security.

"Right then, son, there's the phone. If you can get yourself a club in the next five minutes, you can leave for nothing. If you can find anyone desperate enough to take you, that is."

This was a great opportunity for the player.

"Right, I fucking well will," he replied.

The player picked up the phone and dialled a local club who, according to press reports, were interested in signing him.

Player asked to speak to the manager.

Manager came on the line.

Player gave his name and explained the situation.

Manager asked who it was and if he could spell his name.

Player spelt his name.

Manager asked if he was a goalie.

Player slammed down the phone and said to Sacko, "Pass me the fucking pen."

And that was how it was back then. No agents and the club held all the cards. The upshot was players were paid less than they should have been. To be fair to Rovers, though, they were barely keeping their heads above water as it was and the other local clubs were just as bad. The money just wasn't there, so the reward packages were based on everybody getting pissed at the expense of the club.

This was the bonus scheme: a top-six finish would almost

certainly get you the five-star, all-expenses-paid, piss-up of the century that was Magaluf. Top half, and you could be heading for the all-night cabaret at the Douglas Palace Hotel on the Isle Of Man during pre-season. A disappointing season, and you could look no further than a long weekend in Morecambe, taking in pre-season friendlies in Lancaster and Workington. Drink was the currency of the day.

We probably did drink too much, but I don't care what anybody says – I know for a fact the players back then were as fit as the players today. Yes, the game is much faster but that is more down to the rule changes than anything else. We had players in that team as fit and as fast as they are today. Fact.

The only caveat to every boozing session was that you had to get up and train hard the next day. Everybody. No excuses. Whatever the hangover. And training back then with Sacko was very hard – particularly pre-season. You ran until you could no longer move your legs. Heart-rate monitors, training zones, recovery, bottled water – forget it; you just kept running. You ran until you dropped. We did half a dozen cross countries through Witton Park, Blackburn's big country park, as part of pre-season and we dreaded them.

There was none of that, "After you, Claude, let's all run together in a nice pack" rubbish. No, this was eyeballs out, winner-takes-all stuff. Waiting for nobody. Because we had the same team for so long, the cross countries became a familiar feature of pre-season and some players would spend the close-season break training just for those races.

I still feel ill when I think about it now. We stood by the blue bridge, Sacko's hand raised in the air, feeling sick with fear knowing how hard it would be. The smells of fresh cut grass and honeysuckle only added to the feelings of nausea. The hand dropped and we were off.

I was a good runner and won all the races. There was a park section, a road section and then we went back into the park for the last couple of miles. I liked to get a good lead so I could quickly get Max out of the car at the end. I finished in extreme distress every time, as did the runner-up and third-placed player. But further down the field it was noticeable that the players became less and less distressed until finally Garns strolled in last, fresh as a daisy.

That taught me a lot about fitness, running and, more importantly, the psychology of running and would prove to be an invaluable asset when I became a physiotherapist. I think the greatest asset a physio can have in elite sport is the ability to run with the players, to encourage and inspire them.

If ever you needed an example of how much I changed as a player and as a man at Blackburn, it came against Manchester United in the FA Cup at Ewood Park one Friday night in 1985. The game was live on BBC1, the only time I ever played live on TV. After just a few minutes, I made a terrible mistake. I trod on the ball in our penalty area, which let Gordon Strachan in to score. All fell silent except for the distant rumble of euphoric United fans at the far end of the ground. I had made a shocking error in front of 26,000 fans and countless millions around the world. And do you know what? It never fazed me, never affected me, never touched me. I just kept demanding the ball, running for the ball, enjoying the ball. Now that is progress.

However, my favourite and best memory came a few months earlier. Birmingham had been relegated into the Second Division the previous season (they shouldn't have sold me, should they?), and the day came to return to my own personal killing field – St Andrew's. That walk again, those smells again, but not the stuttering footsteps of a shrinking violet again. No, the purposeful striding of a strong, confident man. Waiting patiently and excitedly for that ELO record to start up again. Those familiar opening bars that sucked the final drops of energy from my teenage legs in the past now made the hairs stand up on the back of my neck. On we went. A quick superstitious touch of my club badge – the red rose of Lancashire – and into battle.

We won 2-0 and went top of the league. I played out of my

skin. The fans shouted 'reject' but I just laughed back at them. I showed them all. Afterwards I got out of the shower and some of the Birmingham apprentices asked if they could come in and start cleaning up. History repeating itself. It's a pity I didn't have my flip-flops.

Bob Saxton was one of the key reasons why I could move on from my Birmingham nightmare and become a proper player as I showed that day. I am forever indebted to him. Thanks for caring, Bob. Thanks for being a father like figure to us. Thanks for giving us great and long-lasting memories. We loved your no-nonsense, cut-through-the-bullshit ways. It was a simple game, all about the players.

The philosophy was simple too: if the players cared for you and respected you, then they would play for you. And we played for Bob.

One story in particular sums up Sacko's 'old school' approach (I prefer to call it 'traditional'). We were playing down at Brighton and Sacko rushed into the dressing room as we were about to get changed. "Fuck me, I don't believe it, I have just seen one of their players turn up with a fucking hairdryer. If we can't beat these fucking pansies, I will show my fucking arse in Burtons window."

We won.

Great times, great memories – I still have my blue-and-white-halved No. 3 shirt in my wardrobe. It has magic powers, but everything has a shelf life.

After Sacko left, Don Mackay came in. He was a decent bloke and manager, but he brought in new players, which of course he had to do. Inevitably, though, as he did, the old guard dwindled and gradually died out.

At the end of the 1986/87 season, I decided, after eight years at the club, it was time to move on. Although we had constantly been reminded by Sacko that if any of us decided to leave we would never get another club, I took my chance, turned down the offer of a new contract and was pleased to have my choice of a number of interested clubs.

I chose Preston North End in the Third Division, because they were up and coming, famous founder members of the league, full of proud tradition and, most importantly, just eight miles down the road. New experiences were waiting but, as I found out several times in my career, nothing in football was simple.

This was, of course, the pre-Bosman days, which meant that although my contract was about to expire at Blackburn I couldn't simply go and sign for another club for free.

Players were restricted in their freedom to move between clubs and make decent money. People frequently ask me if I feel resentful that I missed out on the big money era. No, not when I used to see Tom Finney at Preston, arguably England's greatest-ever player, who probably never earned more than a tenner a week. If he wasn't resentful, then how could I be?

So it was a date at the tribunal courts for me that summer and some acrimony between the Blackburn and Preston as a tug of war for my services ensued.

Chapter Six

REALITY BITES

It was June 1987 and I was a man in demand. Yes me, Mick Rathbone. The same Mick Rathbone who was once so terrified of playing in the Birmingham first team he chose not to wear shinpads in the faint hope of getting injured. Preston wanted me and Blackburn didn't want to let me go. It felt good to be in such a position.

I had agreed to sign for Preston but, unlike in today's game, it wasn't as simple as that. The whole deal had to go before an independent Football League tribunal at Lytham St Annes, so the amount of compensation Preston would be required to pay Blackburn for me could be decided.

It had been a bit of a shock to the hierarchy at Blackburn when I announced I wanted to leave – and it was flattering they were shocked. I think the club felt it was a knee-jerk reaction from me after not being selected for the Full Members Cup final the previous month. Maybe there was an element of truth in that, if I am being honest, but I do believe it was more a feeling the time was right to move on – Lassie would have understood.

It was also flattering that Rovers had tried so hard to get me to stay at the club, but I had this inbuilt clock telling me it was time to leave. Unfortunately, however, there was some acrimony between the two clubs over the fee involved and, to be fair, I was dreading the tribunal.

Blackburn had insisted Preston pay £60,000 for my services, arguing I was talented, versatile, a credit to my profession, coming into my best years etc. I nearly didn't recognise myself. On the other hand, Preston had offered a measly £5,000, arguing I was past my best, and that Blackburn, in paying only £40,000 for me back in 1979, had certainly got their money's worth.

I travelled to the tribunal in Preston chairman Keith Leeming's Jaguar, along with 'Big John' McGrath, the Preston manager. Rovers were represented by Don Mackay and Bill Fox. We were all put in the same waiting room. Nobody spoke – it was an absolutely awful state of affairs, especially as I loved Rovers so much.

First up, I was called in to face the panel. Essentially they wanted to know what I thought I was worth. I wanted the fee to be as low as possible to ease the pressure on me (that's me, Mr Confidence), so I said about £5,000, citing the service I had given Blackburn and also the fact they had only offered me a one-year extension and I wasn't exactly being paid a fortune.

I was sent back out and went to sit in the chairman's car. I waited and waited – my fate was being decided and I hoped the clubs wouldn't fall out too much. I didn't want to leave Rovers under too big a cloud.

The clock ticked and ticked and ticked. Why the delay? Is that a good sign or a bad sign? Please don't make me an expensive player.

Finally, Big John and Keith appeared and got in the car. They sat there for what seemed like ages, not talking – you could have cut the atmosphere with a knife. Finally, Keith took a big drag on his cigar and said, "Never mind, John, you can't win them all."

Big John turned around and fixed me with a stare that could reduce the strongest of men (a group that by now you have probably realised I do not belong to) to shivering wrecks.

"Fucking hell, son. Fucking hell. Twenty fucking grand you just cost me. That's the most I have ever paid for a fucking player.

You'd better fucking well produce the fucking goods, son."
(Managers tend to swear a lot.)

What was that about pressure?

So, Preston it was. Personal terms a formality – you should know
that about me by now. I had hit the magical £300 per week.

It was the summer of 1987 and the first hat-trick of the season
had already been claimed by Maggie Thatcher as she was voted
in for a third term. English football was still ostracised from any
involvement in European Football, while on the home front we
were about to be blown away by the storm of the century and
the town of Hungerford was soon to achieve notoriety.

With my signing-on fee, I bought a super-smart Ford Escort RS
Turbo in all white. It cost me £8,000 – a fortune but proof I was
now a success. I was approaching 29 years of age and was considered a good, consistent player, equally comfortable at left or right
back. I was reaching my prime. The only problem was that I was
going bald and looked about 50. (Why, oh why, didn't I pay the
two quid extra and get the deluxe perm?)

Who says you can't put an old head on young shoulders?
Anybody who has gone bald will agree it is not a very enjoyable
experience but, funnily enough, the lads at Blackburn took the
piss out of me to such an extent I had to take it on the chin and
accept it. Today, people say I look better without hair which is
the ultimate back-handed compliment. Strangely, I only started to
realise I was losing my hair when I saw a clip of myself on TV
running back to my own goal. At first I thought it must have been
somebody else as I stared at the bald spot but then, to my horror,
I recognised the magic No. 3.

My fitness levels by now were legendary and I considered my
body to be indestructible. I had developed an inbuilt confidence
on the pitch after eight years of regular football at Rovers. I had
plenty left in the tank but not much left in the bank.

Now I was a Northender (or Nobender as opposition fans used
to call us). Another great club steeped in tradition – Finney,

Shankly, the Invincibles. What an honour to pull on the lilywhite shirt. At the time, they had a plastic pitch which I used to slide-tackle on. That resulted in two things – I became a hero to the fans but had no skin on my hips and elbows for four years. I used to wake up every Sunday morning and peel the sheets off my plastic burns.

Sometimes, before a game in winter, they would sprinkle a salt solution onto the surface to prevent it from freezing. This was an astonishing breakthrough for medicine as you could slide-tackle, get a friction burn and have it cleaned all at the same time.

The most memorable aspect of playing for Preston during that period was the opportunity to play for Big John McGrath – and what an experience it was. Big John was a legend. It would take a whole book to do him justice. When they made Big John, they threw away the mould. He terrified and inspired us in equal measure. You did not fuck with Big John, full stop. He bought players cheaply and sold them on for big money. Think John Wayne, toughen him up a bit, swap the southern drawl for a strong Manchester accent and you have just about got the description of the legendary manager – he inspired us, he scared us, he made us laugh, he made us cry, he made us better players.

His methods would seem anachronistic today and he would probably be ridiculed by the modern football intelligentsia, but he had a very good track record, especially in the development of players and getting bargains. He worked on players, improved them and sold them on to bigger clubs for the profits that are the lifeblood of the smaller clubs.

Big John took over at Deepdale when the club was at death's door, applying for re-election and playing league games on weekday afternoons in front of a few thousand fans because they had no floodlights.

I wasn't there at the time, but word has it he came in and stopped the rot with sheer willpower and determination, taking the place by the scruff of the neck and almost singlehandedly dragging the club back up the league and into a position of respectability. Sam Allardyce, who played for Preston at this time, speaks in glowing terms about Big John's impact. Sam now has a reputation for employing the most modern and forward-thinking ideas in terms of coaching, scouting and sports science, but I am sure some of his success as a manager has owed more than a little to the Big John effect.

McGrath was the undisputed, unchallenged, Commonwealth, European and world champion of one thing – the bollocking. Nobody bollocked you like Big John. When he bollocked you, you stayed bollocked. His bollockings were spontaneous, unrehearsed, non-selective and, above all, meant. These bollockings were dished out during marathon team meetings which were held with terrifying regularity in the home dressing room at Deepdale.

So regularly, in fact, that there was even a meeting on my very first day at the club. As I quickly found out, a meeting could only mean one thing – some poor bastard was going to get a fucking rocket from the big man. Everybody sat in the dressing room in total silence, nervously waiting for the door to open. That first time I noticed all the other players were sitting on a towel. Two hours later, when I emerged from the meeting with a numb arse from sitting on the hard wooden bench, I knew why and wouldn't be making the same mistake again. There would be many more such meetings, but each time I made sure I got a nice thick towel to sit on.

Those meetings were the stuff of legend. Big John would talk for over an hour. Each meeting would carry a slightly different theme. He would bollock, praise, criticise, amuse, inform and entertain. He would never stumble over a word, never repeat himself and never lose his thread. He was a truly amazing orator. In a bygone era, he could have stood on a soapbox on Speaker's Corner in Hyde Park and stopped every car (or horse) in London. I assume he had no formal qualifications, simply because he had been a professional footballer himself and left school at an early age (he was a legend at Newcastle back in the '60s), which made his speeches all the more remarkable. I had certainly never heard anything like it.

When a meeting was called, an element of fear quickly spread through the ranks. Somebody was getting it. We sat on our towels. The door opened slowly and first Les Chapman came in. Les was our player-coach – a good player, a great bloke and very, very funny.

Les would pull funny faces to try and defuse the situation and ease the tension. Then the big man would enter. Each meeting, without exception, would start the same way and follow the same pattern. Big John had a habit of not finishing his sentences.

"Les, just get the err."

That meant Les had to go into the shower area and turn off the noisy fan.

He would then continue: "Gentlemen, there are one or two things I am not too, eh hum…" (that was the precursor to the unleashing of the fury).

All hell would break loose as he singled out the poor defenceless victim. He would round on his prey and the mother of all bollock-ings would commence. You just closed your eyes and prayed he wasn't coming for you.

Sometimes it was difficult to see precisely who was getting it if his victim was at the other end of the dressing room, but I am ashamed to say nobody really cared who it was, just as long as it wasn't them.

Of course, there was much more to the meeting than the initial bollocking and, when that was dispensed, he would settle nicely into the theme of the day and we would be richly entertained.

Each meeting had a different theme and after the well-rehearsed opening – "Les, get the err… gentlemen, there are one or two things I am not too…" – and then the ubiquitous savaging of the unlucky individual, he preached the gospel according to John, usually with the same tragic ending.

Once he strolled in and (after the bloodletting) announced: "Gentlemen, this team is like a huge fruit salad. Mooney (Brian Mooney, our star player), you are the strawberry because you are the most tasty and expensive. Tony (Tony Ellis, our top scorer), you are the slice of kiwifruit on the top because you finish things off. Big Sam and Alex (Sam Allardyce and Alex Jones, both big, strong centre halves), you are the slices of orange because you add a bit of bite when necessary."

The meeting went on in this vein, comparing all the players to types of fruit, when his eyes finally fell on Warren Joyce and me, both good 'bread and butter' type players. "You two are bananas – nobody is ever going to pay anything for you, but something's got to hold the whole fucking thing together." Then he would laugh and laugh and we would all join in. What a treat.

"Right," he finished off. "I have had so much fruit I have given myself diarrhoea. I'm going for a shit!" Off he went, leaving us amused and entertained, but more importantly inspired and motivated. How many of today's managers could do that?

Once, after the team had gained an incredible result in the FA Cup at Middlesbrough, he called a meeting the following Friday prior to the next league game at Swansea. Same format, Les in first, pulling faces, then Big John.

"Les, the err" followed by, "There are one or two things, eh hum…" before imparting that day's nugget of wisdom.

"Gentlemen, what you did last Saturday was the equivalent of going on a date with Miss World, wining and dining her at a Michelin restaurant, taking her back to your five-star hotel and spending the night making love to her. Now tomorrow you are going on a date with the ugliest old scrubber in the world but, gentlemen, she still wants fucking!"

And with that he just turned and walked out. I couldn't imagine Arsene Wenger using that one.

Big John's pet hate was the players over-eating on the day of a game and, legend has it, he once dropped a player for eating too much toast during the pre-match meal. This anti-gorging policy presented a problem to the big match-day scoffers like me, driven on by my nerves to eat huge amounts of comfort food. I just made sure I sat well away from Big John and ate two pieces of toast at the same time.

After one bad performance in London, he called a meeting. He was clearly in a very bad mood.

"Gentlemen," his voice full of menace, "stand up if you had a pre-match meal on Saturday."

Well, of course, everybody stood up. He eyed us up and down, his demeanour full of threat.

"Right, remain standing if you also had a cooked breakfast."

Everybody quickly sat down except our naive centre half Alex Jones. He just hadn't seen what was coming and remained standing – alone, isolated and vulnerable.

Big John unleashed his fury on the poor lad. "Jonesy, Jonesy, you fucking greedy, greedy bastard. The fucking waiter covered more distance than you last Saturday."

One great thing about Big John, though, was that for all his ferocity, he showed some remarkable human touches, which explains why the lads loved him so much. He never, ever fined players. His rationale was it would be impacting upon the player's family and their lifestyle and it wasn't fair that they should suffer.

"I am not taking the bread out of their mouths for something they haven't done," he would explain.

But if somebody did step out of line (and trust me, very few people did), he would make you stay behind after training and clean out the toilets. A really interesting and radical approach to discipline.

Once, however, we did get into a little bit of disciplinary hot water with the FA as a result of the lads constantly backchatting the referees. A meeting was called, usual format (Les, fan, eh hum, gentlemen).

"Right, listen you've got to stop all this fucking foul language to the referees. The board are fucking fed up with it and it's got to fucking well stop. I won't fucking well tolerate anybody calling them wankers or arseholes or twats any more."

"What shall we call them then?" asked Sam Allardyce, prompting a few sniggers from the lads.

"It's simple," he said. "Call them bananas."

Big Sam again. "Bananas? Bananas? Why bananas?"

"Because when they start out they are a bit green but basically straight, but they soon become yellow and fucking bent!"

You couldn't make it up.

Sadly, that great man died in 1998. He was a giant and a great loss to the game. Thanks Big John. Thanks for the memories I can still recall, word perfectly, more than 20 years later.

I enjoyed my time at Preston and I think I gave the club great service – I am sure the fans would say that. However, after a couple of years, things started to go wrong with my previously super-human body. Whether because of my age or, more likely, the unforgiving astroturf pitch, for the first time in my career I started to be hit by injuries – a ruptured medial (inside) ligament in my right knee, surgery on my left knee, a fractured cheekbone and a broken wrist.

I can still feel and hear the crack in my right cheekbone as a Bolton player caught me. I went to head the ball but, unfortunately, the opposing player went for it with his foot and kicked me full force in the face. There was lots of blood and I tried to get up and carry on (because I am such a hero), but the physio dragged me back to the ground and put me on the stretcher. It was a nasty injury which required surgery and, even now, two decades later, the right side of my face is still numb.

The fractured wrist cost me another three months on the sidelines. We were staying at RAF Leuchars on a pre-season trip to St Andrews in Scotland in July. It was a really hot day and the airmen at the base had asked me if they could have a bit of a game against us, so I tried to whip up a team. Most of our lads weren't keen, though, because their pitch was as hard as concrete and they were concerned about getting injured.

Eventually, I persuaded about eight or nine of the lads to play as a thank you for the hospitality we had received at the base. Lo and behold, somebody pushed me over on the hard surface and, crack, broken wrist.

Suddenly, it seemed I was always injured. I was becoming injury prone. I was spending a lot of time in the treatment room. Where were all theses injuries when I really needed them back in the '70s?

Physiotherapy in those days was machine-based and necessitated hanging around seven days a week waiting to go and sit under the various machines without any rehabilitation, gradually becoming physically deconditioned and psychologically demotivated.

The only good thing about that period was that it taught me a valuable lesson for my future career as a physio. I learned to do the job very differently. My players come in early. They work very hard to retain their fitness and motivation. I do not keep them hanging around all day just to sit under a machine that is not likely to have any effect on their injury anyway. Look it up – physiotherapy: treatment by physical means. It's bad enough being injured without the treatment itself being a nightmare. As long as the players are in bright and early, train very hard – in the pool, in the gym, on the bike, on the track etc – they can go home to their families. Why punish them by keeping them hanging around all day?

All the hanging around in the treatment room was gradually eroding my love for the game. In all those hours waiting between treatments, I probably should have started planning for the next part of my life – post-football. I was losing my desire to carry on playing. I was certainly losing my match fitness and sharpness.

Part of the reason for my relatively sudden demise was the fact that several times I tried to return to action when I hadn't received complete and thorough rehabilitation after a long-term injury. I had ruptured the medial ligament in my right knee in a tackle and had been out of action for nearly four months. Eventually it got better. I joined in my first full training session on the Friday and was promptly selected to play in the first team the next day – despite having done no training of any significance or intensity for months.

I am not criticising the physio because he was a brilliant bloke, really caring and kind, it was just he had 40 or 50 lads to look after and that machine-based approach was the thinking of the era. However, there is no way that would happen nowadays. Any long-term injured player I look after would have done so much hard training during the rehabilitation period that, when he eventually rejoined the squad, he would actually have been fitter than before he got injured in the first place. In addition, he would have had to train for at least a week with the squad and played maybe 60 minutes in a reserve game and then a full 90 minutes before being considered to be anywhere near ready for the first team. But not back then. After almost four months out, it was one training session and back into the starting line-up.

My return game was on the Deepdale astroturf. There is an old saying in football that one day your legs will 'go'. It can happen all of a sudden – you lose that essential speed and power in your legs, usually as a consequence of either injury or age or, in my case, a bit of both. I had always considered the whole idea of your legs going to be nonsense and merely a myth, but sadly on the day in question, it happened to me and I can still vividly recall the exact moment when I realised my career was on the wane.

I was playing right back. We were losing 1-0 and there were only a few minutes to go when we won a corner. Everybody went up except me. I stayed back to guard against the counter-attack. The ball was crossed into the box and there was an almighty goalmouth scramble before it was cleared – a huge, towering clearance that sailed high over my head, rolling and bouncing along the sideline towards our own corner flag. I turned and gave chase, running as fast as I possibly could. I was aware, though, that I was being pursued and, more worryingly, I was being caught. The foot race was on. I could feel the presence behind me, catching me. I was sprinting as fast as I could but felt like I was running through sand. I could hear his footsteps now as he closed in on me. I kept running but my legs felt like lead. I could hear his breathing now as he inexorably gained on me. Finally, just as he got level with me, I got to the ball and in the nick of time managed to gratefully poke it out of play for a throw in. There was a huge groan from the crowd. To my horror, when I looked up, I realised my panting pursuer was the linesman.

That might make a somewhat amusing anecdote but the harsh reality is much more profound and the message is clear – rehabilitation after injury must be comprehensive, exhaustive and exhausting.

In my fourth and final year at Preston, I played very few games due to a serious injury to my left knee that required cartilage surgery. The thing I remember most was trying to leave the hospital as soon as I could after the operation because it was my wife's birthday. I made it to the hospital reception, but then fainted and fell, disturbing the stitches around the wound. The injury and subsequent surgery had a profound effect on my knee and, even today, it is constantly swollen and gives me quite a lot of discomfort.

I was released by Preston at the end of that season, even though I hadn't fully recovered from the injury. I didn't make a fuss. I could have gone to a couple of Fourth Division clubs, but no, that was it. Seventeen years or so was plenty.

My four years at Preston were eventful mainly for the toll the Astroturf took on my legs. I gave good service and left a good impression, but not as good as the impression that artificial pitch left on my poor skin.

So the football career rather fizzled out. After that torturous start at Birmingham, I had persevered well and ended up being relatively successful, a regular at Rovers and North End for more than a decade. On reflection, I should have, and would have spent my whole career in the top division if I'd had more confidence. But, let's be honest, that's like saying I would have spent my career playing at the highest level if I'd had more ability.

Confidence can be somewhat elusive and short-lived but, at the same time, vital, innate and essential. You can't just give somebody confidence; it has to be nurtured and encouraged. You can't be something you are not. In some respects, you either possess it or you don't. With it, everything is possible; without it, nothing is possible.

But this was no time for regrets. Off with the old and on with the new. The world was my oyster. What direction would fate take me? It was time to sit back and weigh up those job offers all the hangers-on had promised me when I was a player and seemingly worth knowing. No problem, I'd take my time, take my pick and consider all my options.

How wrong I would be.

I sat back during the summer of 1991, awaiting the executive offers. I couldn't understand it. I kept checking the phone to see if there was a fault on the line. What had gone wrong? I was very bright, seemingly popular, a good personality, famous (keep dreaming), always seemed to get on well with others. Where were these offers? Come and get me – £25,000 per annum and a car would suffice.

Except the phone didn't ring. Why would it? In reality, I had never actually done a proper day's work in my life. I had no real qualifications and, most importantly, I wasn't Baz any more, charging down the wing with the fans chanting my name; in fact, I was nobody. It was one hell of a shock, let me assure you. I was in a real tight spot.

I soon realised I was ignoring a couple of harsh facts of life – as soon as you take off that shirt for the last time, you are instantly Joe Public. Once you are no longer a player, you are nothing. Being a footballer is, in itself, not a qualification. If you are a doctor, lawyer, plumber or electrician, you are these things for life but, once the last ball is kicked, a lower-league footballer is unemployed and seemingly perceived by some to be unemployable.

I kept thinking back to my schooldays. I was very lucky I was born with a high level of intelligence. That is not me being big-headed; it's just a fact. I had determined early on in life to go to university and gain a high academic qualification. I knew that would mean a great deal to my dad who was also a very intelligent man but, having been born on a farm and left school at 14, never had the opportunity to achieve anything. I had wanted to be a doctor but, of course, also had the chance to be a footballer, which I wanted even more. My father and headmaster implored me to do my A-levels and go to university and medical school – but that was easier said than done when the club you'd supported all your life was banging on your door.

Sitting here now as someone who spent eight years as head of the medical department at one of the biggest football clubs in England, I have no real regrets about my decision. But I'll tell you this, during that long, unemployed summer of 1991, I was beginning to think my dad and headmaster had been right and I might just live to regret my decision as I faced unemployment, obscurity and financial hardship.

Apart from the obvious difficulties, I felt a definite loss of self-esteem. I had loved the kudos of being a professional footballer – who wouldn't? When my wife and I met people back in those days, maybe on holiday, the conversation would always come around to what I did for a living and, when they found out I was a professional footballer, you could see their faces light up with a mixture of respect, admiration and envy. Every bloke at some time has kicked a football and millions of people love football, but only the crème de la crème can call themselves professionals.

In my kit, I was Baz – autographs, interviews, a somebody. But now stripped of my magic No. 3 powers, I was plain old Mick Rathbone – a nobody.

I had no qualifications. My usual working day had run from 10am until noon. I had lived all my adult life in a cosseted world of free travel, free food and free equipment. Everything had been arranged for me, I'd had no responsibilities.

After sitting by the phone for the duration of June and July, I realised I was in a mess. I had two young girls to look after so I had to find a way of making some money. My wife had not worked since our eldest daughter was born three years earlier. It made me feel proud that I'd provided for them, and enabled her to stay at home and concentrate on being a great mum without having to drop the kids off at a childminder and somehow do a full-time job as well. I feared she would have to return to her job at the bank and I would feel like shit. A loser again.

Then I had a brainwave. A friend owned a clothing shop in Blackburn. He used to flog the end-of-season items that hadn't even sold in the sales really cheaply. He said I could try to sell some if I wanted. I thought if I took some of this gear to football clubs I might be able to shift some of it and make a bit of cash. Actually, it went really well and I was soon making as much money as I had when I played for Preston, but I found it hard psychologically.

What a comedown. The great Baz reduced to trying to make a living by selling cheap tat out of the boot of his car. But it paid the bills so I just had to swallow my pride. Beggars can't be choosers and all that.

It was a tough period in my life and I was just keeping my head above water through July and August when something happened that transformed my life beyond my wildest dreams. That break. That opportunity. Fate.

The Professional Footballers Association had instituted a four-year part-time course at Salford University to encourage ex-professional footballers to qualify as chartered physiotherapists. The thinking was that if you could combine a chartered physiotherapist with an ex-player, it would raise the standard of medical attention throughout the leagues. After some early teething problems, it began in September 1991.

The plan was to get 12 'guinea pigs' to start the inaugural course. Naturally, such an august organisation as The Chartered Society of Physiotherapists demanded high standards and the course would be identical in content to the one undertaken by full-time undergraduates.

The PFA were having trouble recruiting the dozen candidates because, without being unkind, not many professional footballers possessed the seven or eight GCSEs required (that was back in the day when GCSEs were hard to get unlike today where it seems everybody has at least ten – even the people who can't tie up their own shoelaces). As a result of the lack of candidates with the required qualifications, I was contacted by the PFA and invited on to the course. I politely declined their kind offer because I had no intention of going back to school at the age of 32 and, besides, my fashion empire was about to take off – watch out Hugo Boss, here comes Hugo Baz.

Then an incredible stroke of luck – again. It was Bank Holiday weekend at the end of August 1991, and my brother Martin and his family came up from Birmingham to visit for the weekend. I told him about the course and how I wasn't interested. To my amazement, he begged me – yes, begged me – to do it. I had never seen him like that before. He kept on and on and wouldn't stop until I promised him I would at least go over to Salford University for an interview and find out more about it. Martin is a dustman and said he wanted more for his younger brother. Of course, there is nothing at all wrong with being a dustman; it's a good, honest job and certainly better than walking the streets (notwithstanding the fact I nearly ended up working for Dyno Rod all those years ago). He just felt I could do more than selling gear out of the boot of my car (not that kind of gear...).

So Martin, thank you for when I travelled five-star around the world with Everton; thank you for when I worked with the likes of Wayne Rooney; thank you for when I jogged along Bondi Beach with Tim Cahill and crossed balls for Tim Howard at Soldier Field in Chicago; and thank you for when Lee Carsley scored the winning goal in the Merseyside derby and the roof came off Goodison. Thank you, Martin, you changed my life.

What if he hadn't come up that weekend?

What if Julie hadn't gone out that night?

What if Jim Smith hadn't sent me out on loan?

I sailed through the interview, dug out my 1970s pencil case with the 'Ban the Bomb' insignia on it and started university that September. For two days a week I sold my gear to the football clubs to pay the bills, and the rest of the time I was at Salford. I was about to embark upon the most momentous period of my life.

And so the years rolled on and on. It was the early '90s now. Techno music was deafening everybody, civil war looming in Yugoslavia, the economy teetering on the brink of recession (again), Ralph Lauren shirts and, most significantly, the start of the Premier League loomed. The 1991/92 season would be unique in that it would be the first period in my life when I hadn't been involved in professional football since I was a teenager.

It's amazing how your attitudes shift. When you are inside football, you just don't realise how fortunate you are. There is no better place to be, trust me on that one. The only problem is that you just don't appreciate how good it is until you are on the outside looking in. Football totally insulates you from the harsh realities of life and forms a protective screen around you and your family. Let's face it, if you sign a three-year contract, then you know no matter how you perform you are guaranteed that money. You know you will receive generous remuneration for the duration of that contract – yes, even during the summer when you are sat on your arse at home.

I was 32 years of age when I got my first taste of the real world (that's what I call insulation). I had to get up in the morning and go out and sell some clothes. If I didn't sell any clothes, I wouldn't be able to buy anything because I wouldn't have any money – simple enough, but it took some adapting to. One thing I quickly realised was that I had to try and get back in football ASAP.

During my career I have met a number of players who have come into football late, after doing a 'proper job' for a couple of years. They all seem to share a greater love for the game, nurtured as they grafted on the factory floors for a living wage. These lads never seem to moan about pre-season training, long coach trips, injuries, a bit of pressure. No, they have tasted the real world. They know this is paradise. Maybe all of us could have benefited from a taste of the real world to put things into perspective and help us realise just how lucky we really were. But now, belatedly, I was getting my taste of reality and I did not like it.

For a lot of the players today, everything comes too easily and I doubt if it is really, truly appreciated. It certainly wasn't by me. Perhaps sending some of these young players to work for a living for a couple of months during the off-season would focus their attention better than even the very best sports psychologists are able to do.

I have tried to learn from all of my experiences in life and I think I have been able to learn something from every facet of my football life but, believe me, that period – 1991/92 – was the steepest learning curve of all.

Looking back on my playing career, it was such a rollercoaster ride, the ultimate switchback. From the horrors of St Andrew's to the camaraderie at Blackburn to the injuries at Preston and, finally, the realisation that, for all those highs and lows, I had emerged with no money, no qualifications, and a potentially bleak future.

Why? Why did things turn out the way they did? Was it just fate or more likely the life choices of a young, oversensitive and somewhat immature man?

I can honestly say that every single day something happens – an incident, a thought or a random word – that instantly propels me back to the unhappy period all those years ago at Birmingham. Paradoxically, for all the flashbacks, deep thinking and soul-searching, I still don't really have any firm conclusions as to the reason why things went in the direction they did.

Sometimes I just think I was a coward, a quitter who didn't have the moral courage to go out and play in front of a big crowd. It's a pretty simple conclusion to draw. No need for in-depth soul searching or deep Freudian character analysis – I just didn't have the balls. End of debate.

Even writing this now, so many years later, those words – coward, immature, over-sensitive – carry weight and hurt. A form of self-punishment and self-flagellation – a sort of Alcoholics

Anonymous, but for people with no confidence where you just want to stand up and shout out loud, "I am Mick Rathbone and I am a fucking coward!"

I would prefer that not to be the correct evaluation of those painful teenage years, but if it's the truth, then it's the truth, and I will have to live with it.

Then, on other days – better days maybe, when everything is going well – I can see things very differently. I draw very different conclusions. These are the conclusions I prefer. These are the conclusions I want to be the truth, I want to believe. My only crime back then was to be oversensitive to sustained and vitriolic public criticism. I don't think at 18 years of age that is so unusual or unacceptable – especially when that criticism is coming from 30,000 supporters plus your own coaches and team-mates.

I accept I slowly but surely came apart at the seams during that period, yet seemingly not a single person noticed or, more worryingly, if they did notice, they didn't care or try to help. In my defence, if my father had been alive, he would have put his arm around me, told me to stand up straight and be a fucking man. And you know what? That is probably all it would have needed.

Why didn't the coaches help? They could have done a fairly simple thing – stop shouting at me every five minutes and look at what was happening to me. Spot the fact that this kid, who you all thought was so good the previous season, had now become a shell, incapable of putting one foot in front of the other. Use some common sense. Surely they could see I was struggling to perform to anywhere near my potential? Surely the fact my name alone was booed when it was read out before the kick-off should have given them a clue? Where were the sports psychologists?

Sometimes, I do feel a bit resentful of the whole Birmingham experience – that was my team, for fuck's sake. Now I can't even look at that famous badge without feeling faint. Just a little bit of sympathy, a bit of encouragement. For pity's sake, it can't be such an unusual thing for a young lad to be lacking in confidence. I am sick of hearing the same old bullshit from so-called experts

– "some players need an arm round them and some people need a bollocking". That is so wide of the mark it's frightening. From all my experiences in professional football for so many years, I can honestly say that for every player who needs a bollocking there are a thousand who require encouragement.

I feel bitter when I am in this frame of mind because I know I should have played at the highest level for my whole career and, with slightly more sympathetic management in those formative years, would have had a much more successful playing history. On days when these thoughts prevail, it's sometimes difficult not to resent that period or, more pointedly, some of the main protagonists who so influenced it.

When I am in full flow and blaming everybody else but myself, it's so easy to rationalise it differently and paint myself as the person wronged: it couldn't have been cowardice because, if it was just that simple, then why did it change so dramatically at Blackburn Rovers? Surely a coward is a coward? But at Rovers I wanted to play, I wanted that shirt, craved the adrenalin rush. I felt wanted at Blackburn – and there it is in a nutshell. I felt wanted. Maybe, because they had paid for me, I had some intrinsic value that could provide a framework to support my innate, fragile self-confidence. Birmingham had got me for nothing, I lived just down the road, perhaps that's why I did not feel valued. The money Blackburn spent on acquiring my services would prove to be a tangible and permanent boost to my self-esteem.

The money they spent gave me self-worth, which boosted my confidence, which made me play well, which made the fans like me, which boosted my self-confidence, which ensured I continued to play well. It was an ever-upward spiral.

Or is all that a load of bollocks, invented by my subconscious to spare me darker, more self-critical analysis? Did I do better at Rovers just because there was less pressure, the crowds were smaller and there was virtually no national scrutiny? Maybe, maybe not, but then again when we had big cup ties and they were the focus of national interest and on the television, I still relished them – but was that because we were underdogs so the pressure was off any way?

So, as you can see, I don't know whose fault it really was, who is to blame. Almost certainly it was a combination of several factors. The important thing is, by and large, it all worked out OK in the end. I was really lucky I never ended up out of football altogether and, indeed, if I hadn't failed so miserably at Birmingham (for whatever reason), then I wouldn't have met my wife and had my family.

Over the years I have met nearly all those players from the Birmingham era who were my collective nemeses. And you know what? They are all really decent people. I am positive none of them deliberately set out to destroy my confidence. In their eyes, it was just harmless banter and I completely accept that now. It was cutting, near-the-knuckle banter, but without real malice. It was my interpretation of those remarks that, distorted by my fragile mindset, caused the problems.

Either way, you can't turn back the clock, you can only try and learn from your experiences. What is the saying? That which doesn't kill you only makes you stronger. If that is indeed the case, then I would like to take this opportunity to thank all the fans who booed me and the coaches who persistently bollocked me for ensuring that when I arrived at Blackburn I was a very, very strong person.

If you haven't had bad times then you can never really enjoy the good times, can you? Those years at Birmingham were bad, bad times, but they paved the way for such great times at Blackburn. Being a player at Blackburn was just how I always dreamed being a professional footballer would be when I was a young boy – camaraderie, fan appreciation, a winning team, a joy to be at training every day. As bad as that period at Birmingham was, the subsequent years at Blackburn made up for it – cleansed the spirit, reignited my faith in the game and restored my shattered self-esteem.

The only blip was the heavy drinking spell and I readily put that down to immaturity, the novelty of being away from home for the first time and the almost obligatory mistake-making and poor choices of adolescence. Luckily, I wasn't too badly damaged by that stupidity; on the contrary, it taught me some valuable lessons about striking a balance between relaxing and letting one's hair down at the right time and being professional and preparing for matches in the correct manner.

Finally, the Preston years, and the increasing realisation that it was nearly all over, nearly time to hang up the boots for the last time and turn my thoughts to other things, other opportunities.

And when those opportunities didn't fall into place as expected? The overwhelming panic that the last pay packet had been delivered and I was on my own, alone and treading water in the big scary world outside football.

Enough reflections, self-analysis and amateur psychology – let's cut through all the crap and sum up the whole playing experience in 50 words. Here goes:

Immensely talented player, sadly lacking in innate self-confidence and moral courage and hence unable to play at the level his talent dictated. Not helped by the harsh regime at the club he initially played for. Finally finding his true level in the lower divisions.

There. I can live with that.

PART TWO
MANAGER
(1992-95)

Chapter Seven

HISTORY BECKONS

If I am being totally honest, I felt a bit of a prat (and a failure) sat in a classroom in my thirties with all those young students. Fortunately, there were a total of ten ex-professional footballers on the course and we would be invaluable as friends and motivators to each other to get us through those difficult first few months. Every one of us, at some point, had a personal crisis of commitment and threatened to quit, but the rest of the gang held firm and eventually, albeit four years later, we all graduated.

The course has helped many ex-professionals over the years, including Southampton boss Nigel Adkins, Mark Taylor, head of medicine at Fulham, ex-Oldham winger Rick Holden and Aston Villa physio Stuart Walker. Nowadays, though, the wages are so mind-blowingly good for the current pros I doubt the likes of Torres or Beckham will be enrolling.

I found the actual studying quite easy – if time-consuming – as I had been highly academic at school in Birmingham, but it seemed almost pointless at the time, when you needed a bloody job, to be sat in a classroom earning nothing, four years from being in the position of even applying for a job.

Having said all that, I did understand where the PFA were coming from. No doubt the idea of training ex-professional footballers to be chartered physios was a sound one and, while I could fully understand it might lead to great opportunities, the four-year wait seemed like a life sentence. The thought of living a life of selling clothes a couple of days a week and going to study the rest of the time did not impress.

Cue another piece of luck.

I went to sell my gear at Halifax Town, where the legendary Big John McGrath was now manager. It so happened that the club was looking for a physiotherapist and he asked me if I was interested. Obviously, he said, they would give me the time off to study. I was grateful but explained that, even though I was desperate to get back into full-time football, I really had very little experience in the field of physiotherapy after just a few months of study.

"Don't worry," he said. "We will pay you a shit wage and then you won't feel so bad."

To their credit, they kept their word, and I started work at Halifax Town in the summer of 1992 on a paltry £200 per week plus win bonus (win bonus? This was Halifax – they don't win). Those awful wages notwithstanding, the bottom line was that I would be heading back for another pre-season.

I was so happy and excited, probably more so than at any other time in my life. Yes, the wages were crap, it was a long way to travel, the club was struggling financially and I had to somehow combine it with completing my degree at Salford University, but it didn't matter. I was back. Back in the bosom of the Football League.

I was quite optimistic and confident. I really felt I might be perfectly suited to being a club physio. I was still extremely fit, always got on well with the other staff and players, enjoyed the prestige of being 'the one with the brains' and knew that I had the enthusiasm and work ethic to be successful. This work ethic was driven by the financial difficulties my family and I had endured over the past 12 months. Although we had managed to hang on to our nice family home, we had very little cash and I had had to downgrade to an old Nissan Micra to run around in.

During that period, we had to tighten our belts significantly. Like every other breadwinner, I judged my worth, up to a point, by the amount of money I could provide to make their lives comfortable. Yes, I know money doesn't make you happy *per se*, but I've been relatively well-off and relatively badly off, and I know which one I prefer. I think it was a famous golfer who once said, "Some people say money isn't that important, but for me it's right up there alongside oxygen."

From the first day of pre-season training with Halifax Town in 1992 to the day I left Everton in May 2010, I am confident that nobody, probably in the whole of Britain, worked as hard and for as many days. I think over those 18 years I worked, on average, 350 days per annum. Honestly.

My first day at Halifax Town would be the first step on the ladder that would take me to a top Premier League team, and all the prestige and rewards that came with it. But please don't begrudge me what I went on to achieve because I gave total commitment, day in day out, and most of my motivation was spawned during my 'gap year' when I was out of football, skint and my self-esteem hit rock bottom.

So I was back in the environment I knew and loved. OK, fair enough, I was getting paid peanuts and had to leave at noon three days a week to go to the university. It was slightly different this time, though, because for the very first time I was employed in professional football as a member of staff and not a player. They say nothing in football is as good as actually playing, and I would wholeheartedly agree. Being the physio is not as good as playing; it is better. If I thought I had enjoyed a rich and varied career as a player, then it would be nothing compared to what was to come as a physio.

The sport I returned to was beginning to change. It was the early '90s. Football was emerging from the inertia of the '80s. We were on the verge of the Premier League and Sky TV and we were all about to start sticking our quids in every Saturday for the National Lottery. Bit by bit, the old-fashioned, archaic stadiums were being ripped down and rebuilt or replaced. Some smart new rule changes were about to be implemented that would help re-energise our lacklustre product and drag the fans back in.

Baz was reborn, all kitted up and ready to go. Ready to give his all for the Halifax Town cause. I can't tell you how good it felt to be back in training kit, back in the inner sanctum that is the dressing room, and back among those familiar smells.

Close your eyes, open your nostrils and instantly step into the time machine that is selective memory. It had been a year – a whole year, a long year, and a tough year. Reacquaint yourself with those heady aromas and promise never to let them go again. Leather, Vicks, Deep Heat, shampoo – I am back.

Never again would I take being involved in professional football for granted. The only slight blot on the landscape was that I was a physiotherapist who didn't have a clue how to do the job.

And what of Halifax Town? They were going through a losing period that had started in 1911 – the year they were formed. The smallest club in the Football League, based in a predominately rugby league-supporting town, they had only ever known struggle. If it's true that money talks, then Halifax Town were mute. The smallest average crowd in the Football League generated the smallest income which, in turn, gave them the smallest budget, which afforded them the cheapest players and, hence, the worst team. It was ever thus.

But it was a terrific little club. I loved it from the first minute I walked through the door. Talk about homely and friendly. In many ways, Halifax's *raison d'être* was to struggle. That's what they did. That's what defined them. I don't think any club had applied for re-election to the Football League as many times. The fans, however, were unbelievable. OK, there were only between 1,500 and 1,800 of them, but anybody can support Manchester United; it takes a very special fan to follow Halifax Town.

If only Villa fans knew how close they came to ending up with me! Blues never had a Sunday team so I played for Villa's. Circa 1972, aged 14.

17-years-old going on 50 (that's me – middle row, centre). Kenny Burns (bottom left) is already laughing at me, and Howard Kendall (bottom, second left) and Jimmy Calderwood are discussing my poor form in training.

Anybody seen the ball? If so, don't pass it to me. (Against Man Utd in 1977).

Trevor Francis, Birmingham's best-ever player.

The legendary Sir Alf Ramsey told me I was "fucking crap".

BIRMINGHAM CITY

Just me (front row, far left), Trev (second row, third from left) and Tarantini (third row back, fourth from right) chilling with the Bald Eagle one afternoon.

'Mike Rathbone, DEFENDER'. You wouldn't be able to say that now because of the Trade Descriptions Act.

Birmingham's worst-ever player!

(Right) Flares and curly perm, must be the '70s. The dog is Roscoe, named after tennis player Roscoe Tanner. He was the only one who didn't give me stick during that decade.

Number one? You can tell caretaker manager John Pickering has only just met me, on signing for Blackburn Rovers on loan in 1979.

Russ 'The Full Mog' Coughlin – my drinking buddy, roommate and partner in crime.

Warming up as sub for Blackburn Rovers at Upton Park in 1980, when Howard Kendall was Rovers manager.

Oh my God it's the ball – get rid!
(Against Chelsea, 1981).

'Sacko' – manager and father
figure during my playing heyday.

Band of Brothers: Blackburn Rovers 1986. The total weekly wage bill was probably
about equal to the average modern Premier League player's monthly mobile phone bill.

The mid '80s and the beginning of the end for the hair. That's Max by my side and it looks like he's pulled.

"Hello, hello, Rambo Rathbone!"

"Hey Faz, I'm Rambo not you!" Derek Fazackerley tries to steal my thunder.

Big John McGrath, an absolute legend.

Playing for Preston North End,
circa 1987.

Bald people often have moustaches
or beards.

When I became Halifax manager the *Halifax Courier* dressed me up as Sherlock Holmes (who was played by Basil Rathbone in the films) for a cheesy photo-shoot. I think the theme of the article was the mystery of the disappearing fans!

"What they singing Kammy?"
"Rathbone out, Rathbone out!"

Player/manager/physio/kit man/ youth team coach/bus driver – and failed at every one.

COURIER SPORT

Presented with the 'Evening Courier,' Halifax on Monday, May 10, 1993.

Football League soccer leaves Shay after 72 years

END OF AN ERA

WHEN THE NOISE HAS DIED DOWN THERE'S JUST A MANAGER ALONE WITH HIS THOUGHTS . . . .

● SHAY BOSS Mick Rathbone has a consoling drink in a deserted dressing room as he reflects on what might have happened on Saturday and what lies ahead for Halifax Town.
PICTURE: Alan Barton.

Done it! Achieved what two world wars and the depression couldn't.

Back to Preston as physio and Colin Murdock's lost an eyelash! (Sorry Colin, couldn't resist that...).

A true living legend, and that's Sir Tom Finney on the left. Sir Tom presented me with the 1996 Employee of the Year award at Preston, my first trophy since the early '70s.

That's me at 19!

Getty Images

Preston celebrate reaching the play-off final with victory over Birmingham and Jasper Carrot in 2001. From left to right: Jimmy Lumsden, David Moyes and Kelhan O'Hanlon – a great bunch of guys.

August 2002, my home 'debut' for
Everton, with Oliver and Lucy along
for support at this nervous time.

'Big Dunc', who greeted me to the club
with the immortal line, "I've finished a
few physios in my time!"

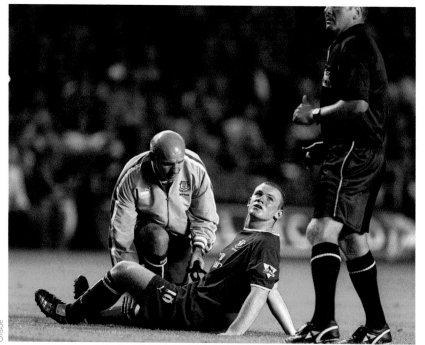

Working with Wayne, the highlight of my career. A great bloke.

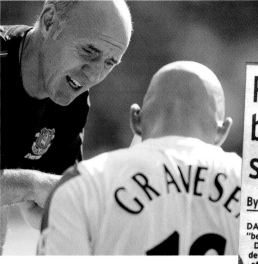

Oh no, Tommy's injured again!

Physio is my best signing, says Moyes

By DAVID PRENTICE

DAVID MOYES paid tribute to his "best ever" signing today.

Despite Sunday's shocking home defeat by Blackburn, Everton are still eight points clear in an unexpected Champions League place.

And the Blues' boss believes physio Mick Rathbone deserves much of the credit for his unsung work in keeping a small squad fit and free from injury.

"I have said all along that 'Baz' is the best signing I have made at the club," he

STAR MAN: Everton physio Mick Rathbone

explained "not just for his top quality physio work, but for his personality as well which keeps everyone going at Bellefield.

"He and his team have done a great job. Of course we have been fortunate as well, although you tend to find that the less players you have in a squad, the fewer injuries you have as well.

"Without naming anybody, there are players here who have

● Turn to Page 47

The Yak runs up to me to celebrate scoring on his return from long-term injury – I was just pleased I hadn't drowned him.

Pass me the handkerchief.

I think he's OK...

I hope he's OK...

Colorsport (3)

Well go and bloody ask him! The great David Moyes and I on the touchline during the 2009 FA Cup final v Chelsea – my greatest day in football despite losing 2-1.

It just doesn't get any better! I hate name-dropping but that's me and Becks in LA where we went for a pre-season tour in 2005. He has that amazing ability to make everybody feel special.

Smile please! I took this photo at a Miami Heat basketball match during a mid-season break in 2007. From left to right: Simon Davies, Gary Cahill, James Beattie and Phil Neville. Business class flights, five star art deco hotel, free tickets and Nev bought the pizzas – what more could anybody ask for?

An absolute honour and privilege to work with him (said Steve).

Another perfectly timed punchline!

That season would be one of the first in history where the team that finished bottom of the division would be automatically relegated into the obscurity of the Vauxhall Conference and non-league football. Halifax were odds-on at the bookies to achieve that dubious feat.

It was great being the physio. It all just clicked into place. I knew a bit more than I thought, based mainly on my experiences as a player. I got on really well with the lads and I think they looked up to me because I had also been a player – in fact, a player who had played at a much higher level than them. All the treatments were based purely on rehabilitation. No fancy machines; just hard work to invigorate, motivate and stimulate. Get them to the training ground early, work them hard and then let them go home – it is still my mantra today. It works. I know – I was a player.

In practical terms, it was great. The players had one of the few physiotherapists who could kick the ball, dribble the ball, and control the ball as well as them, if not better.

I even played in all the reserve games. And then, for the crowning glory, I was asked if I could possibly run in the pre-season cross country and try to keep up at the back just in case somebody sprained their ankle or something. Keep up at the back? I won it by 200 metres to the astonishment of everybody. That was definitely it; I had found my true calling in life. I knew, sadly, I'd had the character defects which stopped me from being a top-class player, but not now, not in this situation. I was born to be a physiotherapist.

Oh, and another thing, as I'd had every injury known to mankind over the past 16 years, I could empathise with the players, get inside their injury, understand it and instinctively know how best to reha-bilitate it. Although I considered myself to have been generally lucky with injuries, over such a long career you do tend to get a wide range of them.

I suffered loads of relatively minor injuries – broken nose (numerous times), stitches, minor strains to nearly every muscle over the years and repeated sprains to my right ankle that has left me with a very odd-looking joint. I have suffered with years of back pain and sciatica due to long-term disc problems, and so many concussions that I can't even remember them (probably due to all those concussions).

Being a footballer can be a dangerous job at times, but I was uniquely qualified to be a physio after all those experiences as a player. Clearly, God had put me on this earth to be a physiotherapist. All right, that might sound a bit over the top but I was at peace and had found my calling.

After a couple of weeks, I heard it for the very first time – the sentence that would define me. "Fucking hell! Don't get fucking injured here whatever you do because Baz will work the fucking bollocks off you." It was, however, always said with affection and respect and I would hear it many times over the years, and each time I would fill with pride.

The medical room at The Shay was an old portakabin. The medical equipment consisted of an ancient ultrasound machine that looked like it had been invented by Thomas Edison and hadn't been serviced since the last war – and I don't mean the Gulf War.

No gym, no pool, no cardiovascular (CV) equipment, no ice machine, no strappings, no weights, no energy drinks, no energy bars, no supplements, no heart-rate monitors. No nothing.

And do you know what? I was glad. You don't need all that fancy stuff to be a good physio. No electrotherapy machines? Good – they have never been proven to work and are time-consuming. No weights? Good – we can do press-ups. No CV equipment? Good – we can use the terraces. No ice machine? Good – we can get in cold baths. You don't need fancy equipment to be effective. Extrinsic stuff like those things may look impressive and modern, but it is the intrinsic things that are more important – enthusiasm, energy, personality, lifting the morale of the players when they are injured, shaking the cobwebs off the long-term injured, getting them off the treatment tables, out of the treatment room, into the fresh air and on the way back to full fitness. Physio for the mind as well as the body. Lift their spirits, motivate them, work them hard, and they will love it, respond to it and start to get better. The mind holds the key to the body's healing.

Big John hit the nail right on the head on my first day when I asked him where all the rehabilitation facilities were. He took me over to the window and pointed to the nearby fell.

"You see that big fucking hill over there? You have my permission to use as much of it as you want."

It was quite funny (the big man still had it), yet it was not without an element of truth. The point is it's not the facilities, it's the personnel. And the personnel at Halifax Town were brilliant. Good people, a fantastic little club and, without doubt, the most loyal and long-suffering set of fans ever.

I was happy and proud to be there and was looking forward to the first League game of the season – the local derby at Rochdale.

I had never actually run on to the pitch to tend to an injured player before the game and I must admit I was quite nervous. Although 99 per cent of the time you were attending to trivial stuff, there is always the potential to be called on to deal with a life-threatening situation. I took my responsibilities very seriously. I took a first-aid course. I thought I was prepared for every eventuality. However, with all the preparation and rehearsal in the world, I still didn't know how I would react when the occasion actually presented itself. Before every game, I spent a few minutes going over all the emergency procedures in my mind. I was still very nervous, though.

I quickly learned that when somebody does get injured, there is a simple rule of thumb that should quickly help to judge the severity of the situation. If players are screaming and rolling around on the floor, then – contrary to what you might think – they are usually OK. It is the ones who just lie there motionless you need to be concerned about.

In my very first game at The Shay it happened – the dreaded serious one. Jimmy Case, our ex-Liverpool legendary hard man, went down over on the far side of the pitch and didn't move. He was quickly surrounded by the referee and some of our very concerned players. They frantically gestured to me to get on right away. Oh, shit. This is what I had been dreading, and for it to happen in my first home game spooked me even more.

I sprang from the dugout. My legs were like jelly (just like that night at Tottenham back in 1976 – shit, I thought all that stuff was history) as I raced across the pitch to the stricken figure. As I ran, I went through all the emergency drills in my head – secure his cervical spine, check he's not choking, airway, breathing, circulation, 15 chest compressions and two breaths with his head extended. Or should that be 15 breaths and two chest compressions, and shouldn't I flex the neck?

By the time I got to Jimmy, everything I had ever learned had totally evaporated from my memory and all I could do was lean over his motionless figure, shake him and plead, "Jimmy, Jimmy, please Jimmy, are you OK?"

He opened one eye, winked and, with that dry Scouse humour, whispered, "Did I get him booked?"

That was a cruel practical joke he played on me that day and I later found out the lads had been planning it all week.

We won 3-2 and it promised to be the year Halifax Town would finally make the headlines.

They would, but sadly for all the wrong reasons.

Fortunately, since that inauspicious start, I have attended many such incidents and, amazingly, nobody has died.

Jimmy was a great fellow. On the pitch a snarling, aggressive, fearsome character, but off it an absolute gentleman, especially when you take into account how much he had won with that great Liverpool team. He would always be helping with the kit and taking his turn to brew up. Always encouraging, never bollocking, a great team player.

And hard? You are not kidding.

After one game down at Cardiff, he came up to me and whispered that he had got a 'scratch'. He rolled down his sock to reveal a huge gaping wound about three inches long and right through to the bone.

"Jesus! Don't worry, Jim, I will take you down to their doctor and he will sort it out."

We went through to their medical room where the doctor started to get his suturing kit out. He sent me down the corridor to the kitchen to get Jim a cup of strong sweet tea. When I got back, he was ready to start stitching, but his needle was so blunt he had to force it through the skin with considerable might. It was stomach-churning stuff and there was a lot of blood.

"Seven, eight, nine, last one, son," said the doctor.

The last one was the most difficult one because it was the area where the wound was most open and, as he forced the needle through the skin for the last time, it embedded itself into the shinbone. Finally, and for the first time during the whole gruesome procedure, Jimmy grimaced.

"Wow," I said, "you *are* human."

"No lad," he said, "too much fucking sugar!"

Those first few months of my first physiotherapy job were so good they were even on a par with my initial 12 months at Birmingham City all those years ago. I loved being the physio. I loved being the physio more than I had loved being a player. Why? Well, even though I finally overcame my early fears and went on to have a career I could be proud of, I had remained a very nervous player and used to start getting butterflies that gradually built up from Thursdays onwards. That's one hell of a lot of butterflies in 16 seasons as a professional player.

But physios don't have to get quite so nervous, as the pressure is so much less on them than it is on the player – or so I thought back in those early days of innocence.

Being the physio was just as I had dreamed it would be – all the involvement, but none of the pressure. I was even thinking of growing my nails.

The only fly in the ointment was the fact that, as ever, Halifax Town were struggling – on the pitch as usual but, more worryingly, off the pitch as well. As they were losing so much money every week, the club started a 'Save the Shaymen' appeal. The message was simple: without the support of the town, the club would go out of business. This was real, not a bluff. The only trouble was that the townsfolk had heard the same line so many times before it was all wearing a bit thin.

When a club is struggling financially, it affects everybody involved. If it goes bust, you don't get paid. Simple as that. OK, I was only getting £200 per week, but at least it was paying the majority of my bills.

That autumn of 1992 was tough for Halifax Town and it was by no means guaranteed they would still be competing in the Football League come Christmas. As ever – and such is the nature of football – even in the midst of that dire financial situation, there was still a funny side to life at Halifax.

We used to get paid on the last day of the month when the club secretary would drive down to The Shay from the little club offices just up the road and pay us all by personal cheque. Sadly, such was the parlous financial state of the club that sometimes there weren't sufficient funds to honour all those cheques when paid in, and only the first players to present the cheques would be guaranteed any money. You should have seen those lads exiting The Shay, like bats out of hell, to be the first to present their cheques at the nearest bank. As Big John would, somewhat harshly, comment, "That's the fastest some of those cunts have moved all season!"

To the eternal credit of the board and the fans who kept digging and digging ever deeper into their pockets, everybody got every penny that was owed to them. It must have been so difficult just to keep the club's head above water. It's all too easy for outsiders to sneer and criticise the directors for being stingy and not investing enough money into the club, but these guys were not millionaires; many were just small local businessmen who kept putting up the cash to keep their beloved club afloat.

On one occasion, I witnessed first hand the financial commitment the directors were prepared to make to the club. I had been invited to a board meeting on a different matter, and they concluded their business while I was still in the room. As ever, the main business of the day was Halifax Town's sorry financial state, and Jim Brown, the chairman, basically asked all the directors to put some extra cash into the kitty or the club would not survive the week.

To a man, those guys got their chequebooks out and donated money – donated, not invested, because they knew they would never see it again. One guy gave £8,000. He was only a small businessman – and, don't forget, this was nearly 20 years ago. I would see this blind altruism many times over the years, at every level of the game, from these often maligned club owners – all for the love of their teams.

Thankfully the fans, board and town collectively came up with the necessary cash, the latest financial crisis was averted and the club breathed a huge sigh of relief when they were cleared to continue playing at The Shay until the end of the season.

It meant the medical budget had to be cut back by 50 per cent. Not that it mattered – what is 50 per cent of nothing? We had no strappings, scissors, bandages or other standard equipment. I used to scour the away team dressing room after every game to see if I could pick up a few dog-ends. I know it's a cliché, but… we were poor but happy.

I developed a great relationship with the players. To be a successful physiotherapist, I think the relationship with the players is the most important part of the whole job. You need compassion, but you can't be soft. You need a relaxed environment, but it can't be a holiday camp. You need to be a friend and confidant to the players, but not to the point where respect is compromised.

The physiotherapist occupies this unique middle ground between the players and the staff. I never betrayed the confidence of any player to the manager and, equally, I never commented on a player's performance. Psychologist, medic, friend and motivator – the good physiotherapist is all of these things.

But on the field, the results just wouldn't come. I shouldn't have been surprised. We had a tiny squad, poor facilities, players who, with respect, only came to Halifax because they couldn't get in at any other club. Inevitably, Big John came under pressure for his job. But what more could he do? It was ever thus.

It was a well-worn joke at Halifax Town that the manager's name was written in chalk on the wall next to his car park space. A shocking 4-1 defeat to non-league Marine in the FA Cup, followed not long after by a home reverse to Barry Fry's high-flying Barnet, and the chairman reached for the duster.

It was the safest bet in soccer that Halifax Town would sack their manager every 12 months, so it was no great surprise when Big John 'resigned'. What was a surprise – in fact, an almighty shock – was their next choice of manager: me!

We'd all had an inkling that Big John was on borrowed time. The players hadn't really bought into his no-nonsense, somewhat off-beat style of management (although he had enjoyed success elsewhere and, as I've said before, I considered him to be an excellent boss). Morale was very low and there had been an all-pervading sense that something had to give. Jim Brown had phoned me a couple of times during that final week of Big John's tenure, asking what the problem was, how the lads felt and what the atmosphere was like. He told me he'd had a meeting with some of the senior players and they weren't happy. What did I think?

To be honest, I really didn't think too much. When you lose every week, morale is always bad. Big John was merely the latest victim of the ongoing problems at the club – a chronic cash shortage. The chairman then told me I was very popular with the players and that they all wanted me to be the next manager. And he agreed.

Fuck me. I nearly dropped the phone. Me, the manager. The manager of a Football League club. I had never even taken a training session, team talk, press conference (they didn't really have press conferences at this level; it was more a chat over a cuppa with a local journo). What did I know?

"But the lads like you, Baz."

"They probably like Kylie Minogue too, but she won't be offered the job, will she?"

Why me? I think the simple answer was that I was there, got on well with everybody, had nearly 20 years of experience in football and, probably most importantly, I was cheap. In Halifax Town's annual turnover of managers, they had tried young, old, experienced, inexperienced, tactical experts, disciplinarians, everything – except clueless. So it was probably worth giving me a go; everything else had failed.

One factor I knew I would require above all others – and this applies to every manager who has had any success – was luck. When asked if he preferred brilliant or courageous generals, Napoleon replied, "Neither. I prefer lucky ones." To be honest, I think even a guy who was confident and optimistic enough to try to invade Russia in winter would have thought twice about taking on this task.

Then it happened, a similar feeling to all those years ago when Trevor first approached me. I started sweating, the hairs stood up on the back of my neck. It had been such a long time since I'd last experienced these unpleasant feelings but, even after all this time, they were unmistakeable. This time, though, I embraced those sensations, determined they would not exert a negative effect on me at a seminal time in my life.

I was winning the fight. Those emotions and physiological responses to stress that had so paralysed me before now began to excite and stimulate me. This was adrenalin, this was positive arousal, this was me overcoming years of conditioning. This was my fate, this was my calling – I was born to be a manager. (Yes, I know a week earlier I'd been born to be a physiotherapist, but people can change, can't they?) I wanted it, I wanted it so badly. I knew I could do it, get those lads playing for me, more motivated, fitter, faster, stronger (it sounds like the bloody Olympic motto).

The chairman's voice interrupted my thoughts and brought me back to the matter at hand.

"Why don't we just make you caretaker for a short period and see how it goes?" he suggested.

"OK yes, I will give it a go."

And that was that. The next day, when Big John resigned, Jim Brown called a meeting and everyone awaited the announcement of Jimmy Case as the next manager of Halifax Town. It was assumed, due to his legendary status, seniority of years and expressed desire to go into management, that Jimmy would take over. What a bloody shock when they announced me.

It sent reverberations around the whole football world – OK, just Halifax then, with a few ripples spreading to the rest of West Yorkshire. The players were jubilant, cheering and back-slapping. The club had placed its future in my hands. A high-risk strategy. The true implications were just about to start sinking in – just like when Napoleon felt the first few snowflakes on his head in Russia. Christ almighty – it's Baz the boss.

I pulled Jimmy Case to one side.

"Jimmy, I thought you wanted to go into management?"

"Yes, I do."

"Well, I didn't and you did, so why am I the manager and you're not?"

I can still see his face with its half-smile as he put his arm around me, pulled me close, and whispered, "Baz, if you start your managerial career here, you will finish it here. You have got no fucking chance."

How profound those words would be.

So that was it. I was now the manager. The youngest in the league, certainly the least experienced and, without any shadow of a doubt, the worst paid. The club, to be fair, immediately put me on a wage commensurate with my new high-powered role – they gave me a £100 a week pay rise (you know me by now, I accepted without a word). At least I was on slightly more than the first-year professionals. I am not afraid to admit my wife actually phoned up the chairman and got me an additional £100 per week on top of that.

My club-issued Ford Escort became a club-issued Ford Sierra and I moved from the tiny spartan medical portakabin to the slightly bigger spartan portakabin next door. We didn't have a game for another ten days (thank God), so I had a bit of time to settle in and get my name chalked up on the car park wall.

I will be perfectly honest – it felt great. Great to be in charge. I decided what to do, when to do it, who to pick, who not to pick (not such a big deal with only 14 players to choose from).

I set the tone of the club. My aim was to learn from Ramsey, Smith, Kendall and Saxton – take something positive from each. Generate that electricity. I knew I was in a high-pressure situation – Halifax Town were facing the unthinkable. If they finished bottom, they would be out of the League for the first time since they were founded in 1911. Would I achieve what two World Wars and the depression couldn't and consign little Halifax Town to footballing oblivion? What responsibility.

I would give my all.

Yes, I was still sensitive, easy-going and gentlemanly, but I had grown up a lot over the years as a result of my various experiences – both good and bad. I was not going to shirk my duties, not this time. Time to stand up and be counted.

I saw this huge challenge as a great opportunity to redress the balance and wipe the emotional slate clean. Deep down I had always felt a sense of regret and, up to a point, guilt at what had happened to me at Birmingham. I was about to enter another very high-pressure situation, but I felt if I could prevail here in these fraught circumstances and emerge triumphant at the other end it could, psychologically, go a long way to exorcising those Birmingham demons.

In fact, the pressure wasn't really that great – we had no money, very few players, even fewer points and no facilities. I was only the caretaker manager anyway. I hadn't asked for the job and the feeling in the town was that I had very much been left holding the baby. The players had pledged their public support, as had Jim Brown and the board. I wasn't stupid. Jesus, if I could succeed here, the world would be my oyster. Forget physiotherapy; a successful manager could earn 50 times more. I saw this as a golden, once-in-a-lifetime opportunity.

What could I offer this beleaguered club? I made a mental promise to myself on that first day: none of my players would dread coming into train, like I used to. Training would be enjoyable. I would always treat players as I would wish to be treated myself. They would be as fit as possible, motivated as possible and, most importantly, they would wake up on the morning of the game and want to play.

Was that achievable, realistic or naive? I would soon find out.

We had no designated training ground as such and rotated between two or three of the town's cabbage patches, depending on the weather. We used to get changed at The Shay – or the 'Stadium of Shite' as we called it. It was very run down in those days but the playing surface was immaculate. I would compliment Bill the groundsman on the quality of the pitch and the cheeky sod would always reply, "Well, there's been a lot of shit on it over the years." Quite funny, to be fair.

From now on, though, it would be nothing but the best for my lads. I told Bill we would be training on the pitch at The Shay.

"OK," he said. "But it is £40 per hour." Amazingly, it turned out to be true – £40 per hour to use our own bloody pitch. Unfortunately, as the council now owned the ground, they were entitled to charge us that amount. Fair enough then, but not too much goodwill.

Nevertheless, we broke the bank and hired the pitch to prepare for the next game – my first game as manager.

The training was brilliant, exuberant and stimulating – it started with a warm-up, then a small-sided game, shooting and finally a few simple shuttle runs, but at an intensity and with a feeling and determination that showed me these lads would give their all for me. I wasn't going to weigh them down with tactics (I didn't know any anyway). We would play with smiles on our faces – well, until the first game anyway.

The first step on the managerial ladder that would probably end up with me lifting the World Cup would be on a Tuesday night at Huddersfield Town in the Autoglass Trophy (at least I think it was called that – the competition has changed sponsors so many times no one ever knows for sure). They were our nearest club geographically, so it would be another local derby.

However, they were in the division above us, so it would be a tough baptism. As the fixture was local, I allowed the players to make their own way to the match (I say I allowed them to make their own way to the match, but we had no choice because the club refused to pay for a team bus).

To say I was nervous would be the understatement of the century. I actually picked the starting XI by drawing numbers out of a bag – only joking – but I did have a unique plan up my sleeve to motivate the players. Cue the ghetto blaster and Tina Turner's *Simply the Best*. I put that timeless classic on, full throttle, just before the team went out on to pitch and we roared out the chorus at the top of our voices.

Wow. What a rush. What emotion. Bring them on. We are invincible.

We lost 5-0.

I was absolutely devastated. We actually played OK, but without much luck, as Russ Bradley, our skipper and best defender, was stretchered off in the first minute – and I will swear to my dying day their fifth goal was offside.

Unless you have been a manager, you will never know the feeling of absolute and total despair every time the ball goes in your net.

1-0 down – we can still win.

2-0 down – we can still get a draw.

3-0 down – we need a consolation goal.

4-0 down – we are fucked.

5-0 down – please don't let it be six.

Talk about being brought back down to earth with a bump. It was time for changes. Tina Turner had played her last game for Halifax Town.

I drove home alone, deep in thought and deeply, deeply depressed. Not since those times at Birmingham had I felt this low. Why did this setback make me feel so bad? I had been on the losing side many times before. Beaten 6-0 at Manchester City, my name being booed by the Birmingham City fans, roasted by Leighton James, sent off in 1979, getting four out of ten in the *Sunday People* – all previous lows.

Jesus, I had never realised just how many lows I'd had. But this was different, this cut deeper, this was me taking the collective responsibility for the whole team – the whole club. Previously, all the bad times had been personal and individual. This failure was on a different scale. At least when you are a player on the end of a bad result you can console yourself with the fact that you gave your best, tried your hardest and, in that pure physical effort, worked the bad feelings out of your system, thus salving your conscience.

But not as a manager. I felt impotent, incapable, unable to stop thinking about the loss. I tried to rationalise the performance and result (you might call it making excuses?). We were away from home, against opposition from a higher division, and lost a key player in the first minute.

Stop kidding yourself.

I soon realised the reason I felt so utterly bad may have been nothing more than the simple case of my ego being deflated. I had been naive in the extreme to think, even for a second, that I could transform little old Halifax Town by simply allowing the players to enjoy their training. I had to be strong now, stronger than I'd ever had to be before in my life.

I have assumed the responsibility, I told myself. I cannot shirk it. I am not the same pathetic person I was all those years ago. Think Howard Kendall. What would he have done? He would have rolled up his sleeves, marched back into the club and lifted the gloom. Sadly, though, I am not Howard Kendall; I am Mick Rathbone – with all the associated bad memories and baggage.

I slept badly that night, tossing and turning, dozing off only to be woken up in a cold sweat by bad dreams – players in blue-and-white shirts (Huddersfield Town) scoring goal after goal against us. Cries of "Rathbone out". The next day the players were off, so I went into the club alone and got changed with the intention of going for a run. Instead, I just sat in the dugout at The Shay. I was hurting like I hadn't hurt since the horrors of St Andrew's all those years ago.

There was, of course, a very simple solution which was becoming more appealing by the minute – just jack it in. Right now. Phone the chairman and tell him you have changed your mind and it's just not for you. He will understand; everybody will understand. This is the ultimate no-win situation. The club is in dire straights, hanging by a thread financially and staring at the footballing oblivion that would be relegation from the Football League. Why take on the burden? What chance do you have of turning the situation around anyway? One phone call and it's over. You could probably even revert to being the physio (when I say revert, that's not technically true because I was still doing the physiotherapy).

Go to your office now, pick up the phone, call the chairman and get out. Breathe a huge sigh of relief. Save yourself a world of pressure. Don't let your legacy be that you were the man who took Halifax Town out of the Football League.

Or, in other words, bottle it, shit yourself, and chicken out.

No!

No!

No!

I am not that man now. I have changed. Once is enough. Time to stand up and be counted. The lads need me. At the very least

I can ensure they stay united, shielded from the pressure, looking forward to coming in every morning. I will not let them down.

The decision was made.

I felt euphoric, invigorated, and reborn. We had mountains to climb. Many difficult times lay ahead. It would be rough. I knew I would be under intense public scrutiny. I would almost certainly be criticised – again publicly. The chances of a good outcome for me and the club were remote.

But all of a sudden, those things no longer mattered. Sat there in the dugout, all alone in that empty stadium, I had just won my finest ever victory. I had finally conquered all my fears and insecurities. I felt a bit like Carton at the end of Charles Dickens's *A Tale of Two Cities* (just prior to him getting his frigging head lopped off). Sacrificing himself for the good of others, his finals words were: "It is a far, far better thing that I do, than I have ever done; it is a far, far better rest that I go to, than I have ever known."

I just hoped it would work out a bit better for me than it did for him.

Chapter Eight
MY PLACE IN HISTORY

The die was cast then. I had made my bed. I would see it through to the bitter end – and I feared it would get bitter. Although I lacked any experience, I actually felt I could be the right man for the job. These lads had been battered mentally. In all likelihood, any player who ends up playing at the bottom club must have, by definition, been through some tough times and faced numerous rejections. The players needed somebody to care for them, to protect them from the harsh realities of the situation we were in. Somebody to rally them, lift their spirits, breathe life into them. If we were to go down, then we would go down fighting. We had a few days to prepare for the visit of high-flying Bury. We would be ready.

Twenty-four games to play with the future of this fine little club in my sweaty hands.

Match 1
Halifax Town v Bury
19/12/92

My first league game in charge. I am introduced to the crowd. Warm applause. Faint chanting of "Mickey Rathbone's blue-and-white army". It is a very small army, but a very determined and loyal one.

I walk into the dressing room at 2pm. With such a small squad, the team has practically picked itself. Even so, the lads are all sitting around nervously, waiting for me to name the starting line-up.

"Right. I have selected a team I think can get us a result today… and it is AC Milan." That lovely little joke breaks the tension and the players visibly relax (I am a bloody genius).

My team talk concentrates on doing ourselves justice, not freezing, trying to enjoy the game as much as possible (some hope). I don't want to be putting too much pressure on the lads by hammering on about the importance of the game or the position we are in. Christ, as if we don't know already.

The game is a blur – stand up, sit down, out of the dugout, back in the dugout, kick every ball, question every decision. The lads huff and puff – and lose. Bury's goal comes from a throw-in that almost certainly should be ours. Everybody can see it. We are robbed.

I barge into the referee's room after the game.

"That should have been our throw-in. That should have been our fucking throw-in."

"Maybe," the referee says candidly. "I didn't get a good view."

"Didn't get a good view? Didn't get a fucking good view? That cost us the fucking game!"

"Sorry, but that's football."

When I calm down, I realise I have learned two important lessons. Number one: Blaming the referee for your team's and your own shortcomings is pathetic, pointless (just like us) and unworthy of your status as manager and leader. Number two: Football matches are often decided on such marginal decisions. Of course, when I say I have learned those things, I already knew them; it's just they have really hit home today.

Count to ten, go see the lads, tell them well done, comfort them and pick them up. No matter how bad I feel personally, this is my job. You promised to see it through – don't weaken now after only one league game.

Next, the two worst jobs after defeat, neither of which I have really thought about. First, the press conference – talk the lads up, we will fight on, lots of positive points (Winston Churchill would have been proud). Then, report to the boardroom to be debriefed by Jim Brown and the directors, who remind me we need to be winning home games. That comes as a surprise; I thought we needed to fucking well lose them. But to be fair, I shouldn't have a go at them; they are good guys who love the club and are just worried and frustrated.

I tidy up, put the medical equipment away, and lock up. I'm pleased to see my car has not been vandalised. Name still there – in chalk.

Match 2
Halifax Town v Doncaster Rovers
26/12/92

This game really spoils my Christmas.

It is cold and the pitch is quite hard. I have to be the physio as well as the manager (my friend Stewart Walker performed the duty at Huddersfield but he can't do it today). We enter uncharted territory – we are leading 2-0. There are only two minutes to go. Two lousy, fucking, poxy minutes.

I run on to tend to an injured player and the referee whispers into my ear, "Two minutes to go, Baz. It looks like your very first win as manager."

Magic words. My first win as a manager – savour it.

By the time I return to the dugout, it is 2-2. Unbelievable. The final whistle goes, the crowd boo. I am shell-shocked.

Nobody speaks in the dressing room. I feel like my very innards have been sucked out. I want to curl up in a little ball and cry. Cry like a baby.

No, come on, take it on the chin. It was never going to be easy. Lift the lads, throw an arm around them, it's a good point earned, we are off the mark, one point nearer to survival and all that. Of course, nobody is buying that bullshit. It is an absolute disaster to drop two vital points in such a manner.

Off to the press – bring out Winston Churchill again. Back to the boardroom where I am reminded we can't afford to give goals away in such a manner. Really? Why not?

Match 3
York City v Halifax Town
29/12/92

Yes. Yes. One of the great nights.

The pitch is frozen. John Ward, manager of in-form York, is gracious enough to seek our opinion on the state of the pitch and if we are happy to play the game on such a surface.

We are really short of players tonight.

"No, it's fine, we play on," I say. No excuses.

We play really well. The lads slide-tackle for the cause on the frozen tundra. One hundred per cent effort and grit. York are outplayed, we deserve to win and even hit the post late on. The final score is 1-1. We are clapped off by the fans and praised by John Ward.

A great performance, a great night, restoring pride in the badge. Everybody is happy. I sprint up the terraces to speak to Pete Barrow, a reporter from the *Halifax Courier*. I give Winston Churchill the night off.

Match 4
Darlington v Halifax Town
9/1/93

This job is easy and I am definitely born to do it. We win 3-0. My new signing Dave Ridings (from non-league football, for the grand fee of nothing) scores two. My new assistant (sounds great, doesn't it?) Alan Kamara, who has just retired from playing, is brilliant. A strong, silent type who is popular with the lads, he helps get the tactics just right – kick the ball into their goal and stop them kicking it into ours.

There are wild scenes of celebration in the dressing room after the game. The lads are excitingly discussing goal celebrations for the next time we score and one of them asks, "Baz, what celebration should we do next time we score?"

"Well," I say, "What's wrong with the one that we have been doing all season? Wrestle the ball off the keeper and sprint like fuck back to the halfway line!"

I light up a big cigar.

"You are all off Monday." Loud cheer.

"Fuck it, and Tuesday." Even louder cheer.

"Don't come in Wednesday either!" A cacophony of noise.

The chairman comes in, grabs me, drags me outside and says, "Don't get so bloody carried away over one win."

It is a bit late for that.

Match 5
Halifax Town v Northampton Town
16/1/93

This team cannot be beaten. We are 2-0 down with less than 20 minutes remaining and Dave Ridings does it again. He scores two goals to salvage a draw. These lads no longer know the meaning of the word defeat. Is this how Bill Shankly started?

Match 6
Scarborough v Halifax Town
23/1/93

We are on a run. A very un-Halifax Town-like run of four games unbeaten. We stop at a roadside café on the way to Scarborough for a cuppa and a bacon butty – our nutritionist can't make it today. Steven Hook, better known as 'Hooky', is playing the fruit machine. (Hooky is Halifax Town's striker, our Johnny Haynes – Johnny was the first £100 a week player and Hooky was probably the last. He was born in the medieval town of Todmorden where public hangings used to take place – and possibly still do. I would pick him up every morning and we became close friends.) He wins the jackpot, but it is paid in tokens only, so we have to hang on a while so he can gradually reinvest his tokens into the machine (the smaller wins are paid in cash).

I feel good sitting at the front of the bus. At the head of my team – my unbeaten, and now unbeatable, team. I wonder if we can get to the end of the season without losing another game.

We lose 2-0.

We actually play quite well and deserve more. I am still doing a good job. The players are doing a *great* job.

Match 7
Halifax Town v Cardiff
26/1/93

Another outrageous conspiracy by the officials to halt my rise to the top.

Cardiff win 1-0. What is wrong with the goal? Well, it's offside, the ball goes out of play, it's well past the time for the final whistle, and there is an element of handball. That's all. Take your pick.

Into the referee's room. Shouting and arguing. Hating myself. Knowing it's too late. Not behaving like a man. If you can't stand the heat, stay out of the referee's room.

By the way, I should mention they completely outplayed us and should have won by three or four. Never mind, Cardiff are one of the top sides; no disgrace there.

I go back to the dressing room to lift the troops. Who's going to lift *me*? I am starting to find the going a little bit tough.

Match 8
Scunthorpe United v Halifax Town
30/1/93

Ouch. What's that hissing noise? The sound of an ego being deflated.

We are beaten 4-1. Well beaten. We never get going and are three down after 30 minutes. The fans are starting to have a go. Somebody shouts, "Resign Rathbone." Or is it "Re-sign Rathbone?" Probably the former.

For the first and last time, I go mad at the players after the game. Why? Because that's what you do when you lose heavily, don't you?

Shouting and screaming at the players is pointless and counter-productive. They have done their best. I know they have. I am beginning to feel the pressure. I have a go at the players in the press conference as well. Again, a terrible betrayal of their efforts. Screaming at the players is just not me. I am surprised the lads don't burst out laughing. I apologise to them later.

Into the boardroom. Jim Brown says, "I don't need to remind you how serious the situation is now, do I?"

No, but you just did.

Match 9
Halifax Town v Rochdale
6/2/93

Right, I am preparing for this game like it is the World Cup final. I go to watch Rochdale play and note they are dangerous from corners due to the height of their centre halves.

We change our preparation for this game. Instead of the lads just reporting for the game one hour before kick-off, we meet at The Shay at 10am, do a light training session, go through their team individually, noting the danger from set pieces, have a pre-match meal at the ground and enter the match perfectly prepared.

Their centre half heads the ball in from a corner in the second fucking minute. I sit in the Perspex dugout and can feel the sides closing in. This is becoming almost unbearable. I am waiting for that famous Halifax Town chant to start – "Rathbone out, Rathbone out."

It never comes, and the fans get behind the team. We rally, get back to 2-2 and then, tragically, concede a third and decisive goal.

What a sickener. I don't know how much more of this I can take. I happen to be wearing some new shoes today – Brogues, with a big toecap. After everybody has gone, I lose it and proceed to kick a big hole in our dressing room door. (So there it is. The secret is out. It was me who kicked that hole in the door. I am very sorry.)

Match 10
Halifax Town v Lincoln City
10/2/93

Hallelujah. Praise be to God, peace on earth and goodwill to all referees. We win, our first home win since October, I'm told (I am assuming that is October 1992).

Jimmy Case scores his first goal for the club. We don't play very well, but am I bothered?

I am very happy and proud of myself because, even though I'm starting to feel the pressure, I have kept my promise to behave, at all times, in a manner that inspires respect and confidence in my players. I think I'm doing well on that front (no one saw the door incident). I am holding up well, especially on the outside. The league table is starting to look a bit better, although we are still hovering a few places above the foot of the table.

What if we pull it off? I don't dare to dream what that could lead to.

Jim Brown is happy and relieved; I even get to stay for a drink. His parting words are, "Don't forget, Baz, two swallows don't make a spring."

Isn't it: "One swallow doesn't make a summer?" Never mind.

Match 11
Halifax Town v Crewe Alexander
20/2/93

Crewe are far too good for us. They win 2-1, but it could have been more. A lot of their players have come through their youth ranks. Halifax Town, meanwhile, have just abolished their youth scheme, which has caused a degree of bad feeling in the town and alienated a lot of people. I decide, at the end of the season (lynching permitted), I will organise some trials and start the youth policy again. That will be my legacy to the club.

Deep down, I am worried it won't be my only legacy.

Match 12
Colchester United v Halifax Town
26/2/93

Big Roy McDonough, my very close friend, old team-mate from all my schoolboy teams and a former Birmingham City apprentice (he was a member of the daily 'kick the ball into the farmer's field and avoid training with the first team' routine I had perfected) is the manager of Colchester. It is quite odd because Roy, Ian Atkins and I are all from Sheldon, all played tennis together in the close season and all have gone on to become Football League managers. We are probably the last three people on the planet anybody would believe would become managers. (I am sure all the fans of the teams where we got sacked would agree!)

Some friend Big Roy turns out to be. We lose 2-1. We are leading, then our goalie is sent off, and that's that.

Roy and I have a few beers after the game and reminisce about the good old days at Birmingham City. Good old days? Fuck me, how much have we drunk? He's a great bloke and a lifelong pal but right now, at this very moment, I hate the fucker's guts.

We are sinking fast, games are running out, we need results. On the exterior, I remain calm, the personification of dignity and relaxedness. Team spirit and training are still very good. Morale is still high. In these respects, I am doing a great job.

Everybody, however, is getting very worried now.

Match 13
Halifax Town v Carlisle United
6/3/93

We lose 2-0. No excuses. We don't play well. The fans' complaints are growing louder. That's to be expected, but I am not going to crack up now. No way. I will be strong and meet the challenge head on. We are in deep shit now. We have dropped down to 20th, just two spots off the bottom of the league. It's getting hairy now. I merely exist during the week thinking only of the games coming up. Eleven to go. Running out of games, running out of time.

Match 14
Torquay United v Halifax Town
13/3/93

When you look down the list of remaining fixtures, it seems very, very short. When I took over, I reckoned we needed six wins from 24 matches. That sounded relatively easy. Now, though, I feel we need four wins from the last 11 games, or more than one in three. It suddenly sounds very daunting.

More worryingly, I am starting to get angry letters from the fans. The secretary puts them on my desk. I know what they are, sitting there looking at me all day, their Halifax postcodes a dead giveaway.

One is addressed to Mick Rathbone "manager" Halifax Town. I don't like the look of that, the way the word manager is written in quotation marks. I chuck that one away without even opening it. (If you wrote that letter all those years ago to say I was doing a great job, then I do apologise. However, if you just wrote to me, like several others, to say I was a wanker, then too bad, mate.)

One letter starts: "Dear Mr Rathbone, where is the attacking football you promised us?" (That opening sentence has stuck in my mind even after all these years. I don't know what came next because I filed it in the same place as the other one.)

Some are constructive and encouraging, to be fair. I have no complaints, though. These people are understandably concerned about the future (or lack of it) of their beloved club. As I have said before, anyone can support Man Utd or Chelsea, but these Halifax fans are truly the most stoical and long-suffering set of fans in the country, and I greatly respect them for it.

We are down but not out. In terms of team spirit, motivation and organisation, I know I am doing a good job and, crucially, I feel I am sheltering the lads from the pressure of the situation.

I can't get the results I'm hoping for, but I am getting the commitment from my players I've asked for.

And so, with hope in our hearts, we set off on the long journey to Devon to face Torquay, who are also struggling. We leave on the Friday for a rare overnight stay. We play very well and should be awarded a penalty but then, soon after our appeal is denied, Torquay get a penalty at the other end when Chris Lucketti makes a perfectly timed challenge on one of their players. In short, we have been robbed again (is it all starting to sound depressingly familiar?) and then they double their lead and put the game beyond us.

Right on cue, Mr Predictable storms into the referee's room after the game. Shouting, arguing, not recognising myself – anybody who knows me would be astonished by my behaviour. But that's what pressure does to you.

The situation is getting ever more desperate. They are oiling the trap door.

A few days later, I am invited to be the guest speaker at the monthly meeting of the Halifax and District Referees Society. I decide to do them a favour and grace their little get-together with my presence. (That's another thing about being the manager; you can get a big ego even when you are getting beaten every week.)

To my surprise, I get quite an unfriendly reception, presumably due to my constant criticising of match officials. To cut a long story short, I am asked a lot of questions, the upshot of which proves I don't even fully know the rules regarding the incidents of which I have been so critical.

It is a sobering experience and I learn an awful lot from the evening. Firstly, the guys who are reffing the games are the very best in the country. If you can start with that mindset, then it makes it much easier to accept their decisions. Secondly, the players make far more mistakes than the officials and earn up to ten times more money (OK, maybe not at Halifax). Finally, managers who criticise officials are not behaving in a manner appropriate to their status at a football club.

I learn all these lessons as the refs exact their well-earned revenge. From now on, I will never again question any decision by any official – even the short-sighted, bent ones.

Match 15
Halifax Town v Shrewsbury Town
20/3/93

A 1-1 draw. Fair result, decent performance. One point closer to survival (to the lads and press). Two more home points dropped (if I'm being honest).

Match 16
Chesterfield v Halifax Town
23/3/93

Midweek game. Usual story: we play well, we miss chances, we go 1-0 up and lose 2-1 to two late goals. In the wake of this defeat, we sink to the bottom of the league for the first time. It is a truly shocking and sobering experience to look at the table and see Halifax bottom of the pile.

Worse is to come. I am 'invited' to travel back to The Shay in the chairman's car. With him is the gentleman who has been putting the lion's share of the money into the club and he, understandably, wants some answers.

Never has a journey taken so long. Of course, I understand their concerns and admire the directors for giving their money to the club, but I just don't need that grilling, especially on the night when we slip into bottom place. They ask if I want them to get another manager in. Somebody more experienced to help me?

"Yes please."

Or should they just replace me with another manager?

"Again, yes please."

Or should I just resign?

"Yes please. Do what you want; I am only trying to do my best."

Ironically, my job is saved on this occasion by the feeling that it is so late in the day, in terms of games to go, that in many ways the die is already cast. Besides, they aren't sure they will find anybody of any repute prepared to put their name on the line in such difficult circumstances. So, it is decided – somewhat by default – that I will fight on.

Thanks for the vote of confidence.

They then remind me that tomorrow is transfer deadline day and it is imperative I abandon training and spend the whole day in the office (portakabin) on the phone, from 9am until the close of the transfer window at 6pm.

I am somewhat taken back. "But I didn't think we had any money available for new players?"

"No, you don't understand. If we don't sell a player or two tomorrow, there will be no money to pay the March wages."

That's it then. We are surely dead and buried.

The next day, we sell our top goalscorer, Ian Thompstone, to Scunthorpe for £10,000. March's wages are guaranteed; Halifax Town's future certainly isn't.

At some point during the nine-hour ordeal in the portakabin, I get a call from an agent. He has a player, a very, very good player – no, a great player. A Cameroon international called Godfrey Obebo. He will come and join Halifax Town for nothing (how many truly great players could you say that about?). What the hell? Why not? We are fucked now, we have nothing to lose, so we sign him. His agent says he has been playing in Serie A. He is a lovely man, deeply religious, and very muscular.

Match 17
Halifax Town v Wrexham
26/3/93

We are beaten easily. The final score is 1-0, but it should, and could, have been 6-0. The coaches, Brian Flynn and Joey Jones – both good fellows – don't rub it in when Wrexham score (that always stuck in my mind).

I'm running out of things to say now to the press, the players and the chairman. How about we are the strongest team in the Football League – propping up the rest? At least I can still laugh.

Match 18
Barnet v Halifax Town
3/4/93

This fixture causes controversy that puts both clubs in the head-lines. Normally we would have travelled down to London on the morning of the game, getting to Barnet at 2pm after a five-hour journey (traffic permitting). However, a mystery benefactor, thought to be linked to one of Barnet's promotion rivals, has paid for us to stay in a hotel on Friday night. (It caused quite a furore at the time and I think Barnet may have complained to the Foot-ball League about this interference.)

Fortunately for us, all the great preparation pays off and sets us up for a battling performance, and a deserved point, as we draw 0-0. We could even have won it, but we missed a late sitter.

We are still 22nd in the league, but daring to dream.

Match 19
Doncaster Rovers v Halifax Town
10/4/93

Time to unleash our secret weapon – Godfrey Obebo.

We go 1-0 up after three minutes. But then one of our players gets injured, so I ask Godfrey to warm up. Godfrey takes this a little too literally and goes to the dressing room to sit by the radiator – no kidding. We have to send the other sub to go and fetch him. Godfrey then produces a virtuoso warm-up on the touchline that resembles something between somebody performing a breakdance and somebody having a fucking seizure.

Play stops, allowing us to make the change, when the ball is kicked clean out of the stadium. As Godfrey jogs into the fray and play restarts with a replacement ball, the original ball reappears, bouncing off the stand roof and onto the side of the pitch. There then follows one of the funniest things I have ever witnessed in football, as Godfrey latches on to it and speeds off in the direction of Doncaster's goal with one ball, while the other 21 players play on in the opposite direction with the correct ball.

Sadly, it transpired, he was not even a footballer's cousin. And Serie A? I think I misheard. He actually said Syria!

This hilarious incident, coupled with an excellent 1-0 away win, make it a memorable day for us. We climb off the bottom. I am starting to believe we can do it.

Match 20
Halifax Town v York City
12/4/93

I feel this game is crucial. If we win, then I think we can stay up. Mind you, if we'd won our last 20 games, we'd be top of the league.

We lose 1-0 to another disputed goal although, to be fair, I am disputing every goal by now – and every free kick and every throw-in too (so much for my promise to the refs).

If only. Those words should be engraved on the Halifax Town badge in Latin.

Match 21
Bury v Halifax Town
17/4/93

Four games to go.

We win 2-1 against promotion-chasing Bury. It is our best result, and best performance, of the season. Absolutely marvellous. Scenes of jubilation in the dressing room. What a celebration. This could guarantee survival.

But wait.

Jesus Christ! What a complete and utter choker. Torquay have unbelievably won 1-0 at in-form Shrewsbury. Our party stops dead in its tracks. For the first time there is a look in the eyes of the players that says we are doomed. We get three points, but then the unthinkable has happened. This is it. It just isn't meant to be. I must stop them thinking like that. It's so self-destructive. The only problem is, deep down, I now believe it myself.

Match 22
Halifax Town v Walsall
24/4/93

Three to go.

We are trounced 4-0. A really desperate performance at a time when we needed to produce something special to lift everybody at the club and give ourselves some hope.

Again, our home form is the problem. A combination of the players freezing at The Shay, the small pitch and the lack of atmosphere caused by the large speedway track around the playing surface, which forces the fans into the far corner of the stadium where they can't be heard, culminates in this almost certainly being every team's favourite away ground (you can add shit manager to that list).

Our performances and results on the road have not been that bad – three wins, two draws and six defeats would have kept us out of trouble if we'd had any semblance of form at home. Our form at The Shay, though, is disastrous. One win and three draws since I've been in charge is putrid and relegation form in anybody's language.

After the game, I am really choked and can hardly bring myself to talk to the players until I compose myself. All those rallying words now just seem empty rhetoric – everybody has been listening to the same old shit for more than four months now.

Match 23
Gillingham V Halifax Town
1/5/93

Last but one game. Drinking in last-chance saloon now. This game at fellow strugglers Gillingham is the real crunch match of the season.

Here is the situation (and it's not great): we are bottom of the pile on 36 points. One point ahead of us are both Gillingham and Torquay, while Northampton have 38 points but only one game remaining. So, the good news is that if we win, we'll be off the bottom. The bad news is, if we lose, then we'll still be bottom and it'll be out of our hands.

I am so far behind with my studies it doesn't even bear thinking about. How can I cope with what I am going through on a daily basis and then go home and write an essay about somebody getting a bloody hip replacement?

On the Friday before the trip down to Gillingham, I should be spending the afternoon doing a clinical placement at Burnley Hospital. They have gone to the considerable trouble of arranging special patients for me to see, but when the club find the resources for us to go down to Kent on Friday morning, I have to let them down. I don't turn up. How can I? I feel terrible, letting all those people down, but I have to travel to Gillingham with the team. It is as simple as that. The hospital are understandably furious, and who can blame them? I will be marked down severely for not turning up. I am now in grave danger of completing a horrific personal double – taking a team out of the Football League and flunking my course.

Saturday is a lovely warm spring day in Gillingham. Roughly 1,000 Halifax fans have travelled to the south-east. We completely outplay them, going close to scoring on many occasions. However, we lose 2-0 to two speculative long shots. The thousands of home fans packed into the compact and atmospheric Priestfield Stadium go crazy. They are mathematically safe now.

Glenn Roeder, the Gillingham manager, comes into our dressing room after the game, congratulates us on our gutsy performance and sympathises with our plight. He is emotional – and mightily relieved. He knows the luck has been with him. They are safe; we are anything but.

Many times over the ensuing years, I would see Glenn with England, Watford, West Ham and Newcastle, always behaving like the perfect gentleman, and I would think: what if? What if our shots had gone in on that warm spring day and theirs hadn't? We would have been safe and they might have gone out of the Football League. Would I have gone on to greater managerial things than him? But that's all pie in the sky. The fact remains: we lost again.

Worst news follows. Torquay have won 1-0 at Carlisle. We can't catch them now either.

We will go into the final game of the season against Hereford United next Saturday at The Shay, needing to win to survive while also praying Northampton do not win at Shrewsbury.

I am about to enter the most turbulent and emotional week of my life.

Chapter Nine

THE FINAL RECKONING

Match 24
Halifax Town v Hereford United
8/5/93

Andy Warhol said, "Everyone will be famous for 15 minutes."

Well, this is my 15 minutes. For once the cameras of the football world are pointing in the same direction – Halifax. Well done me. What an achievement.

This small working-class town, nestling in the foothills of the Pennines, is about to be the focus of seven days of intensive media interest. Everybody likes a good tragedy and this is a classic in the making – famous, proud old club on the verge of Football League extinction after an almost constant struggle since its formation in 1911.

The ghouls are out in force. The club has received hundreds – maybe even thousands – of requests for the match programme from collectors from, literally, all over the world. The ground is only able to accommodate 7,500 spectators due to safety laws, and these tickets have gone like hotcakes. Our average home gate of less than 2,000 will be nearly quadrupled for this game.

To my horror, early in the week I notice a scaffold is being erected by the main stand. I am mightily relieved to discover it is for the TV cameras, and not my lynching.

Just how do you prepare a set of young players for a game of such importance? How can you try to diffuse the pressure of such an occasion? How can you possibly get the lads to relax and treat it as just another game in such difficult circumstances? All we can do is train and prepare and go home and come back the next day, and train and prepare again and keep looking anxiously at the clock as the hours tick by to our collective date with destiny.

The mindset of the players during this final week of training? Shitting themselves. And the manager? Shitting himself too. What do you expect? I think I am hiding it well. I believe I am exuding a calm, confident persona, despite my shaking hands.

Finally, after a relentless round of interviews and photo opportunities, the day of destiny is almost here. The day that will decide the future of little Halifax Town. Needless to say, I don't sleep at all on the Friday night – not a single minute. The last time I managed that was on a foam party night back in the early '80s in Magaluf. I lie awake, hardly daring to contemplate the two alternatives – carried off shoulder-high, the hero and saviour, or booed off as the man who had taken Halifax Town out of the Football League. What a stark contrast.

On the way to The Shay on the day of the match, I very nearly stop at a church to pray. Pathetic really, as I'm not even remotely religious and, even if I was, I doubt the Lord would have any great interest in Halifax Town's plight with so much other shit going on in the world. (To this day, though, I do wonder if the outcome would have been different had I stopped).

When I arrive at The Shay, it is so unlike a usual home game – there are lots of people there, for a start. There are also a host of TV vans from Yorkshire TV, BBC and Sky.

There is a carnival atmosphere. It is quite nice really and I start to relax and get carried along by the whole thing. Of course, many of the 7,500 people are only here to witness the end of an era, to be able to say they were there when Halifax Town played their last home game in the Football League. All we need now is a couple of old hags knitting and the picture of impending doom will be complete.

The lads arrive one by one, looking pretty ashen-faced. For any professional, to play in a team that gets relegated from the Football League is the ultimate embarrassment, the ultimate shame. But somebody has to finish bottom, don't they?

I have thought long and hard about my team talk, but decide to keep it simple. I tell the players I am proud of them, thank them for their efforts, and urge them to go out there and do their best. I reassure them that the situation they find themselves in is not their fault, but the inevitable consequence of being at a club with the lowest financial resources, year in year out.

Tick tock, tick tock, the referee looks at his linesmen and the biggest game in the history of Halifax Town kicks off.

It is like a cup final. Who would have thought it – little old Halifax Town in a cup final?

The players are up for it and so am I. I kick every ball for them. The atmosphere is electric. Dave Ridings nearly scores early on.

At half time, it is 0-0. A loud cheer goes up at the interval as the score from the Shrewsbury Town v Northampton Town game trickles through. It's 2-0 to Shrewsbury! Fantastic. All we have to do is score one solitary goal and we will be safe.

At the start of the second half, the noise is deafening. We go close again. Bad news elsewhere, though, Northampton have pulled one back.

The reports from Gay Meadow get progressively worse. Northampton equalise and then, incredibly, go 3-2 up. They only need a draw to be safe, regardless of our result. The Shay falls into stunned silence. It doesn't even seem to matter when Hereford score a late goal.

We have lost. We are out.

When the referee blows the final whistle that signals the demise of this marvellous, homely, proud, little club, there is an almost tangible gasp of despair.

The scenes after the game will stay with me for the rest of my life. The fans invaded the pitch – one, two, three generations of Shaymen, most in tears, singing, "There will always be a Halifax Town." It was the most emotional thing I ever witnessed in professional football.

And recriminations?

Surprisingly none. They chanted for me to appear and say a few words. I muttered some rubbish about coming back stronger, that sometimes you need to take a step backward before you take a giant leap forward etc. It was hardly William Shakespeare. It turned out to be empty rhetoric.

Back in the dressing room the players, to a man, were in tears. I felt a strange mixture of emotions – despair at what had befallen the club, of course, and terrible pity for the supporters. I felt a great deal of pride in the efforts and commitment of the lads, as well as sheer relief that the whole ordeal was over.

But my overriding feeling was that I had been a winner.

A winner? A winner who had just got relegated from the Football League? Yes, I felt a winner. I saw it through, through all the pressure. I stood tall, the lads never let me down and, more importantly, I never let them down.

Call me a loser if you want, but I knew I was a winner, especially when judged in the context of those awful experiences at Birmingham City all those years ago. I had laid that ghost well and truly to rest.

All the excitement, passion, sorrow and emotion were suddenly gone, to be replaced by… lots of litter, actually. I stood alone by the dugout. Everybody had gone home. It was eerily quiet. It was over. So was my job probably. The board usually weren't too backward in coming forward with the P45 for their managers. Surely the duster would be brandished by the chairman? I was bracing myself for the phone call.

What did the future hold? I was light years behind with my studying, but I didn't really give a damn. I knew those last few turbulent months, and the manner in which I had coped with everything thrown at me, had given me the strength of character, mental toughness and self-confidence to get to the top in anything I did. My self-esteem was sky-high and the whole fraught experience had proved to be a catharsis that finally vanquished any lingering demons from my past.

Amazingly, that dreaded phone call never came. I kept my job – or should that be jobs. Maybe it was a matter of simple economics and they couldn't afford to get rid of me and replace me with a new manager, physio, reserve team coach etc. In fact, it turned out the club's major concern regarding my position was that with all the studying I was doing I would find it increasingly difficult to commit the time to my roles at Halifax Town.

I had a meeting with the club and they were very fair. They were concerned about how much work I had to do and suggested they should appoint a joint manager to share the job and the workload. Somebody older, a bit more experienced, who knew the Vauxhall Conference perhaps. They felt if they retained me solely as the manager for the next season and we didn't start well, then they would have to sack me quite quickly.

I told the board I would prefer to take my chances on my own because I actually felt I could be a decent manager, especially the following season when we would have one of the best teams in the league. I felt confident my methods would bring success, given a level playing field and a fresh start.

In terms of results, I held my hands up and accepted I'd failed as a manager – although for reasons previously explained, I also felt a winner. In pure footballing terms, taking a team out of the Football League doesn't look too good on any manager's CV. What was my managerial record? Won four, drew five, lost plenty. It was hardly going to put me on the shortlist for the next England job, was it?

The board said they had taken my views on board and would get back to me.

During that spell as manager, I realised just how fine a line there is between success and failure – a crucial refereeing decision, a key player getting injured, that quintessential rub of the green and run of the ball.

How much can the manager influence things anyway? OK, he picks the team, but if he only has a paper-thin squad and no cash to buy players, what can he really do? He takes training every day, fair enough, but you can't make a silk purse out of a sow's ear.

John Bird, one of many recent Halifax Town managers, was equally philosophical about the true value of the manager. He reckoned if a team had no manager then, by the law of averages, they should still win one, lose one and draw one throughout the season. If his theory was correct, then there are plenty of so-called top managers who should be looking over their shoulders. Indeed, if you follow his rationale even further, then Halifax would have been better off without either John or me. It's a sobering thought.

Of course, there are some truly wonderful managers in the game, some of whom such as Kendall and Ramsey I was lucky enough to work under, but undoubtedly some teams succeed in spite of their manager. Management presents the ultimate footballing paradox. If it is supposed to be the crucial all-important appointment, reserved only for the best of the best, then how is it that people whose only qualification is that they were great players or just happened to be at the club working in a lesser role (me) can become managers of top clubs?

In what other industry would this happen? If you were an exceptionally good mechanic, joiner or plumber, and the head of the large corporation you worked for got the sack, would you have even the remotest chance of getting that top job? Of course not. But in football, this is common practice. In fact, many top ex-players who have been fast-tracked into management have proven conclusively that good players seldom make good managers. But why should they? Playing is playing; managing is completely different and encompasses such diverse factors as man-management, tactical acumen, discipline, dealing with the press, organising training, and buying and selling players. Yet still, this complex and difficult job is offered to people with virtually no experience in any facet of the job.

Ironically, some of these guys do sometimes succeed. What does that tell us about management? That these people unearthed from within the actual club happen to be, by an incredible coincidence, the right ones for the job, or is it more likely that sometimes the best men for the job just never get a chance?

While the Halifax board was deciding if I'd get another chance as a manager on my own, I had the opportunity to take a break from football and get a breather from the tumultuous events of the past few months.

However, that summer following the relegation was tough. I had just been to hell and back emotionally, but even so there was no respite – two days after the season finished, I was off on a six-week work placement at Bolton General Hospital. I started at 9am and finished at 5pm before getting in my club car and driving over the Pennines to Halifax to spend a couple of hours doing club business, such as sorting out players' contracts and organising pre-season. I would finally arrive home in Blackburn at around 9pm – knackered and smelling of old people. So there were no holidays for the Rathbones for nearly four years. In fact, there were virtually no days off for the best part of four years.

But you know what? I wasn't bothered. I could, and would, do it because I knew it would all be worthwhile in the end. Nothing was going to stop me.

Over the previous two decades, I had experienced so many good and bad times that I had developed a strong and resolute character able to survive this football rollercoaster – I wouldn't take the highs and the lows for anything other than the transient and shifting sands they were.

Nothing phased me now. My personality was fully rounded, resilient, confident and, I hope, still humble and gentlemanly. I got my head down and kept going, day in day out.

I was called in to another meeting with Jim Brown in early

June. He reiterated the board's preference for me to be employed as a joint manager, and introduced me to Peter Wragg, the ex-Macclesfield manager and a man whose non-league CV was second to none.

I still told the board no, I wanted sole control. With my methods I so strongly believed in (and still do), I thought we would be successful.

They reluctantly agreed, but reminded me that if we had a poor start to the season, they would have to act quickly.

Several days later I had just come out of intensive care (all part of the physio course, don't worry) when I picked up a copy of the local paper and was horrified to read the headline on the back page: Wragg and Bone. It was a *fait accompli*. They had appointed Peter over my head and without my agreement (to be fair, though, it was an absolutely fantastic headline).

Although I smiled at the headline, I felt hurt, betrayed and let down. I knew I could have done it on my own. I deserved to be given the chance to do it on my own, I needed to be given the chance to do it on my own for reasons you should know by now.

Peter was a good guy and we became great friends, but the worst ship that ever sailed is a football managers' partnership. As I was away throughout June doing my work at the hospital, Peter started to assume more and more control. I couldn't blame him for that – I wasn't there. However, he made a lot of changes I wasn't happy with. He changed the pre-season schedule that I had organised, signed some of his own players and, most worryingly, found the hidden stick of chalk and put his name on the car park wall.

We ended up having a no-holds-barred meeting with Jim Brown, who made it clear he saw Peter as the senior figure in the partnership and, essentially, that was it. I could like it or lump it.

So I lumped it. I still had two years to go until I qualified and I needed that wage. Beggars can't be choosers, can they? And to be fair to the club, they were as good as gold and allowed me to stay on, on my manager's wage of £20,000 per annum plus club car.

Nevertheless, going back to Halifax at the beginning of July for the first day of pre-season training, having effectively been demoted to the role of assistant manager, was a bitter pill to swallow, believe me. Talk about a loss of face; I just wanted to walk out. But I didn't, I couldn't.

The players were very upset, as were the office staff (both of them). The players all felt that with me still as boss we could have achieved promotion at the first attempt. However, it was done. We had to support 'Wraggy' now. The club had to come first. We all had to pull in the same direction. We owed that to the fans.

It was another knockback for me, but so what? I was invincible now. I would take it right on the chin and come back for more. It's not the getting knocked down that matters; it's the getting up – and I bounced right back up off the canvas.

Chapter Ten

AFTERMATH

I stayed at Halifax Town for two more years. Peter Wragg came and went after nine months, while the club struggled to cope with the Vauxhall Conference. They remained fully professional, but had to let the best players go. As a result, the team became weaker but, as the only professional club in the league, they were everybody's favourite scalp. The opposition always raised their game when they played the professionals.

I concentrated on looking after the full-time Youth Training Scheme (YTS) lads who had just joined the club's new programme that I was proud to say I instigated. Looking after that group of young players was one of the most satisfying jobs I have ever done in football, for all the obvious reasons such as being involved in their football development, working outdoors on the grass, gaining their confidence and trust. But, as ever in the thread of my life, there was a deeper reason – creating an environment for players to enjoy their football free of the criticisms and pressures that I was subjected to. I felt like I was their guardian angel, the man who would ensure they loved coming into work every day.

Of course, I was having to combine that work with all my other roles at the club. I was still the first-team coach, assistant manager, reserve-team player-coach and physiotherapist.

John Bird took over as manager. Again, I liked him very much. He, like Wraggy before him, did his level best to turn the club around but, like the rest of us, failed. The club was in a desperate financial plight again. 'Birdy' and I were often asked not to cash our pay cheques until after the next home game.

It was bloody tough, but I was creeping ever closer to finishing my degree. Only 12 months to go. Once I got that qualification and became a fully qualified chartered physiotherapist, I knew I would be successful. Just keep going. Keep going. Keep banging out the hours.

Towards the end of my third season, with the club again struggling to survive, a new chairman, John Stockwell, came in. The club looked like they were going to have to become semi-professional. They certainly could no longer afford to pay both Birdy and myself, so I was made redundant or, probably more accurately, sacked, in April 1995. It's all a matter of semantics at the end of the day.

So ended a tumultuous three seasons at Halifax Town. Sometimes, even today, I sit down and think, "What the fuck was all that about? How did all that happen? How did so much happen to me in such a short space of time?"

But right at that moment in time, I was faced with the question so many people working in football have to answer: what now?

If I was to graduate on time in June 1995 then I would have to fit another eight-week work placement in during April and May. Fortunately, by making me redundant, Halifax had done me a massive favour because I now had just enough time and opportunity to finish all those laborious hospital placements before sitting my final exams at the start of June.

So, to the Halifax board who decided they no longer wanted me, even though I had worked so hard and done so many different jobs on such a poor wage, don't feel too bad (I am sure they never did anyway); you did me a big favour.

And John Bird? He bucked the Halifax trend and lasted more than two years.

I left Halifax with a treasure chest of precious memories: the lads and the camaraderie; those first few months when I was just the physio and developing my own personal style in that role; being the boss, setting the tone, stamping my own personality and set of standards on the club while taking the pressure off the lads; resurrecting the youth policy; taking training every day and winning all the cross-countries; providing an environment not ruled by fear, an environment I would have thrived in as a player, an environment to encourage, reassure and give confidence to the players.

There were so many special people at that club, from Godfrey Obebo (a loose cannon, capable of flashes of inspiration followed by flashes of desperation) and old Cyril, the lovely tea man who, despite playing his part in building the Bridge on the River Kwai, could never manage to brew up without breaking a couple of cups, to Ossie who looked after the stadium and Bill the groundsman – all terrific people who worked so hard for the club.

But what was my best memory? Easy. My 30-yard goal. During Birdy's reign, I used to join in training. I was 36 at the time, but I was still superbly fit and turning out for the reserves so he persuaded me to play in the first team.

I made my debut at Gateshead on Boxing Day 1994, and we won 2-1. Ironically, it was the first time since I was 16 that I'd played in midfield. I enjoyed it so much, and more than all those games I played at full back. I could just run and run, and tackle and tackle, and get involved in the game all over the pitch – not like at full back, where you waited nervously for the game to come to you, frightened of making a mistake in the defensive third of the pitch. Much as I had enjoyed tearing down the wing as a full back, especially for Blackburn, there was always the fear of messing up at the other end – and if you made an error, that often meant a goal. I played four or five games (just before I was made redundant) and was even awarded Vauxhall Conference player of the month – fame at last!

My finest moment came in our 4-0 drubbing of Dover Athletic

at The Shay in my home debut. Obviously the fans, up until this point, had only known me as the physio who became manager and then took the team out of the Football League. But there I was in front of them in playing kit. It took all my courage to put myself in such a vulnerable position, and even Birdy shook his head in admiration and said, "Fucking hell, Baz, you have got some fucking balls to pull on a shirt at The Shay."

If you want hard evidence of just how far I had come as a person, just contemplate those words.

I played a blinder and scored a sensational 30-yarder. I turned and ran the full length of the pitch towards the far corner where the Halifax faithful were congregated. I stood in front of them with my arms raised above my head. Their wild applause was, I felt, for the great goal I had just scored of course, but also an appreciation of my previous efforts and commitment to what had ultimately, for me, been an impossible task. I think and hope, in that performance, goal and shared celebration, they accepted me as a true Shayman – somebody who genuinely had tried his best for the good of the football club.

Every player on the pitch ran to me and dropped to their knees as one, to give an impromptu 'hailing' of the goalscorer. It was one of the greatest moments of my life. People in Halifax (I am told) still hold me in the highest regard and talk about that goal and the subsequent wild celebrations to this day.

It wasn't all good, though. Some of the experiences I suffered at Halifax Town were among the most painful of my football career – quite literally when it came to injuries.

The injury that pissed me off more than any other was a broken right fibula in 1994 after I'd come out of retirement to play in a pre-season friendly against Tadcaster Town. It was so unnecessary. This fucking arsehole deliberately did a two-footed tackle on me about three weeks after the bloody ball had gone. I tried to carry on but was in terrible pain. The leg swelled like crazy and I could actually feel the ends of the bone grating. However, in a tribute to my namesake and erstwhile alter ego, Rambo Rathbone, I determined just to soldier on and keep working.

Obviously, I had a good knowledge of sports injuries so I knew it would heal up OK with time. More to the point, as I was doing so many different jobs at the club I was in no position to take any time off anyway. I managed to get by, though, and in fact I never even missed a single day. It's amazing what you can achieve if you really have to.

Even so, that injury was an absolute nightmare because I still had to do my physio duties and run onto the pitch when a player got injured, so I had to dose myself up with strong painkillers before every match. I really resent what that twat did to me. He caused me so much pain and suffering, and all for a bloody lousy pre-season friendly.

The day I suffered a nasty concussion also sticks in my mind (no pun intended). We were playing at Altrincham and I clashed heads with one of their players and was knocked out. A situation of pure farce then unfolded as the referee, seeing my plight, frantically started to blow his whistle to summon the Halifax physio onto the field of play.

Nobody came.

Eventually the concerned and exasperated referee turned to one of our players and demanded to know where the physio was.

"That's him on the floor".

Eventually, I was taken to hospital by ambulance. I started to regain my faculties in the hospital and, as I came round, could hear a conversation going on outside my cubicle. It was one of the club directors who was questioning the doctor. "How bad is it, doc? We really need him."

"Well, he was out cold for a few seconds, so I am afraid to say he must not play football for the next two weeks."

"Oh no, we ain't worried about that. He was playing shit anyway. Will he be fit enough to drive the minibus back to The Shay in about half an hour?"

Sadly, I was not able to drive the minibus back to The Shay

and, to this day, I still feel sorry about letting the lads down so badly.

Injuries aside, relegation and the heartbreak it brought to the fans was naturally my most painful experience at the club. The lack of almost any facilities made training a daily challenge, but not half as challenging as releasing the young players, reliving that same scenario I had witnessed all those years ago at Birmingham. But this time it was me breaking the hearts and shattering the dreams of others. A different time, a different era, a different level, a different generation – but the tears were still the same.

Such was the strain on finances during my final 12 months that the team bus would not move from the club car park until the driver had been paid – and no, he would not accept a cheque. Cash only. We had to do a few whip-rounds. We had no training balls, so we used to telephone Mitre, who were based in nearby Huddersfield, and they would kindly provide us with a couple of bags of their prototype footballs – all colours, shapes and sizes. Some were heavy, some light and some not particularly round, while some would just explode if you kicked them too hard.

Once we stopped at a motorway service station en route to a game for a pre-match meal. We had to sit in pairs so we could share our beans on toast with another player. That is the definition of skint.

Another time I was driving my club car back from one of the local cabbage patches where we had been training when I was stopped by the police. They had noticed neither I nor my passenger in the back, one of the YTS lads, were wearing a seatbelt. The copper, spotting our training kit, decided to take pity on us.

"OK," he said. "I will let you off, you have suffered enough, ha ha."

I had to take my documents to the police station, though, so I went to the club's offices to get my insurance details. The club secretary, somewhat embarrassed, informed me that as money had been so tight they hadn't been able to afford to insure my car. So, two weeks later I was up in court on the charge of driving with no insurance (luckily the club took responsibility and I was exonerated).

Similarly, after I left the club, I enquired about signing on the dole for the duration of my final hospital placement as I had no way of getting any income. I presented myself at the DSS office in Blackburn.

"Sorry Mr Rathbone, but your previous employer, Halifax Town, have not paid full National Insurance contributions for you for the last couple of years and, as a result of that, you are not entitled to unemployment benefit."

I had to laugh; they had been taking it out of my wages and keeping it. I bore no grudges, though; they were always great to me and I still hold the club, board and fans in the highest esteem.

Halifax Town always had a special place in my heart and I followed their progress closely over the ensuing years. They actually regained their league status several years later, but soon lost it again, before finally going bankrupt a few years ago. But now, like a phoenix from the flames, the club have reformed as FC Halifax and are on the up again.

During my whole time at the club, and notwithstanding all the failures we endured, there was only really one unsavoury incident, and that came near the end of my final season. We had lost 5-1 at Kettering, a truly shocking result and performance, and the Shaymen were understandably having a right go at the players and manager as we trooped off.

"Bird shit, Bird shit, Bird shit," they chanted at Birdy. I was walking off behind Birdy with my physio bag in my hand and, even though I liked him, I had to stifle a smile at the nature of the invective hurled in his direction.

It was a shame he was getting so horribly abused but, at the end of the day, that's life as a football manager. Rather him than me. I had done my stint as manager. It was the club's decision to relieve me of those duties.

But then, just as I was walking up the tunnel, somebody from up above screamed, "Sort it out, Rathbone, you fucking wanker!"

What a shock. If you don't know what it's like in those circumstances, take it from me – you have to look up. I raised my eyes in the direction of those foul expletives and there he was, his face all twisted with hatred and with a little strand of spittle hanging off his lower lip, one of the bloody directors. I assumed that was not a traditional vote of confidence.

What an experience I had at Halifax Town. In fact, what a lifetime of experiences. Even years later, when I sat on the Everton team bus as we made our way to the north-east (we flew everywhere else – I told you I would get to the top) and passed the town of Halifax – just off junction 23, take the M62 down the hill through Elland – every time I saw The Shay's floodlights, all the memories would come flooding back and I would often have to wipe a little tear from my eye.

But it was time to move on. The dream of being a manager had been strangled at birth and I had once again reverted to the belief that my true calling was to be a physiotherapist. I don't think I ever actually got beyond the caretaker manager stage. I did go to see the chairman about it once and asked him to remove that temporary prefix and officially define my role as permanent. "OK," he said with complete sangfroid, "from now on you are the caretaker." To be fair, that was a fucking great joke and we both laughed.

Having said that, though, I firmly believe, with a bit more luck and a few more players, things could have been so different. When people find out that I, of all people, was once the manager of a Football League club, the reaction is usually laughter followed by incredulity.

"Baz the manager, you must be joking."

However, when I had been the physio at Preston North End for about six years, we signed a player called Chris Lucketti. This was the same Chris Lucketti who had been my skipper at Halifax Town during that fateful season.

When the players found out he had played under me, and seemingly lived to tell the tale, the first question everybody asked, with a large dose of incredulity, was: "What was Baz like as a manager?"

This is what Chris said: "It was without doubt the best five months I ever had as a player. There was a great buzz about the place, training was brilliant and, most importantly, you looked forward to playing."

Thanks Chris for those kind words. On that note, my conscience is clear and I am proud of my role as manager of the Shaymen.

PART THREE
PHYSIO
(1995-2010)

Chapter Eleven

THE ROAD TO GLORY

There was no time to sit and reflect after saying goodbye to Halifax Town. It was straight back into the hospital environment, 9am until 5pm, for the eight weeks of my final placement. Long days, no wages, revising at night for my finals in June. Not much fun.

The Ford Sierra company car had gone back – it wasn't insured anyway. We had to make do with the old Nissan Micra we had bought a few years earlier and were dipping into our meagre savings. It was the spring of 1995 and Blackburn Rovers had just won the Premier League. Great for the club and great for the town but, if I am being totally honest, it left me feeling both envious and totally distanced from the football world I adored. Critics may say the title was bought with Jack Walker's money and they may be correct, but others have tried and failed whilst spending more money. Either way, it was still an incredible achievement for a small provincial town with a population of roughly 100,000.

But there was no point in me worrying or getting frustrated about my situation; I just had to get through the next few months, grind it out, get the qualifications, and then all would be fine. I was confident that once I got those revered letters after my name I would soon get a job, and I was very confident my highly individualistic style of physiotherapy would become popular and eventually make me successful.

Then a phone call changed my story. Once again – and this is a common thread that has run through my story – something out of the blue occurred and propelled me in a new and exciting direction.

I was working in the outpatients department of Blackburn Infirmary and had just put an ankle strapping on an old bloke with the most rancid feet I had ever seen (or smelt). I remember feeling particularly low that day, feeling so far away from the environment I loved and yearned for when that life-changing call came. I was surprised anybody would call me at the hospital. In fact, I was surprised anybody even knew I was at the hospital.

It was Gary Peters, the manager of Preston North End. He offered me the job of physiotherapist at the club on £20,000 per annum, starting on July 1 on a three-month trial basis.

Since I had left Preston, they had dropped back into the bottom division but, excitingly, they had just been purchased by Baxi Heating, a large local company which had vowed to rebuild the famous old stadium, buy some better players and try to take the great club back up to the higher reaches of the Football League where it deserved to be.

"Yes, yes please," I said. "Yes please, thank you so very, very much."

If I sounded desperate, then that's because I was. This was a great opportunity for me. I had just put my foot on the bottom rung of the ladder, but this was a proper ladder – this ladder went right to the top.

Suddenly, the last few weeks of the placement sailed by effortlessly. The final exams were easy and, hey presto, after four years of solid work and commitment, I was finally a fully qualified chartered physiotherapist. It was somewhat ironic now, at nearly 37 years of age, that I had finally got the medical qualifications my dad and the headmaster had urged me to get all those years ago.

So, I walked back into Deepdale on July 1, 1995, barely four years since I had left. The world was only days away from reeling from the horrific massacre in Srebrenica and a bloke in Seattle released something called Windows 95 with MSN and Internet Explorer (it will never catch on). You could now flog anything you wanted on something called eBay, and Oasis, Pulp and Blur were locked in their own little war for chart domination. And me? Still bald, but now with grey sideburns.

The Preston North End I was returning to had changed. It was a very different club to the one I had experienced. Why? Money. The lifeblood of any football club. It doesn't guarantee success but it at least gives you a fighting chance.

Baxi had pledged to invest £10 million pounds into the club, rebuild the famous but dilapidated ground and give the manager the funds needed to achieve success on the pitch. They were in the process of turning this founder member of the Football League into a Public Limited Company – a bold and exciting move for a non-Premier League club.

I reported for duty a couple of days before the players were due to return to pre-season training and went straight into the home dressing room where I had spent so long sat on those bloody towels. I closed my eyes, drank in the memories and inhaled the aromas – *the smells of football*. Yes, they were all here as before, as at every club, as in every dressing room, those heady, intoxicating, nostalgia-inducing smells. The smells of home, the smells of belonging – leather, polish, heat rub, Deep Heat and Vicks. Bliss. Admittedly, they were not as strong during the summer, but they were still there, in the lino, in the faux-wood panelling and in the polystyrene ceiling tiles, pervading every nook and cranny of the dressing room and my mind.

Gary Peters took me into his office and said he wanted me to go down to the big, local country park and sort out all the running sessions for the players when they returned later in the week. He told me he was thinking of promoting one of the senior players to a player-coach role, and that I should take him with me so we could devise the running sessions together.

So off we went on the short drive to the local park. It was a lovely sunny day and I was really looking forward to this task. I had always loved running. When we got there, we agreed we would do the cross country first, so we ran a lap of the entire park. It took about 20 minutes and was perfect for what we needed. We were both happy, but my companion felt that if we ran in the opposite direction then the hilly bit would be at the beginning instead of the end and that would make the run harder.

"OK, I will make a note of that on my pad."

"Well, I think we should do it again in the other direction, just to be professional," he said.

So we did it again as he suggested. Phew, that's two cross countries then.

Then we found the biggest hill and decided to sprint to the top 12 times, with each run taking 15 seconds, with a one-minute recovery in between. We did them and it was fine, but he felt a one-minute recovery was too long and 50 seconds was enough. Guess what? Yes, we did the lot again. We then went to the flat area between the hills and used the trundle wheel to mark out the 200 yard strides. Again, we did them all, but then he decided he wanted the distance to be 200 metres instead of yards so we did the whole fucking lot again.

Finally, several hours later, we slumped into the car, both knackered. I turned to this guy and said, "Wow, you are keen. Is that what you want to do when you finish playing – go into coaching?"

He looked at me and said, "Baz, by the time I am 45 I firmly believe I will have been manager of the season in the Premier League."

It took me all my self-control not to laugh in this poor deluded fellow's face. And, of course he was wrong – by the time he was 45, David Moyes had been named the LMA Premier League Manager of the Season three times.

It felt great to back in the football fold and, crucially, back in the dressing room. Yes, it was a different dressing room, but in many ways it was just the same – no matter which club, which level, which set of players, the dressing room is reassuringly the same. The same cross-section of personalities – the funny one, the good-looking one, the cocky one, the nervous one (guess who?), the tight one, the crazy one, the one who is aggressive after two pints, the one with the good physique and the one who crawls around the manager. Anybody who has played at any level of football will surely recognise this diverse bunch of characters. And all those superstitions – must go out last, must go out fifth, must put left boot on first, must wear same underpants if we won the last game. Ridiculous and pointless, but try telling that to the players. It's just so bloody important to win the games, to guarantee a good week ahead, that players cling on to anything, no matter how bizarre.

One lad had a particularly strange superstition. When the dressing room bell went, I had to throw him the smelling salts. Not pass them, throw them. I had erroneously passed them on a few occasions and he had become quite irate, almost as if I had, at that moment and by that deed, destroyed his chances of playing well. Crazy I know, but it meant the world to him, so I made sure I threw him the smelling salts (not passed them) just after the bell went (not before).

Unfortunately, he had a poor run of form, lost his place in the team and was consequently given a free transfer at the end of the season. He drifted into non-league football and became depressed. Sadly, his marriage broke up and he was unemployed. He asked Gary Peters if he could play in a few reserve games for us just to keep fit, as his non-league team had also let him go. So, a year after he was first released, he came back for a game in the second team.

You know what's coming, don't you? Sure enough, I had long forgotten about his ritual and handed him the smelling salts.

"Fuck me, Baz, fuck me. Throw me the fucking things, don't pass them to me!"

Only in football.

'Proud Preston' – a proud club with a proud history, and a proud physio – had always had a great fan base and everybody was buzzing as they kicked off their first match of the new era.

Our first game of the 1995/96 season was at home to Lincoln City. The first time I ran on to tend to a player I got a fabulous reception – I was choked. Unfortunately, we managed to lose the game 2-1, leaving everyone at the club with that 'put the suits away' feeling. I was starting to think I might be football's equivalent of Jonah. Was it my fault things kept going wrong at the clubs I worked for?

Fortunately, we recovered and won the league by a country mile – clinched at Leyton Orient the following May. Simultaneously, the huge and impressive new main stand, named after Preston legend Sir Tom Finney, with a brilliant mosaic of his head and shoulders made out of different coloured seats, was completed.

The success was great for the club, the town and me. Wild celebrations, champagne, and an open-top bus to the Town Hall. It was the first taste of success I'd had in nearly a decade. I could get used to this.

Personally, it was a great year. I had only been at the club a couple of weeks when Gary Peters called me into his office and told me he was absolutely delighted with both me and my particular brand of physiotherapy, and so were the players. He gave me a £100 per week pay rise and a special one-year 'rollover' contract to ensure I couldn't leave and go anywhere else without giving the club a year's written notice.

Was I happy? What do you think?

Professionally, it was going really well. I did all the conditioning work as well and even took the reserves for training. Perfection. I even played in a lot of the reserve matches that season, as well as tending to the players during games. I would put my physio bag on the halfway line and, if one of the players got injured, I would run to the touchline, pick up my bag and run back to the stricken player. What about if I got injured? I suppose we would have been in the shit, but it never happened thankfully.

I was playing really well in the reserves in centre midfield, but I felt a bit guilty because my career was over and I didn't want to stand in the way of the development of the young players at the club who needed those reserve games. I shared my concerns with Gary Peters and, reluctantly, he saw my point of view, but insisted I remained at least a substitute for the games. That seemed like a reasonable compromise.

In the next reserve game at Deepdale, though, Kevin Kilbane, who was only a teenager himself at the time, sprained his ankle quite badly. I carried him down the tunnel to the medical room and carefully removed his boot to assess the injury.

Gary Peters burst into the dressing room in a highly agitated state – Kevin, who went on to become a regular for the Republic of Ireland and play for several Premier League clubs, was Preston's greatest asset.

"Don't worry, boss," I said. "It looks worse than it is. It's not broken, only sprained."

"I don't give a fuck! Stop fucking about with him and get your shin pads on, you are going on."

That was typical Gary Peters – no nonsense, hard as nails, but still an exceptionally good manager who achieved good things with Preston.

That whole season was a roaring success. The players responded to my style of physiotherapy – energy, hard work, enthusiasm, fun and positivity. The same treatment room which had been a dungeon for me as a player was now a vibrant, noisy centre of optimism and hope.

I worked 358 days that year (virtually part-time compared to Halifax Town) and I can honestly say I enjoyed every one. Everything had worked out so well and I looked forward to the next season with great anticipation.

When you mention Preston North End, the first thing most people say, even now more than 50 years since he last graced Deepdale, is, "Tom Finney – the Preston Plumber."

He was, is, and always will be the heart of this great club. He might have come from a different era, a different world, but his skills, grace and humility have transcended time.

Even then, well into his 70s, Sir Tom was incredibly switched on and knowledgable about the modern game. He used to come into Deepdale every Friday afternoon to sit in his office and go through his mail. He was given his own little office as a mark of respect, a reaching out to a distant, bygone era – plus he received 90 per cent of the club's frigging mail.

Quiet, yet friendly, he was always the perfect gentleman. And modest? I'll say. Many people whose football knowledge spans the post-war period agree he was probably England's best-ever footballer. What an accolade. England's best-*ever* footballer.

The story goes that, at his peak, if he was injured and therefore unable to play, the club wouldn't announce the teams until very late on the day of the game after most people had already entered the stadium, otherwise thousands would not have turned up for the match. When I was at Birmingham City, the same strategy was used if I *was* playing.

When I was a Preston player back in the late '80s, Sir Tom was the 'victim' of the TV show, *This is your Life*. As current employees of the club, we were invited on to the show to sit on the stage in our kit. As you can imagine, we felt a little bit awkward, to say the least. The show wasn't live, though, and just as the host, Michael Aspel, was about to start proceedings, the floor manager shouted, "Stop, stop. Make-up, put some powder on that bald bloke's head, it is reflecting off the cameras and spoiling the picture."

How embarrassed was I? It gave the audience a great laugh, though.

The marvellous thing about Sir Tom was his humility and complete lack of resentment towards the modern players – most of whom would not have been fit to lace his boots, yet even the most modest of them was earning many times more than he ever did.

One story perfectly sums Sir Tom up. He would often pop

into the medical room when I was the physio to see how things were going and ask after my health and my family's health. One day, he had some guests over from America and brought them down to the medical room to show them around. As they left, I could hear Sir Tom say to them, "That's Baz, the physio, he's doing a really good job. He was also a very good player when he played for us. He always got stuck in and gave 100 per cent."

How's that for humility then? Sir Tom Finney telling other people what a good player I was.

Those seven years at Preston were idyllic. Again, I accepted the almost impossible workload, safe in the knowledge my acceptance of this, in combination with my highly personalised and successful style of physiotherapy, would take me to the top. Bank Holidays, Easter, New Year's Day – they were all working days but I wasn't complaining. It was marvellous. The club was on the move. The momentum and force were with us. More and more fans were returning to see Proud Preston and it was a great honour to be a part of the club at that time.

There were so many highlights at Preston. Here are just a few:

1995/96 season

Third Division champions! Incredible scenes and memories, as bumper crowds flocked to Deepdale again. We had an open-top bus parade to the town hall steps. There was also the opening of the fantastic new Tom Finney Stand and, best of all, an end-of-season trip to Magaluf. It had been ten years since I had last staggered around those mean streets with Garns and the rest of the Rovers lads.

1996/97 season

A season of consolidation in the Second Division. Plans were approved for the new Bill Shankly Stand behind the goals, complete with a brand new, state-of-the art fitness club. The momentum and Baxi's backing continued to drive the club forward. I got a good pay rise. The club were really treating me very well.

1997/98 season

Gary Peters's reign ended when he resigned early in 1998 as momentum stalled and Baxi PLC became impatient at the lack of progress. The team were in a sticky position in the New Year, but David Moyes took over and steadied the ship.

1998/99 season

The first full season of the reign of 'King David' brought instant results. We reached the play-offs, where we lost to Gillingham, but the Deepdale bandwagon was back on course. The club acquired its own training ground, so there was no longer any need to get changed at Deepdale and drive to the local park to train. I was still working long hours and earned another decent pay rise. Moyes was driving everybody on – especially himself.

1999/2000 season

Second Division champions! We were back on the open-top bus, back at the town hall steps and, most importantly, back in Magaluf. Work started on the third part of the ground – the Alan Kelly Stand (they must be leaving the Mick Rathbone stand until last). The club was a giant snowball getting ever bigger as it rolled downhill. Moyes was relentless. I received yet another pay rise, as well as several offers of jobs at bigger clubs, but I wasn't interested – I was enjoying it too much at Preston and there was still much to achieve. I was still working every minute, but enjoying every minute.

2000/01 season

The snowball rolled all the way to the Millennium Stadium in Cardiff for the play-off final against Bolton Wanderers and the ultimate prize – a place in the Premier League.

That was my biggest game as a physio (or a player) so far

– 60,000 fans, live TV, huge stakes, massive media attention, new tracksuits and new kit, all fresh, all ironed and all laid out in the palatial dressing rooms at the Millennium Stadium. But don't worry, those smells were still there, the smells I had grown up with.

It was an absolutely fantastic experience, but we didn't perform on the day and lost 3-0. After the game, I couldn't help feeling that the Preston star that had burned so brightly and with such vigour had probably reached its zenith and must surely dim and fall back down to earth.

Money talks, especially in football, and Baxi's money had propelled the club from the depths of the bottom division to within 90 minutes of the ultimate prize. However, that final step – up into the Premier League – and more importantly, the ability to survive and prosper there, took the kind of finances Preston and Baxi just didn't have.

I got another pay rise, though, and as always, was still working every hour and still loving every minute. Who is that woman? She looks familiar... oh, it's my wife!

2001/02 season

Given what we'd achieved the previous season, this was a slightly disappointing year, but by no means a disgrace.

The snowball was starting to melt. In March 2002, Moyes left for Everton. It was the end of an era. He was temporarily replaced by assistant Kelham O'Hanlon. I did think of putting in my own CV for David's job but 'Previous Management Experience: Relegation from the Football League' doesn't look too good.

The measure of my success through those years was parked on my driveway. In my first season, it was a clapped-out, ten-year-old Ford Fiesta van with more than 200,000 miles on the clock. Then, after the initial promotion, it was updated to a white Seat Ibiza with our sponsors' name on the side. Promotion to the next tier was marked by a Rover 216 (alarm, central locking, metallic paint) before it was replaced with the final reassurance of my importance, the BMW Coupé complete with cruise control. Fucking cruise control – can you believe it? OK, I never actually used it, but at least I had it.

On reflection, that period at Preston was a sharp learning curve in terms of acquiring the knowledge and expertise required to be a successful Premier League physiotherapist. Working all those hours – alone, in terms of medical support – somewhat isolated at times, and having to make all the big decisions regarding the management of the injuries on my own was a real test of my competence and expertise.

Looking back now, having spent a glorious eight years as head of the medical department at Everton, with their comprehensive medical and sports science teams and instant access to scans and the finest orthopaedic specialists in the world, it all seems a very far cry from those distant days at Preston where I had a much longer job description, to say the least.

In a way, though, I preferred the set-up back then when "good old Baz" did all the jobs, because it gave me that air of indispensability which, due to my borderline low self-esteem personality, I really embraced and thrived upon. It's so different in the Premier League, where there is a fully qualified practitioner for every facet of the job. This complete polar opposite, in terms of staffing levels, reminds me of when Preston signed Colin Hendry on loan from Premier League side Bolton in 2002.

Bolton, at the time under my old team-mate Sam Allardyce, had possibly the biggest and most comprehensive sports science and sports medicine department in the country – maybe even in Europe. On Colin's first day at Preston, after David and I had greeted him and welcomed him to his new club, he was curious to find out the support staff situation and had a list of questions.

"Who is your fitness coach?"

"It's Baz. He's still very fit, so he combines that with his physio job."

"OK, that makes sense. Who is your chiropractor?"

"Well, if you have a problem with your back or neck, Baz will sort it out in the afternoon."

"OK, fair enough. What day is the chiropodist in?"

"Baz is in every day."

"Masseur?"

"Baz will give you a rub."

"Nutritionist?"

"Baz will give you a diet sheet."

"Podiatrist?"

"Baz."

"Strength coach?"

"You know the answer to that one."

We had a good laugh and it makes a good story but, as I said before, I preferred it that way. It made me feel wanted and needed and indispensable. I put in so many hours at Preston during those seven years I couldn't help but learn almost everything there is to know about sports injuries and experience virtually every type of on-field emergency, including potentially catastrophic spinal injuries, severe cuts, concussions and serious orthopaedic trauma.

Of all the serious injuries I have attended on the pitch, one in particular will always stick in my mind. It was a very badly broken leg and it happened at Deepdale to one of our players called Steve Basham. It was one of those injuries that occurs every three or four years when everybody has to look away and is so horrific that the TV channels won't even show a replay of it.

I ran on to the pitch. Steve was lying on his back staring up at the sky with a look of agony and fear in his eyes. Some of our players were actually holding his shoulders down so he couldn't see the state of his leg. Obviously Steve knew he had a bad injury, but he could have had no idea just how shocking it was.

How the fuck was I going to get him on a stretcher with that injury in front of all those people without him screaming the place down?

Cue a slice of luck. One of our players, Rob Edwards, came running over at high speed and yelled at the referee, "Not even

THE SMELL OF FOOTBALL

a fucking yellow card, ref, not even a fucking yellow. Look at his fucking leg, it's hanging on by a fucking thread!"

At which point, Steve conveniently fainted, making his evacuation from the field of play nice and simple. Thanks Rob.

And thanks Preston for seven magical years.

Chapter Twelve
DESTINY CALLS

David Moyes was destined to go to the very top, just as he had predicted on that exhausting training day in 1995 before pre-season started. What is so special about him? A very good coach? Yes. A great motivator? Yes. A master tactician, skilled in the art of preparing his team? Yes.

But it is much, much more than that. There is an intensity, desire and passion about the guy that makes the Reverend Ian Paisley, Sir Alex Ferguson and 'Braveheart' himself, William Wallace, seem meek and mild by comparison. In a nutshell, David does not 'do' failure. This fierce, indefatigable thirst for success is tempered by a genuine modesty and humility that probably only a handful of us have ever seen. David is a very nice man.

As soon as Walter Smith lost his job as manager of Everton in March 2002, in a flash of almost indecent haste David was gone. I knew he'd had plenty of good offers in the past that he felt just weren't quite right, but not this one – he was off. He left the clubs to sort out the compensation issues between themselves and that was that. He called me into his office and told me he was leaving – NOW. He also said he wanted me to come with him to Everton, and that as soon as he got settled in he would contact me.

I rather hoped he wouldn't, if I am being truthful. I didn't really want to go anywhere else. I was so happy at Preston. In fact, I doubt if anybody, anywhere, in any role in the history of football, had ever been so happy. Well-paid, appreciated, autonomous, a great relationship with the players, fans, board, office staff and ground staff – whatever definition of happiness you care to use, I personified it. I hoped that David would get to Everton and forget about me. I intended to stay at Preston for as long as they would have me.

Funnily enough, that intention to stay has been a recurring theme at nearly every club I have worked for and is a true indicator of the vagaries of professional football and the transitory nature of one's involvement at any given club. For long periods I never thought I would leave Birmingham (except for Dyno Rod), Blackburn, Preston or Halifax, but I did, so I could never say never. But this was different; this was perfect.

David kept Everton up with something to spare in 2002. Preston, meanwhile, just missed out on the play-offs and, in May, the board appointed the highly respected, former Scotland boss Craig Brown to the position of manager.

Craig is a great fellow, the antithesis of David in terms of approach to the job. David is intense, full-on, squeezing the last drop out of everyone; Craig is calm, relaxed, unflappable. David finds it very hard to delegate, while Craig is the master of it.

I will give you an example of their completely different approaches. Let's say, for example, that one of the players had come to see me early on a Monday morning complaining of a tight hamstring. I would report this information to David and suggest, in my opinion, that this player should refrain from training for a couple of days, have some light sessions with me and join in with the rest of the squad on Thursday, to be available for Saturday's game.

David's response to this information would typically be: "Tight bloody hamstring? Did he report it yesterday? He can't afford not to train. He just wants a rest. Make sure you work him hard in the gym and get him in the bloody swimming pool. Tight hamstring! That's buggered the whole session up."

Same problem to Craig: "Thank you for that information, Baz. I will leave him in your eminently capable care and look forward to him rejoining the squad on Thursday."

Can you spot the difference?

But that's David, and that's one of his greatest strengths – never letting go, never giving an inch. Destined for greatness. I liked working for David. The man is a winner and I wanted to be a winner too.

However, working for such a great guy as Craig certainly didn't lack appeal. The close season of 2002 was set to be the longest break I could remember, due to the World Cup in Korea and Japan. Even though it was a long summer break for the players, I took just seven days off. During the close season, only the physio and the injured players are at the club, it is a very relaxing and enjoyable environment. This is the 'no pressure' time of getting players fit.

If I am being totally honest, despite not wanting to leave Preston, I was a little bit disappointed that David did not make any contact with me in his first two months at Everton. I assumed he must have been happy with the medical set-up that was already in place. In truth, my ego took a bit of a knock. I would at least have liked the opportunity to make the grand gesture of turning the job down and having the chance to martyr myself on the cross of club loyalty. We all want to be wanted.

So, I remained at Deepdale with Craig Brown preparing for the start of the new season. Everything was going really well as usual and we were all looking forward to the campaign ahead. Then the phone rang. Just a phone call but a potentially life-changing one.

"Baz, it's David. I want you to come to Everton as head of the medical department. Will you consider it?"

I told him I would think about it for a couple of weeks, but it was important he formally approached the club and everything was done in the correct way. He told me he would do it immediately.

How did I feel? Excited, nervous – as ever. Wanted.

David phoned me back soon after and told me there was a potential problem because the chairman of Preston, Derek Shaw (nobody loved that club more than Derek), was being awkward and would not release me from my contract unless Everton paid the one year's notice (£42,000) in full.

So, that was it then. I was worth more as a physio than I ever had been as a player. I was either a fantastic physio or a shit player. I prefer to believe the former.

To be fair to Derek, Preston were well within their rights to demand compensation. I had enjoyed, for seven years, the security of a 12-month rollover contract whereby if the club had wanted to get rid of me, they would have been obliged to give me one year's wages. The flipside, though, was that if I wanted to move on, then they could ask for the same year's wages as a kind of transfer fee.

David wasn't too impressed. He felt that as I had worked virtually every day for the last seven years for Preston they should allow me to 'better myself' without all this nonsense – and it wasn't as if they'd had to buy me in the first place. David also had a point. It was a difficult situation for everybody.

David advised me that I was well within my rights, morally, simply to walk out and join him at Everton, and there was some justification in that. But I wasn't prepared to breach my contract, even if there was a strong moral argument for doing so. Preston had been absolutely brilliant to me. True, if I did walk out then they wouldn't really be able to do anything, but how would the chief executive of Everton feel, when I was over there putting pen to paper, knowing I had just walked out on my last contract?

I told David I would consider coming but only after the two clubs had reached an amicable agreement regarding the terms of my departure. He wasn't happy and assured me there was no way Everton were going to pay a single penny for me.

"OK, David, good luck for the season." I didn't have to call him boss any more.

That worked out well, then. Hopefully, Preston would dig their heels in, Everton wouldn't budge either and I could revel in the role of the poor, innocent victim of club politics and neatly escape having to make a big decision about my future.

Worryingly, though, the two clubs did finally agree some kind of compromise and all of a sudden I was free to talk to Everton. But did I want to talk to them? I loved working for Preston so much. It was only seven miles from my house, I had lots of very good friends there, I had played for the club which gave me a special affinity and, to be honest, I was a bit worried the 'big hitters' at Everton wouldn't really buy into my particular style of physiotherapy – all the running and hard physical training. The whole thing daunted me.

Derek Shaw and I were good friends and I had known him from my playing days. He tried everything to get me to stay at the club. It was very flattering. All the players wanted me to stay and my best pal Brian Hickson, the kit man who had spent almost every day of the last seven years with me, was pretty upset about the prospect too. It was all quite upsetting really (let's be honest, though, I was loving the attention).

And still the phone calls came.

Eventually, in early August, I went to David's house to talk. I had never been there before. I had a brainwave. Because I didn't really want to go but, similarly, didn't want to turn down such a great offer, I would ask for so much money that Everton would tell me to get lost. That would be the perfect solution and neatly save me from making a possibly life-altering decision.

For the first time in my life, I decided to ask for what I thought I was worth (well, slightly more actually). I could afford to be confident and bold. I had walked out of Willie Bell's office in the mid-'70s on a derisory wage. Every year at Blackburn, I walked out of Sacko's office with a pitiful pay rise, despite playing my heart out every week. I managed, coached, played and physioed at Halifax for a pittance. Now, though, it was different because for the first time in my life I held all the cards. They had approached me; I was totally happy and content at Preston.

I had my speech rehearsed. (I had also had my speech rehearsed in the '70s, '80s and '90s, but never had the guts to deliver it.)

"Right, David, you approached me. You know I am settled and happy at Preston. You, and all the players at Everton, are earning a fortune. You know if I come I will do a good job, work every day and inject some life into the department, but I don't come cheaply any more. Those days have gone."

Deep breath. Go on just blurt it out. It's now or never.

"I want double what I am getting at Preston." Christ, I can't believe I actually said it.

"OK," he said, without hesitation. That nearly disturbed my flow, let me tell you.

"And a good quality company car."

"OK, you will get a Jag."

"And a win bonus."

"OK."

I was starting to lose my thread.

"And the same 12-month rollover contract."

"OK."

Jesus, that was so easy. I should have asked for more. I told him I would let him know in the next 48 hours.

As I tried to make a decision, I asked my wife's opinion – she is always right. She just shrugged and said, "Whatever makes you happy. But you will be in the Premier League one day – you belong in the Premier League." (She is my No. 1 fan.)

I didn't sleep that night. As I saw it, I could either be rich and probably unhappy, or not rich but definitely happy. All night I turned it over in my mind – it's too far, I love Preston, money isn't everything, happiness is the most important thing.

Why risk your happiness and professional contentment for a few bob extra? Eventually, I realised my happiness had to come first.

So, decision made. I would be staying at Preston. Phew, what a relief. I told Derek Shaw the next day that I had made up my mind to stay and he seemed genuinely pleased, as did Brian and all the lads. That vindicated my decision. Definitely the right decision, no doubts, 100 per cent. It could have, and would have, been a disastrous move. A real close shave, but no harm done, disaster averted. What was it the Queen said in *Hamlet*? "The lady doth protest too much, methinks."

The night after I'd made my decision, my wife and I went to a dinner party at her sister's house. A chance meeting changed everything. Call it fate if you want. As we only go out about once a year, it made what happened next even more remarkable.

There were two other couples at the dinner party who I didn't really know that well, but they were keen on football and I was busily informing them of the job offer, my decision to remain at Preston and the reasons for it. Once again, I went over the points I'd been tossing around in my mind – I told them all about the travelling situation, how Preston was so handy, how I felt a special bond with the club because I had played for them. I explained that I didn't really think my style of physio would be well received at Everton and reiterated how happy I was at Preston. Everybody was nodding in agreement, seemingly in total support of my decision. I knew it had been the right thing to do.

But then, out of the blue, the husband of one of the couples, said, "Right, let's get this straight, you are being offered twice the money to work at the highest level in professional football, but you're not going because you love it at Preston, it's too far to travel, you might not get on with the Premier League players and you never played for them? Right, fair enough, but at least be honest with yourself and admit the real reason why you are not going is you don't have the bottle."

Cheeky twat! Who the fuck was he to lecture me? What did he fucking well know?

But do you know what? He was 100 per cent right. It just needed somebody to say it. I got up, went outside with my mobile phone and called Derek Shaw. It was very late. I told him I was very, very sorry but I would be joining Everton on September 2.

That guy was called Tim. Thanks Tim – you changed my life.

Chapter Thirteen
BACK TO THE TOP

That was that then. The Preston North End experience was over. My last game as physio of that great club was on September 1, 2002. Ipswich Town at Deepdale, televised live on a sunny Sunday afternoon.

There had been some reports in the local paper saying that I was leaving and the chairman had said some nice things about me. I think Derek knew I would leave eventually – everybody wants to work at the top, to test themselves at the highest level. To his credit, on the phone he had sort of sighed and said, "OK Baz, I understand."

I received numerous letters from fans thanking me for my contribution and wishing me good luck. Brian Hickson sent me a card – it was so unlike him it must have been sincere. He wrote on it: "Good luck, congratulations, I will miss you. NOBODY, NOBODY deserves this more than you."

Needless to say, it was all very emotional. When you spend the amount of time together Brian and I did over seven years, you can't help but become very, very close. We used to jokingly say after the first pre-season game, "One down, 99 to go." We reckoned that with pre-season friendlies, cup games, league games and reserve games we would come very close to the 100-match total.

The players had a whip-round and bought me a beautiful watch which Colin Murdock, the club captain, presented to me on my last day. It's one of my favourite possessions. It means so much to me. Thanks lads.

Monday, September 2 was to be my starting date at Everton, but I went into Deepdale first thing that morning to check if there had been any injuries from the Ipswich game that weren't apparent at the time. Everybody was OK, though, so that was it then, time to go, time to leave.

But first, maybe just enough time to squeeze in one more coffee with Brian. That was it then, time to go. No, just time for a quick walk around the ground to say a final goodbye to the groundstaff. That was it then, all done, off I go. Hang on, forgot to say goodbye to the girls in the office – Janet, Maureen and Margaret. Hugs all round. A few tears. That was it then, all done, time to go. No, hold on, just pop into the gym under the stand to say goodbye to their staff. All done then, or maybe one last coffee with Brian for old time's sake.

Do you think I was trying to put it off a bit?

"Shall we go and get a sandwich, Bri?"

"Baz, just fuck off will you!"

We laughed and hugged and off I went. I closed the big blue door for the last time. It was one hell of a wrench to leave that football club.

I was very nervous. Brian and some of the Preston players had put the fear of God into me regarding the Premier League players and how unfriendly they could be.

"I've heard the players in the Premier League don't respect the physios," he said. "And, in particular, big Duncan Ferguson has a deep hatred of all medical staff."

"Fucking hell – thanks lads."

I pulled into the car park at Everton's training ground on the afternoon of September 2, 2002. I was approaching my mid-forties now and still there had been no breakthrough in the search for a cure for baldness. My grey sideburns had been joined by my chest hair. Brazil had just won the World Cup, Jade Goody had become famous, Eminem was at No. 1 in the charts and British roads were about to be swamped by the 4x4 phenomenon.

I was filled with fear and trepidation. I sat in the car for a few minutes composing myself. At the end of the day, though, I knew I had made the right decision, particularly for the future of my wife and kids, so I took a deep breath and went in.

I was wearing some faded jeans, a yellow checked shirt and a denim jacket. I stood nervously in the foyer, taking in my new surroundings, when I heard a loud voice, in a strong Scottish accent, bellowing from the adjacent room, "Fuck me. Have you clocked the new physio? It's Bob the fucking Builder!"

Oh my God.

That was my first introduction to Duncan Ferguson. He emerged from a side door and swaggered up to me.

"I am 'Big Dunc' by the way, and I have finished a few physios' careers."

"That's OK," I replied. "I'm Baz and I have finished a few players' careers!"

He loved that one, laughed out loud, patted me on the back and walked off.

Then Kevin Campbell appeared, extended his hand and welcomed me to the club, saying he had heard a lot about me and was looking forward to working with me. That was it then. I was in. Simple as that. And I knew from that moment everything was going to be all right.

And everything *was* all right.

I had made up my mind that, whatever happened, I would be just the same as I had been at Halifax Town and Preston North End. The same principles would apply. It was the best way, my way, the only way. If they didn't respond, then I would leave. I was determined not to change my methods – hard work, with me working alongside the players, leading the way, sharing the load, stride for stride. If I could do it at 43 years of age, then they could do it too.

THE SMELL OF FOOTBALL

Believe me, there is nothing worse for an injured player than to be sent out alone to do the rehabilitation. Even worse, to be exercised by the physio who just stands there with a stopwatch and a whistle. That does not inspire the players. Don't ask them to do what you are not prepared to do yourself. Try to lift them mentally. It is not a crime to be injured. Don't make it a punishment. Try to make it a positive experience. Inject some life and energy into the department. No sitting around all day under those machines slowly losing all your fitness and motivation. Come in, be assessed, work hard. Weights, exercise bikes, swimming, running, ballwork, and then let them go home. Quality, not quantity.

And it worked. Beyond my wildest dreams it worked. Why? Because these lads were no different from the lads at Halifax and Preston – all from the same working-class environments but just slightly better at football, and with a lot more money.

What a buzz. Working at the top level in my profession with the top players and earning top money.

Sadly, it is one of life's great injustices that the more successful you become and the higher up the food chain you ascends, then the less you pay for while enjoying ever greater perks. And so it was at Everton. In fact, this was one of the things that struck me most in those early days – the sheer scale and scope of these fringe benefits. The first thing I noticed on my first day was that there was fresh fruit everywhere. Bowls of it – all types, all ripe, all free. There were baskets of the stuff in virtually every room at the training ground.

I really couldn't get over it. As a child growing up in Sheldon, the only fruit I ate was an overdose of unripe apples when you went scrumping after dark in the neighbours' garden in late August, or on the one day a year when the Rathbones went, en masse, to the Pick Your Own farms in Evesham. We forced so many strawberries into our mouths, stomachs and pockets we could hardly walk back to the car.

But here in this modern day land of milk and honey, the Garden of Eden that is the Premier League, it was all free, plentiful and delicious. I used to take handfuls of oranges, pears or peaches home every day to stock up our fruit bowl. It was marvellous and, for the first time in generations, the Rathbone family was scurvy-free.

One day, a bloke from the local opticians came to the training ground and gave everybody a free pair of Armani sunglasses. Who knows why? I suppose that's just how it was in the Premier League. They must have been worth more than £100 each. I remember all the lads laughing at me because I went out to training with my new shades on, even though it was pissing down with rain.

On another occasion, a box full of brand new, latest release computer games appeared. Help yourself, lads. Fill your boots. I grabbed a couple for my son Ollie and thought I had done well until I got home and realised he didn't have the right console to play them on, so I had to go out and buy a new one – hoisted by my own petard.

Then there was the time some ladies came to the training ground and gave everyone hundreds of pounds worth of Clarins skincare products. Fuck knows why, but I took mine and gratefully started rubbing cream into every accessible part of my body. Why not? Perks of the job. The land of plenty.

Tommy Gravesen gave me a beautiful watch, Lee Carsley gave me some boots, Dave Weir got Ollie a couple of brand new pairs of boots, Kevin Campbell gave me a bottle of Cristal champagne, RRP £150. Why? Well because they liked me, appreciated the work I was doing and were generous guys, I assume.

There was a room at the training ground full of Lucozade sports drinks and energy bars that were given out free, and in unlimited amounts, to all the Premier League clubs as part of a sponsorship deal. You could simply open the boot of your car and take boxes of the stuff home. There was a seemingly endless supply. People always used to remark when they saw my son play on the amount of energy he had. "What do you feed him on?" they would ask. If only they knew. He was living on a diet of energy bars, energy drinks and fruit.

There was so much training gear: hats, coats, tights, gloves, thermal undergarments, wet tops, dry tops and hooded tops. Some mornings I would look at Joseph Yobo all wrapped up in about 20 different items of clothing, looking like he was setting off for the fucking South Pole. And you should have seen him on a cold day.

When the team travelled away, the theme continued: the best hotels, private planes, the finest foods and, above all, the ultimate example of luxurious living – single rooms. A room each. A whole room to myself. A seminal moment and a lifetime away from those very rare overnight stays at Halifax, sleeping on the put-me-up bed in a room with the coach driver so the players could have the best beds.

Yes, I could get used to this.

Actually, it did take some getting used to because I had spent so much time at clubs with much less money and hardly any facilities where nobody gave us anything and we could not afford to buy anything. Now we could afford to buy anything we wanted, but people were queuing up to give it to us for free.

I felt I deserved it, though. Nobody had put in more hours than me over the past ten years – both mentally and physically. Nobody.

Those first few weeks were nothing short of amazing – sometimes I had to almost pinch myself. What a thrill when I looked at myself in the big mirrors in the gym, wearing that famous badge with the tower and the Latin logo 'Nil Satis, Nisi Optimum' (Nothing But The Best Is Good Enough). What a thrill when I looked at the contact list in my mobile phone and saw all those famous names. What a thrill on payday. Sometimes, I looked around at the famous faces of the international players sat in my room – all household names – and felt like I had my own personal Panini sticker book.

I made an instant impression (I think). The lads were very impressed by my fitness, my football ability and my sense of humour (I hope). Any fears I might have initially had about the 'big hitters' in the Premier League not buying into my personality or style of physiotherapy were soon dispelled and, within a matter of a few weeks, the medical room at Everton was the same lively, energy and banter-filled social centre of the club it had been at Halifax and Preston.

Any why shouldn't it have been? Players are players and, despite the differences in ability and earning potential, they tend to share those common strands of DNA – those familiar characteristics of wanting to be around each other, sharing funny stories and, in many cases, simply acting daft together.

I'd always felt that kind of almost immature behaviour players displayed (none more so than me) was a defensive mechanism to protect and insulate against the pressure to perform in the rarefied atmosphere of professional sport. I was delighted to see that each morning virtually every single player would make his way into the medical room just to socialise, as they had done at Halifax and Preston. They would sit on the cupboards talking and laughing and generally taking the piss – usually out of me.

This is what I wanted. This is what I had intended. This is the hub of it. This is where it begins. This is where the team spirit is nurtured and grows. This is where we start building for success. Put the laptops away and create the right atmosphere. That environment away from the boss – the pressure, the tactics, the press, the worries. That little enclave just for us; just a bunch of footballers enjoying each other's company.

Although it had been my ambition to engender this team spirit, I was very lucky that the medical staff who were already there were so good. Jimmy, Matt, Danny, Dom and good old Dr Irving were all equally a part of the whole atmosphere, the whole vibe. Just as well really, because when I accepted the job David had told me to deal with the staff – in terms of who to keep and who to let go – as I saw fit. That was a big shock to me. To suddenly be transformed from the ultimate one-man band, jack-of-all-trades model of the club physio prevalent in the lower leagues, to being the boss, the head of the department.

The man who hired and fired.

I honestly don't think I could have ever sacked anybody, but I also knew that at this level you were only as good as your staff and, fortunately, they were absolutely brilliant – thanks guys.

In those early days and months in my first season we had so many good laughs in that medical room. Every day something funny seemed to happen and all the players sitting around would join in the fun. One day Tommy Gravesen, a renowned character, blew up one of Nick Chadwick's brand new boots with a firework and also launched a giant rocket firework through the gym which caused permanent scorch marks to the entire length of the floor.

And then there was the time Wayne Rooney brought a couple of dogs to training. Apparently, he and Alan Stubbs had been to look at some pups. They were chows – you know, those fluffy dogs with purple tongues – and he liked them so much he bought two of them. However, I think Wayne decided that one was probably enough and he was keen to find a home for the other one. He brought them into the medical room to see if anyone wanted to keep one. I was tempted, even though we have a Yorkshire terrier – that must have been around £500 worth of pedigree pup going begging. Eventually I said, "Look Wayne, you're going to have to take those dogs out now because Li Tie is starting to salivate!"

And I'll never forget the time I was in the medical room, enjoying the pre-training banter, when I was summoned to reception for a telephone call. When I got back, Steve Watson and Gary Naysmith had taken my beloved yellow checked shirt (the Bob the Builder one) and gone to the enormous trouble of bringing a small table into the room and laying it using my shirt as the tablecloth, complete with two sets of knives and forks, two plates, a lighted candle – would you believe it – and a salt and pepper pot. Everyone just laughed and laughed. Great days.

I really felt at home. I felt I had arrived at Everton and was actively contributing to an ever-growing sense of team spirit and camaraderie among the lads which could only be beneficial for the whole club. And then, after a couple of months, I got the real welcome, the true validation of my belonging – when I felt the sickening pain in my buttock as a famous international player shot me with his paintball gun. Just like the Steve Kindon fart all those years ago, that piercing pain was a clear indication that I had been officially accepted into the dressing room.

I wasn't at Everton just to foster team spirit; I made some important logistical changes too. I brought in some of the finest specialists in the country and insisted our lads could have consultations, scans and investigations seven days a week, and get the results immediately. We extended the staff in the medical department so that the players could have as much one-on-one time as possible. As it says on the shirt, nothing but the best is good enough. And that was how it was going to be for Everton players from now on.

Make no mistake, Everton is a massive football club. With the greatest respect to Birmingham City, Blackburn Rovers, Preston North End and Halifax Town, this club was on a different planet.

The intensity with which Everton fans support their club borders on the fanatical. I know lots of supporters regularly mouth the old saying about football being more important than life and death but, with Everton, I think they really mean it. You have only to walk past the famous statue of Everton's greatest player, 'Dixie' Dean, and see all the bouquets of flowers and wreaths from the funerals of newly deceased Evertonians to get some idea of how this great club is intricately and inextricably woven into the lives of its fans. The club has an aura, status and function within the community that transcends any idea that the game is simply about kicking a ball on a grass pitch.

It is a truly great club and I felt truly privileged to be a part of it. And the biggest privilege of all arrived during those first few magical weeks. It is one incident that will always stay with me, a moment that will forever rank as one of the greatest thrills in my life – the delivery of my new Jag.

The Big Cat.

My Big Cat!

The club secretary, David Harrison, delivered it to the training ground. Silver, wide-bodied and mean-looking (the car, not Dave), it was the absolute business. Any of my lingering self-doubts were now finally gone, washed away in a torrent of silver metal and black leather. Low self-esteemers need these visible, tangible embodiments of their success to provide continual reassurances of their achievements. And I was no different. That beautiful machine proved I was good at my job, proved I was a winner.

I fleetingly wondered if it would be practical to take the rest of the day off and drive the car down to show Trevor Francis, Jim Smith, all the Blues fans, the Halifax directors who got rid of me, Leighton James, Tommy Hutchison and that fucker who ran all the way down from the back of the Kop to abuse me. Better not – got a lot on this afternoon.

Dave interrupted my daydreaming by starting to show me how to open the boot, how to operate the phone, how to release the fuel cap, how to work the computer, etc.

I wanted to shout, "Dave, just give me the fucking keys before I fucking well explode!"

But I didn't. I retained my dignity and thanked him when he finally passed the keys to me.

My keys.

My car.

My validation.

Oh my God, the keyring has got a jaguar's head on it. That meant, even when I wasn't in the car, people would know I drove a Jaguar and was thus a man of some substance. I couldn't wait for training to finish so I could drive home in my car. I wondered if anybody had ever actually dropped dead with excitement before. Oh the smell of the leather, the purring of the engine, the lightness of the steering.

Halfway home, I stopped at Charnock Richard service station

and got out of the car. I climbed up the nearby bank and sat on the grass in the late afternoon sun, just looking at the bloody thing. After a while, I went into the café, bought myself a cup of coffee and sat at a table, still looking out at the car. I remember wishing I had blocked somebody in – maybe an emergency vehicle – so there would be a call over the tannoy.

"Would the owner of the brand new silver Jaguar with leather seats, walnut dashboard and 20-inch alloys please return to their vehicle."

Then I could have got up, slowly, in front of all those people, and they would have known that was my car and, therefore, that I was a winner.

I'd had dozens of cars over the years and their prestige and newness always neatly mirrored how I was doing at the time – whether I was on the crest of a wave or a slump. In the lean times, I had to make do with clapped out Minis and 20-year-old Ford Anglias while, in the better times, it was Ford Capris and Dolomite Sprints. But the Jag was in a different class to anything I had driven in the past. I deserved it, had earned it and had worked so hard for it. I was never going to let it go (and it was insured).

I soon realised that driving a Jag, big executive wages and a generous bonus scheme were a direct reflection of the responsibility I had assumed as head of the medical department at such a big club – or, more importantly, for the shit I would be in if I messed up.

I got my first taste of the realities of my new role at Everton after just one week. Big Dunc had been out for several months with a muscle problem. When I arrived at the club and reviewed the case – with the benefit of knowing that all usual pathologies had been looked at and ruled out – I felt that the problem was possibly not with the muscle itself, but with the nerve running under it. That would explain why the injury was refusing to get better.

I managed to find one of the very few surgeons in the region who'd had any experience with this admittedly very rare condition, and we all met for a consultation in a private Manchester hospital with a view to the surgical release of this vexed nerve. The surgeon went through the procedure in fine detail but, in his frankness, painted rather a negative picture, explaining that if the operation was not a success, then Dunc's career would probably be over.

Naturally, this made us both feel a bit unsure, so the surgeon told us to discuss it while he went to scrub up and, if we wanted to go ahead, then we should inform the sister who would get one of the porters to take Dunc to the operating theatre. The surgeon left the room and, before I could say a word, Dunc said, "Right, it's up to you. You decide. I will go with what you say."

Wow, that was pressure. The penny dropped: I wasn't getting the big wages for running around the training ground or kicking balls to the players; no, it was to make these crucial, big decisions on the management of the injuries of Everton's multi-million pound assets.

I told Dunc I would go downstairs to clear my head and make the decision. I went outside and had a walk around the car park. I went through the whole thing again: right, he can't play with this injury, it's not getting better and it's not likely to get better with time, so medically it's an absolute no-brainer. The problem was I had only been at the club for a week and wasn't too keen on fucking up Everton's star player after such a brief time in the job.

Fortunately Trevor, Sir Alf, the Blues players, the Blues fans, the 'four' in the *Sunday People*, the Thwaites Bitter, the meat pies, the tribunal, the plastic burns, the coming out of the game with nothing in the bank, the going back to school at 32, the relegation and the crippling workload had all conspired to produce the world's most mentally resilient person. I bounded up the stairs and informed Dunc the operation would go ahead.

I watched the surgery. It was a great success. He was cured

and, after that, did not miss another game through injury for three years. (Sadly, he missed dozens through club and FA suspensions and altercations with local burglars.)

So here I was then at the summit of my profession. Being in the Premier League was everything I could have dreamed of – and more. The recent history of Everton had been one of struggle, underachievement and flirting with relegation. Nowhere near good enough for this great football club.

My first game was away at Southampton and I immediately realised the atmosphere at Premier League games is on another level to that of the lower leagues – the noise, the size of the crowds, the media coverage. The Everton fans never let their team down. Every single away game I attended was the same – as soon as the team bus turned into the main street outside the stadium, it was surrounded by hundreds, sometimes thousands, of noisy Toffees. They made it almost seem like a home game.

My first home match was against Middlesbrough – and it was simply electric. Nearly 40,000 fans packed into that famous old stadium. Goodison Park is the best ground in the Premier League for atmosphere. A proper football ground, with the fans close to the touchline ensuring a fantastically noisy, hostile backdrop to the action.

Even in my final season, when I had been on duty for nearly 200 matches at Goodison Park, I still got the same buzz when I was on the pitch before the kick-off. I must admit, in the early days when we were lining up in the tunnel, I had to resist the urge to stare at the likes of Beckham, Henry and Shearer. It wasn't that I was starstruck or anything like that; after all I had played in the top division myself. I think the reverence and awe I felt, stood alongside some of the greatest players in Europe, was – just like with the Jaguar – a case of me coming to terms with the measure of my success and new-found status.

As good as it was for me to rub shoulders with the stars, there were also benefits and advantages for my family and friends. They too enjoyed mixing with these famous footballers and circulating in this environment – who wouldn't?

Little Ollie was only six when I joined Everton. He is soccer-mad and, on quiet days, I would take him to the training ground to mix with the players. Big Dunc would sit him on his lap and let him steer his Range Rover around the car park, while Wayne would always find the time to have a kick around with him. What a marvellous treat for a young, football-obsessed lad – especially when I think back to the forlorn attempts of me and my brother just to get an autograph from *any* Birmingham City players.

My teenage daughters also came to some games and got photos with David Beckham, and even my wife didn't miss out on the celebrity fest – after one of the games, I went into the players' lounge to find her holding Didier Drogba's trophy with both hands (his man-of-the-match trophy, that is).

I have a German friend who loves English football and once he came all the way from Frankfurt to see Everton play Manchester United. After the match, he was in the medical room having a beer when Wayne came in for a chat, as he always did when he was at Goodison. The look on Wolfgang's face when Wayne sat next to him on the physio bed was priceless and made me feel proud to be in this highly privileged position where my friends and family could also enjoy this fabulous lifestyle.

Sometimes, I must admit, when surrounded by these superstars, I just wanted to grab a pen and piece of paper and get their autographs, but this was frowned upon as being totally uncool. A few years ago, however, when we played United again, Ollie begged me to get Cristiano Ronaldo's autograph on his brand new Portugal shirt that he had just received for his birthday. I really didn't like to ask and did feel a bit of an anorak, but you know what it is like – you will do anything for your kids, won't you?

I kept my eyes open after the game to try and catch sight of Ronaldo passing the medical room. Eventually, I saw him and stepped into the busy passageway, clutching the shirt. I was in my full Everton regalia, so I didn't feel too much of an intruder.

"Excuse me, Cristiano, could you please sign this for my son?"

He didn't look too pleased, but grabbed the shirt and the pen without looking up or acknowledging my existence, and started scribbling.

"Can you write, 'To Oliver, happy birthday' on it please Cristiano?"

He still didn't look up but just kept scribbling.

"It's O-L-I-V..."

I didn't get any further. He just threw the shirt back in my face where, due to the phenomenon that is static electricity, it stuck. He then walked away, leaving me with the shirt on my head.

There were a couple of the Everton press guys in the corridor that day who saw it all, and we absolutely pissed ourselves laughing for the next ten minutes. Never again.

This fraternising with the famous eventually extended into our private lives, perhaps most memorably when Big Dunc invited our family to his son Cameron's christening. The invitation (which only a handful of people at Everton received) asked us to the ceremony at Liverpool's Anglican cathedral – the biggest in Europe – and then back to his house for 'refreshments and entertainment'.

We were expecting a cup of tea, a few sandwiches and a game of pass the parcel for the kids but, when we pulled up at Dunc's mansion in Formby, we soon realised refreshments and entertainment were on a much grander scale in the Premier League. There were people dressed as clowns, people on stilts, people making balloon animals and people face painting. The theme was *Alice in Wonderland* and all the characters were there, even somebody dressed as the bloody March Hare. There was also a huge marquee in the garden.

When Dunc saw us, my wife and I were given a grand tour of the property after he handed us each a glass of Cristal champagne. It was unbelievable luxury. In the marquee, there were fantastically decorated tables. There was a bar made of pure ice spelling CAMERON, with a vodka river running right through it. The food, wine, hospitality and entertainment were absolutely incredible. We sat on the same table as the Parrotts (the snooker player and his wife, not the birds – although they wouldn't have been out of place at this party). Dunc and his wife were the perfect hosts and made us feel so welcome and genuinely part of the proceedings.

A jaw-dropping day. I will never forget it, although I can't remember much about the last bit as my wife tells me I ended up on my back with my mouth open at the bottom of the vodka river.

Soon after this, Wayne invited us to his 18th birthday party at Aintree – red carpet, paparazzi, soap stars and Atomic Kittens. A great night of splendour and famous faces – the high life indeed. But you know what, it was also very intimate, family-like and, despite the free cigars and champagne, unpretentious because the Rooneys truly are the salt of the earth. I feel lucky not only to know Wayne, but also his fantastic parents.

Again, we were really made to feel part of it and Wayne, his parents and then-girlfriend Coleen were so friendly and welcoming. My outstanding memory was that my wife got her picture in *Hello* magazine. When we looked at the big group photo (with a magnifying glass, to be fair) and spotted her right at the very back, we knew for sure we had made it to the very top.

As much as I enjoyed those events off the field, Everton's home games were my personal highlight and I quickly developed a routine I stuck to for every match at Goodison.

I would leave home early on the morning of the match and stop at Charnock Richard service station for a coffee and a cake. This would guarantee victory. I would arrive at the stadium four hours before kick-off because I liked to make sure all the necessary equipment was there and in good working order. It also meant I was in situ if a player woke up with a problem like a stiff neck or a sore throat, so we could get him in early for treatment.

I would park my car behind the club shop and walk up to the players' entrance. There would already be activity around the place – hot dog vans, programme sellers, souvenir stalls being set up for the game, TV cameras from Sky everywhere (that didn't bother me now).

I would once more be asked the immortal question which has transcended every era and to which there can be no definitive answer, "Are we gonna win today, Baz?"

That question had been directed at me in the '70s, '80s, '90s and noughties. It had been fired at me in a Brummie accent, a Lancashire accent, a Yorkshire accent, and now a Liverpool accent. It had been asked of me in the Premier League, the First Division, the Second Division, the Third Division and the Vauxhall Conference. And my answer? Still always the same: "I hope so, because I need the bonus!"

When I got into our dressing room, Jimmy and 'Sagey', the kit men, would be putting the kit and boots out in each player's places. Then the smells would hit home – those familiar friends that had accompanied me on my travels through the years, through the divisions, bringing the comforting reassurance that I was where I belonged, where I was needed.

At the risk of sounding pedantic, it is worth pointing out, while the old smells could never change, there were some minor olfactory tweaks to some of the more cosmetic smells. In the '70s, it was the great scent of Brut, the '80s gave us Aramis, while the '90s produced the sweet aroma of Lacoste Sport. That was, in turn, replaced by Hugo Boss and now I do believe Chanel is the choice for the discerning player. Similarly, the foreigners imported their own exotic aromas to add to the traditional heady mix. Spices from deepest Africa, herbal rubs from the southern Mediterranean and manly musks from our former colonies. All welcome, all embraced, but never could they overpower those time-honoured smells of football.

I would get changed and sit in the medical room waiting for the lads to arrive. They would turn up in virtually the same order every time, wearing their club suits. First Phil Neville, next Tony Hibbert, then Leon Osman. They all looked so relaxed. Maybe I looked relaxed all those years ago at Birmingham?

It would be busy by this point, with groups of sponsors being guided through the dressing rooms, getting autographs and photographs. Then the opposition would arrive, usually wearing tracksuits.

With one hour to go, it would start to get serious – team meeting, get changed, paddings and strappings in the medical room. Forty minutes to go – everybody ready, boots on, out for the warm-up, manager and coaches evaluating their line-up. Fifteen minutes to go – everybody back in the dressing room for a final briefing from the boss.

Then the superstitions. Premier League superstitions were just the same as the Conference superstitions – Phil Neville's lucky socks, Tim Cahill's special shinpad tape, Tim Howard with the smelling salts just before we went on the pitch, Steve Pienaar with his head bowed in final prayer (I know how he feels).

Next, there were handshakes, pats on the back, high fives and words of encouragement, as we headed into the tunnel. Side by side with the opposition who, as at every level of the game, always looked bigger.

There would be a last-minute opportunity for one of the players to tell me they thought they'd picked up an injury in the warm-up. It happened every week and was merely a sign of pre-kick-off tension, and a quick word of reassurance from me would promptly settle their nerves. The buzzer would sound and out we'd go.

And then the roar.

Different grounds have different songs – the magic of the West Ham fans belting out *I'm Forever Blowing Bubbles*, The Kop with *You'll Never Walk Alone*, Manchester City's *Blue Moon*, Wolves with *Hi Ho Silver Lining*, *Delilah*, *Blaydon Races*, *Keep Right on to the End of the Road* – the list goes on and on. All proud clubs, proud fans and proud songs. All belted out with ear-numbing ferocity. *Keep Right on to the End of the Road* was Birmingham City's anthem, their tribal chant. I used to sing my head off to that song many times with my brother Martin next to me. I don't remember hearing it too much when I was actually playing, but

I fear that was because the song is only sung in a celebratory fashion and God knows when I was playing there wasn't too much to celebrate.

Even though I was not a player any more, I still got really nervous before the kick-off. It was a combination of a lifetime of classical conditioning à la Pavlov, the importance of the result in every Premier League game, and the possibility of having to run on to the pitch in any of these fixtures, in front of tens of thousands of spectators, to deal with a life-threatening incident.

Just as my first sortie on to the field to tend to the legendary Jimmy Case all those years ago at Halifax had been traumatic, a couple of my early forays on to Goodison Park stretched my chronically taut nerves to breaking point such as when Tommy Gravesen went down in a heap.

In football, people want to find out who is the fastest, toughest, most skilful, the friendliest, the fittest, etc. Well, Tommy was the maddest. But mad in the nicest possible way and a good friend to me. Once I was taking him for a scan and we stopped for fuel on the way. Tommy got out of the car and stood next to me as I filled up the tank. He then followed me into the shop and stood next to me while I paid. Then he followed me back to the car and got back into the passenger side – without saying a word.

Tommy was a great bloke – but this was only up until the game started. Then he turned into a complete headcase. On the occasion in question, I ran over to him and asked what the problem was.

"What's the problem? What's the problem? You fucking tell me, you fucking idiot, you are the medical man!" he screamed in his perfect English, but with the Danish accent that made him sound even more crazy.

Nothing, no amount of teaching, can really prepare anybody for that kind of reaction, and I didn't have a clue how to react, so I asked Tommy if he wanted a drink. That really infuriated him.

He screamed, "A drink? A fucking drink? The game is only five minutes old, you fucking moron!"

Fortunately, he was beginning to recover from the knock and got up. I took his arm to escort him to the touchline, and he went berserk.

"Take your fucking hand off me! Take your fucking hand off me or I will fucking knock you out!" He pushed me away.

By this time, most of the players and the fans nearest to the incident were having a good laugh at my expense. Eventually, we got to the sideline at which point he politely thanked me for my help and trotted calmly back on to the pitch.

The incident was never mentioned again, but it really spooked me, and I used to sit in the dugout praying Tommy never got injured.

A few weeks after that ordeal, I was subjected to another equally disturbing incident – this time courtesy of the extremely funny and likeable Steve Watson. 'Watto' was playing right back over on the far side of the pitch. He had got a knock and was hobbling a bit, so the boss told me to run round there as fast as I could and check if he was going to be OK to carry on.

I ran about 200 metres in the latest Olympic qualifying time and screamed at the top of my voice, "Are you OK, Steve?"

No reply, but it was, as you can imagine, really noisy, so I screamed the same question again. Still no reply. He must be OK, I thought. I sprinted all the way back around to the dugout and told David I couldn't get any response from him, so he was probably fine.

"That's no good, Baz. I need to know. Go and ask him again."

Fuck me. Off I went again, another couple of hundred metres flat out, and shouted, "Steve, Steve are you OK?" No reply.

I stepped on to the edge of the pitch and bellowed the same question at him. He must have finally heard because he just waved his hand. I sprinted all the way back to the dugout and explained to the boss he had waved his hand, so I thought he was going to be OK.

"Baz, that's no good. I am going to use my last substitute now, so I need to be sure he is going to get through the 90 minutes."

For fuck's sake. Off I went yet again. I was breathing through my arse by now. Another lung-busting run and once more I screamed the same question.

"ARE YOU OK?"

That same wave of the hand again. This time I walked right on to the pitch and yelled, "We need to know if you are OK because we are going to put the last sub on."

Finally, a response. Watto's retort, delivered with full fury – just like all the verbal barbs of years gone by – remains burned into my soul for all eternity, allowing complete word-for-word recall: "Fuck off, Baz, you cunt. You are fucking up my game. Fuck off!"

Then the fans started on me. And when the Everton fans start on you, you know about it. In unison, and with those strong scouse accents that can sound so coarse in such situations.

"Fuck off, baldy!"

"Sit down, slaps!"

"Get back in your box, Kojak!"

And so on and so forth as I trudged back to the dugout. That was gratitude – Premier League style – I raced around the bloody pitch three times, flat out, probably covering more ground than some of the players.

And for what? Stick off the boss, stick off the fans, and stick off the player.

Being head of the medical department at Everton involved much more than just having a fancy title. At Halifax and Preston my role as club physio had been multi-faceted, but running the entire medical department was a different beast entirely.

I loved the job, of course, but it was also tough and extremely high-pressured with few days off. The fact I could cope with it is a different matter and the summation of all the previous chapters. I was responsible for the health and well-being of over £100 million worth of talent. I was responsible for making the final decisions regarding the management of players' injuries. The buck stopped with me.

I had a staff of five to oversee and organise, and I must admit I found it difficult to let go of the craving to do every job. To see somebody else warming up, cooling down and massaging the players was certainly odd. If I am being totally honest, I don't know if I ever got used to delegating the workload.

In this environment and at this level, the days are seldom identical and you are at the mercy of the exigencies of the business. I had to travel the world (often at very short notice, but always business class) to fulfil my duties. For example, after Everton's match against Burnley at Turf Moor in 2009, the boss pulled me to one side and told me we were signing a Russian player the next day called Diniyar Bilyaletdinov and that I had to fly to Hamburg via London the next morning and perform as good and concise a medical as I could in a hotel room in Hamburg. Why Hamburg? Fuck knows. He played for Lokomotiv Moscow!

So instead of enjoying a relatively easy half-day after the match, I boarded the 7am flight from Manchester to London, changed planes at Heathrow, then flew to Hamburg before getting a taxi at Hamburg airport and arriving at the Hilton Hotel at 2pm. I conducted the medical in the hotel and flew back to the UK, via Amsterdam, the same day. I finally arrived home at 3am the following morning and was up for work at 7am.

Now I hasten to add that I wasn't complaining; it was thrilling, exciting and I even learned a few words of Russian – I am just telling you about the fluidity of the job.

My son soon loved 'Billy', as he became known, and wanted his name on the back of his Everton shirt – but not at over a quid a letter. I persuaded him to go for a Brazilian player instead after telling him they were the best players in the world. So, Jo it was. Result.

Those medicals had the potential to cause great stress, especially with the foreign players and agents who didn't really seem to have any preference for the club they joined, as long as the deal was good. I am proud to say I conducted more than 60 medicals in my career as a physiotherapist and only ever had to fail two players. Both players went on to have further significant problems with the joints I had vetoed (phew, what a relief).

One of the players actually played a couple of games against us later the same season. The old doc asked me to point him out. "Right," he said without a trace of irony, "we could do with him collapsing in a fucking heap." Doc, that was very funny.

As soon as there was a problem with a medical, you could see the fucking mood change in around five seconds flat. From the agent saying, "My player, he is a-loving only this club" to, "We are having other clubs, mister, if you push us". One player went from being an Everton fan all his life, as a boy growing up on the continent only ever dreaming of pulling on the blue shirt, to somebody threatening to fuck off to another club if the blood tests weren't back in the next hour. We called his bluff and, guess what? Yes, he waited. Of course he did. He loved Everton, didn't he?

When you failed a player on medical grounds, all hell broke loose. All of a sudden you were a fucking joke and so was your medical department. The chief executives got involved and the mud started being chucked – usually at me. But fuck them all. I wasn't bothered. I was, for eight years, the guardian of the club, and no way was I letting anybody in who wasn't fit enough to be there. I always felt my duty was not to the manager, chairman, agent or player, but to the fans.

One medical I will never forget was that of Marouane Fellaini. It was the last day of the transfer window – September 1, 2008. It was lunchtime, everybody had left the training ground, but I hung around. I knew David was after a player and he would never give up until the clock struck midnight. I sat at my desk by the phone. Everybody was telling me to go home, it was over, too late to sign anybody now. But I knew David better than anybody – he would not give up, he would never give up.

Then the phone rang. It was David.

"Baz, I've got a player, club-record transfer fee. I need a medical ASAP."

"OK."

"Right, Baz, listen carefully. I need you to meet me on the corner of the park."

"OK. Sefton Park or Stanley Park?"

"Hyde Park. He's flying into Heathrow at 8pm."

Jesus! I set off from Liverpool in my car. It was pissing down with rain and the motorway was busy. Then, when I was just north of Birmingham, I got another call.

"Baz, slight problem, he can't get into Heathrow, he's coming to Luton. See you there."

"OK, Dave."

I was glad. Going to Luton saved me a lot of hassle – I wouldn't have to drive through central London.

I had just got to the outskirts of north London when the phone rang again.

"Baz, slight problem, he can't get into Luton, so we are boarding Phil Green's (a long-time Everton supporter and friend of Bill Kenwright) jet to Brussels to meet him there."

"I haven't got my passport, Dave."

"Don't worry, you won't need it."

Now I know David is a powerful guy but I didn't think even he could get somebody out of the country without a passport.

I got to the airport about 9pm. It was chaos – windy and raining. The agents – there were two of them for some reason – were running around, sending emails and arguing in French, and David and Dave Harrison were scratching their heads in dismay. Time was running out as the jet was being fuelled. Of course, I was not allowed to board the plane due to the lack of a passport, much to David's consternation. Suddenly they were off, running across the tarmac, through the rain and wind, to the plane, papers flying everywhere, and I watched amazed as it took off and disappeared into the stormy night back up the fucking M1.

This was surely a mission impossible but, luckily, David Moyes's alter ego is Tom Cruise. It was nearly 2am when I was driving home and the news came through on the radio: Everton had got their man.

It was a lesson to any aspiring person on the value of determination and never giving up. That money (£15 million) which David spent, in such bizarre circumstances, is beginning to look like a fantastic investment now. That's why David is special.

In terms of the medical – or lack of it – we were OK really because Fellaini hadn't ever had a serious injury and we had already received faxes of his cardiac screening, latest blood tests and medical records.

I loved the job but, as you can tell, it owned you, and the hours owned you. Forget planning anything; you did as the job required. No complaints. When Fellaini injured his ankle one day, we went straight down to London to see the specialist. But I knew the nature of the player, knew the nature of the player's agent and knew what was coming. It had been a long day and we were on the way back to Liverpool when the inevitable happened.

"Baz, je voudrais un rendez-vous avec Monsieur Van Dyke à Amsterdam demain s'il vous plaît."

And with that short sentence all your plans were cancelled (for those of you without a basic grasp of French, it basically meant I was off to Amsterdam). Twelve hours later, I was on the early flight to Holland to see the renowned ankle specialist. Again, I am not complaining – I got to visit Ann Frank's house; I am just telling you what it was like (and yes, OK, there was also a bit of window shopping in the red light district). I made the most of my European trips: San Sebastian, Barcelona, Nice, Amsterdam, Hamburg. What a lucky bloke.

Notwithstanding the trips abroad and my extra responsibilities, the rest of the job was virtually the same as before. In at 8.45am, assess the injured players from 9-9.30am, and then climb the stairs to David's office to unload the bad news. Of course, it wasn't always bad news – often it was good news, and we had a relatively unburdened first seven years. But still, I was the man charged with giving the daily delivery of the injury updates. And it took its toll.

Knock on the door, and in I would go, clutching my list. I had learned over the years how to spin the news to my best advantage – where to hide the bad bits, talk up the good news, play down the negatives.

Then David, Steve Round, Jimmy Lumsden and Chris Woods would, in the mode of a top Hollywood courtroom drama, begin the cross-examination. But I never cracked. I had been doing the job too long and I wrote everything down so I could always back it up. They were good guys and didn't give me too much grief; it was their job to question, probe and query. I suppose I was lucky it was not ancient Rome where the bearer of bad news got his fucking head chopped off.

I would then return to the medical department downstairs and discuss with the players their individual treatment and rehabilitation plan for the day. The injured lads would go for breakfast and the medical department would get to work preparing the fit players for training with massages, strappings and stretches. At 10.30am I would go outside to monitor training whilst simultaneously doing the late-stage rehabilitation work with the injured players – it was fucking great.

After lunch the medical department would meet and we would reassess the injured lads, discuss plans for the next day and maybe use the swimming pool for an afternoon session. The day would conclude with a further brief meeting with the boss. And that is how the department worked – smooth as silk, very professional, full of energy and enthusiasm, and stocked with top-class medical staff. I know we had the best medical department in the country and so did the players. I was very proud of all the medical team.

Nevertheless, with respect to the assistant manager, coaches, fitness coaches, sports scientists, other physios, scouts and match analysts (the list has probably got even bigger since I left), it is the boss and the head of the medical department in the senior football environment who really have to make big decisions – the former much more than the latter. Of course, all the others work hard, give advice and make suggestions, but it was only David and I who lay awake at night hoping we hadn't dropped a bollock.

The fact I shared the pressure – albeit a much smaller amount – with the boss, allied to my own desperate efforts as a manager back at Halifax, enabled me to understand better the strain any boss of a Premier League team is under. This pressure would crush most men, most mortals, but David isn't most men. He is exceptional with exceptional talent. If you ask him who the Chancellor of the Exchequer is, he probably won't be able to tell you. But ask him who gave the free kick away that led to Aston Villa's equaliser at Villa Park six years previously and he will get it in an instant.

He is like the bloody Rain Man. David's almost supernatural ability to read, understand, analyse and recount every single passage of play while he is in the dugout is truly amazing. For example, on numerous occasions when we conceded a goal, the coaches would blame the most obvious offender, but David would often argue that the initial problem had started 15 passes and five passages of play earlier when one of our players took a sloppy throw-in. The coaches would argue against him and then sit scratching their heads in disbelief when the post-match video analysis proved the boss right – every time.

He also has the unusual ability of being able to read another human being's mind, which is something of a dying art. I never tried to pull the wool over his eyes with the daily injury report. He could remember everything you said – and yes, everything you had said the previous week as well. If there was an inconsistency, God help you. He would have made a fantastic barrister.

In some ways, Everton is similar to Birmingham City – both big city clubs, both living in the shadow of their more illustrious and successful local rivals, both playing in blue and both with a set of staunch yet long-suffering fans.

I had started at the top as a 16-year-old all those years ago and, after a remarkable and torturous journey, had finally found my way back to the summit. A quarter of a century after ignominiously leaving the biggest football stage, I was back at the highest level of professional football. The big difference now, though, was that I was mentally tough enough to cope.

It had been a hard slog, but I had endured, and as I stood at Old Trafford, Stamford Bridge and Villa Park drinking in the atmosphere, I felt very proud of what I had achieved despite some very difficult and testing times. It had been a rollercoaster ride and, like the best rollercoasters, it had negotiated some very high points and very low points. But I had sat tight and ridden it all the way to the end.

There was another striking similarity between the Everton of this era and the Birmingham of the mid-'70s – they both owned a player who would be considered the best of his generation. Trevor Francis, of course, had been the star attraction at Birmingham (I think I may have mentioned him before), while Everton in the 2002/03 season unleashed one of the greatest talents in the modern game – Wayne Rooney.

I have had so many high spots in my career, but being able to say I worked with Wayne is probably the top one. Everybody knows about him as a player, but I was lucky enough to know him as a lad. He is a very modest, polite young man, always courteous, always on time, hard-working, very bright and switched on.

What sets these once-in-a-generation players apart from the rest? Obviously, much of it is natural ability and athleticism but lots of players are talented and athletic. With Wayne it was those things and – contrary to what many people may think – the most incredible, unflappable temperament.

I remember about 30 minutes before his (and my) first Merseyside derby at Goodison, which was live on Sky Sports, he came into the medical room and started juggling the ball and generally larking about. He was laughing and clowning around. I couldn't believe how relaxed he was. I was shitting myself, as you would no doubt expect even though I was only the physio, because the Merseyside derby is a big, big game. I was fascinated to get an insight into how he really felt, remembering all those fears that wracked my body when I was 17 years of age and about to cross the white line.

So I said to Wayne – just 17, minutes before his first Merseyside derby, live on TV: "Please tell me you are nervous..."

In a strange way, I wanted him to say he was very nervous, even scared, just like I had been. It would vindicate me. We were both local lads after all. This game should be difficult for him.

"No."

"Come on, you must be a bit nervous?"

"No."

"Just the teeniest bit?"

"No."

"It's OK, you can tell me, I won't tell anybody."

"I am no more nervous than if this was a reserve game. I can't wait for the kick-off."

And that was it then, in a nutshell. Born to be great, born to play at the highest level, whereas I was born to be mediocre, born to scrape a living at the lower levels. I think it's fair to say Wayne and I are somewhat different. The players at the very top all seem to have a fantastic mental approach. Vive la difference and all that.

The 2002/03 season was all about Wayne and his effect. We finished seventh (a great achievement) and my enduring memory, other than Wayne's incredible goal against Arsenal that heralded the arrival of the next great English footballer, was the buzz that went round every time he got the ball. Everybody stood up and there was an almost reverential silence as the fans waited in expectation for the magic to be produced – and he seldom failed to deliver.

My first season with Everton was unforgettable. A new super-star had been born. David Moyes was voted Premier League Manager of the Season – just as he had predicted eight years earlier after that pre-season training session at Preston – and I was at last getting the financial recognition that had eluded me for so long.

There were hundreds – yes hundreds – of days that season when I felt incredibly privileged to be doing what I was doing. Some days, when the medical room was quiet, I would go and help Chris Woods fire balls at the keepers. I can hardly describe the feeling of happiness and almost total disbelief that I was being paid by such a great football club to spend my time taking shots at England international goalkeepers such as Richard Wright, Nigel Martyn and even Woods himself. This truly was the Promised Land.

There was a great feeling at the end of the season that the manager and players could take the club back to their rightful place as regular top-six finishers and bring European football back to Everton. There were record season ticket sales in anticipation of Moyes's brave new world.

I was really looking forward to my summer holidays as we went into the final game of the campaign at home to the champions, Manchester United. But, yet again, a totally unpredictable set of circumstances conspired to throw a spanner into the works and ensure a nerve-wracking but somewhat exciting postscript to the season.

Wayne's rise had been so meteoric that he was called into the full England squad to play some friendlies during June and go to South Africa. The club were a little concerned things were happening just a bit too fast for the lad who was still only 17 and, understandably, wanted to protect him from too much publicity too soon.

Wayne hurt his leg against United. It was a totally bona fide injury but was seized upon by the press, who were aware of the club's concerns about the player getting too much exposure, as a ruse to get him out of the trip to South Africa.

The whole thing escalated into a full club-versus-country dispute and the upshot was that I would have to go down to London with Wayne to participate in a joint medical evaluation of the player's injury.

That was pressure.

By now, there was a public feeding frenzy regarding this meeting and it was presented by the press as a power struggle between Everton and the Football Association. It was big news every day and our routine, medical-based meeting was portrayed as something akin to the gunfight at the OK Corral. I was very nervous (but not scared).

Due to the media interest, there was an element of the clandestine about the whole day. Everybody seemed very tense. We evaded the press and all parties met in a top-floor suite in a posh hotel near Heathrow. We were ushered into the room and I presented our case. It was very amicable and the England manager, Sven-Goran Eriksson, was the perfect gentleman. I was very impressed with him – as with Howard Kendall, it was that word charisma again.

It was unanimously agreed that Wayne would miss the South Africa trip because of the injury and join the squad for the latter part of the international itinerary. What a relief.

After the business was concluded, we sat drinking coffee and making small talk. It was almost surreal and a marvellous indicator of just how far I had come up the football ladder when Sven offered me a biscuit.

The fact Wayne was excused from the trip was perceived, in the media, to have been a victory for Everton and our medical team, but it was never that – just a common-sense decision on the management of a genuine injury. And again a stark reminder of the pressure involved at this level of professional sport.

So with that frisson of high pressure comfortably negotiated, it was time for my annual summer holiday. I had two weeks off

(I was getting lazy by now) and looked forward to the 2003/04 campaign with great optimism. This was to be the year when the football giant that had been enjoying a good kip for nearly 20 years would finally awaken and former glories would be restored.

If only life was that simple.

Chapter Fourteen
LIFE AT THE TOP

Pre-season 2003. My first pre-season at the top level and what a great experience.

Previously, the pre-season tours I had been involved in had taken me to such exotic places as Morecambe, Llandudno, the Isle of Man and Devon. Not any more. During my time at Everton, I would be lucky enough to travel the world – from Thailand to Switzerland to Salt Lake City – always business class. It was five-star all the way.

Hopes and expectations at the club were so high, but it just didn't happen and we finished the 2003/04 campaign a dismal 17th, culminating in a crushing 5-1 hammering at Manchester City on the last day of the season. It's hard to put a finger on what went wrong exactly. It was probably a combination of things: high expectations, bad luck in some games, loss of confidence, bad referees. You know, the usual excuses.

The only good thing about the whole situation was that Wayne was selected in the England squad for the Euro 2004 tournament that summer in Portugal. Wayne sparkled on the big stage, scoring four goals as England advanced to a quarter-final against the hosts. His performances certainly cheered all Evertonians up. But then, bang, disaster struck in the quarter-final against Portugal.

The dreaded metatarsal break, an injury that has been the curse of England players in recent times, and one Wayne would suffer again before the 2006 World Cup. The metatarsals are the long, slim fragile bones in the foot and sadly they seem to keep breaking. Why? In my opinion, a combination of reasons: poor boot support, hard pitches, the increased speed of the game and probably the power of the players.

The England doctor called me about 30 minutes after the match and confirmed the nature and severity of the injury. My blood ran cold. Wayne was now the hottest property in Europe – if not the planet – and I knew for the next few months the eyes of the football and medical world would be focusing on him, his injury and his recovery. I would be under pressure and public scrutiny like never before.

Fuck this one up and you are history.

As part of the recovery process, Wayne had to have an X-ray every couple of weeks which we would then take to show to the consultant in Manchester. As you can imagine, there was a huge degree of media interest about these appointments as everyone waited with bated breath for the latest progress report on the game's newest sensation.

On our very first visit, we had just pulled on to the M62 outside Liverpool when Wayne said, "We are being followed."

"Rubbish."

"No, really we are. That Chrysler Voyager behind is following us."

"Wayne, you are watching too much TV."

"Turn off the motorway then."

So I turned off the motorway and, coincidentally, the Voyager also turned off.

"Told you."

"Wayne, that is called a coincidence."

"Turn right here then."

"Another coincidence."

Left, right, right, left, 180 degrees around the next two islands and I had to admit that he was right. Wow, what a shock. A combination of astonishment, fear, excitement and, overall, confirmation of the amount of media interest in this player and the scrutiny the management of his injury had generated. In the end, with a bit of *The Sweeney* circa 1975 driving, I shook off our tail and we ended up in a kiddies' playground. You should have seen the look on those kids' faces as we roared into view and screeched to a halt in front of them. Open-mouthed they pointed at the car.

"Look, it's Mick Rathbone."

I had another stark reminder of the national obsession with Wayne's foot a few weeks later when it was time for his first bit of jogging. We were at Everton's former training ground, Bellefield, which is surrounded by 12-foot high walls and is very private and secluded. We had just started jogging when Wayne said, "Shit" and stopped running. I thought he must have had pain in his foot, so I nearly had a cardiac arrest, let me tell you.

"What's the matter? Is it your foot?"

"No, I've got my old Puma club trainers on but I've just signed a deal with Nike. They will go mad."

"And how will they know?"

"The photographer in the big tree will take a picture."

"Listen son, stop eating cheese before you go to bed. Nobody can see us here."

"He is up there all right, hidden in the tree. You can't see him but he is there."

Talk about paranoia.

However, to my total disbelief, when I looked at the back page of *The Sun* newspaper the next morning, I nearly choked on my cornflakes. There it was, just as he had predicted, a big photograph of me and Wayne jogging with an arrow pointing to his trainers and the caption: "Who's been a naughty boy then?"

Those incidents taught me a lesson, though – when you are with Wayne Rooney, don't pick your nose or scratch your balls.

It's a real shame Wayne is now unpopular with a large section of the Everton fans. He was such a good lad, a great player and a true Evertonian. Hopefully, in time, attitudes will soften and I would love to see him get a good reception at Goodison. I think that would mean the world to the lad.

By July 2004, the air of optimism that had accompanied Everton's pre-season of 2003 was a distant memory. We were at our pre-season camp in Austria and all was doom and gloom. A small, ageing squad, very little money to spend on new players, rumours of Wayne about to be sold, boardroom in-fighting involving two factions struggling for control of the club and an angry backlash from the supporters following the great disappointment of the previous campaign all contributed to a sense of impending disaster.

David, our first-team coach Jimmy Lumsden and I were in a bar having a drink one evening. For that afternoon's training, David had decided to put on a 'fun' session to try and lift spirits a bit. He had taken half of the lads to one end of the training pitch to play a game of 'chip the ball on to the crossbar from the edge of the box', while Jimmy had taken the other half to the opposite end of the field for a game of 'curl the ball in from the corner flag'.

David asked Jimmy how it had gone.

"Yes great, boss. Everybody really had a good time, it was a good laugh and it really seemed to give everybody a bit of a lift."

"Who won, Jimmy, as a matter of interest?" asked the boss.

"Well," said Jimmy, a little embarrassed. "I actually won."

"That's odd," said the boss. "I won our competition."

"Fucking hell," I exclaimed. "You won the chipping the ball on to the bar comp, you won the curling the ball into the goals from the corner flag comp, and I got the highest score in the bleep test despite being 45. We are well and truly fucked. This is definitely going to be our last season at the club so I think we should all agree now to relax, stop worrying, give it everything we have got and just try to enjoy it as much as we possibly can."

I am a strong believer that if you want people in professional sport to perform at their best, then it is essential they are allowed, or even encouraged, to relax and enjoy the whole experience. It's just common sense really, if you are enjoying something you will do it better. I had felt for a while, with all the new technology at the top clubs, the intense, highly scientific approach to the modern game and the days of preparation before a fixture, that we were in danger of throwing the baby out with the bath water. In the drive for thoroughness and professionalism, I felt we were taking some of the enjoyment, spontaneity and, ultimately, level of performance out of the whole proceedings.

That's my theory anyway and I am sticking to it. Either way, the new approach to proceedings, demonstrated by that fun afternoon, allowed the players to relax without too many expectations, and it paid off. The club finished fourth that season and qualified for the preliminary round of the Champions League. It was nothing short of sensational and one of the few times in the decade that the traditional Premier League top-four monopoly of Man United, Chelsea, Arsenal and Liverpool was broken.

I remember we beat Newcastle at Goodison in our last home game of the season and, in front of 40,000 delirious and grateful fans, did a well-deserved lap of honour. We had to wait 24 hours until Arsenal played Liverpool at Highbury – anything but a win for our Merseyside rivals would ensure we qualified and pipped them to the keys to Fort Knox. The game was live on TV and I remember being so nervous watching it. There was so much riding on it for Everton. If we could qualify for the Champions League it could generate the kind of money that might allow David to really compete with the big boys. It was possibly Everton's one and only chance in the foreseeable future to become a club once again capable of winning things, just as they had been so many times in their illustrious but sadly distant past.

Sitting there watching the game at home, knowing how much rested on it, was pure torture. There was nothing you could do but sit and watch, knowing it was completely out of your hands. It took me back to the climax of the 1993 season when I was at Halifax and a similar situation had unfolded. On the Tuesday evening 11 days before our momentous final game against Hereford, Northampton Town had played at home to Wrexham. The upshot was that, if they had won, then we would have been all but relegated that night without even making it to the final day of the season. I recall sitting, glued to the radio, feeling sick with worry.

It was amazing to be involved in two such similar situations – your life in their hands and all that – concerning two completely opposite prizes and all played out almost 90 Football League places apart. It was a fucking big ladder I had climbed.

Arsenal won, we qualified for the Champions League, and we all headed to Liverpool for an impromptu party. A truly amazing feat but, more importantly, a real opportunity for Everton Football Club to re-establish itself among the elite.

Sadly, it ended in tears.

To qualify for the group stages in August 2005 we had to beat Spanish side Villarreal over two legs . After the first leg at Goodison Park, which we lost 2-1, we needed to win in Spain. That match will always stick in my mind for many reasons: it was played at 10pm, it was really warm, Villarreal's ground was very compact with steep sides and, most memorably, the seats in the dugout were leather Recaro seats – beloved of the '80s hatchback.

However, the most remarkable part of the whole experience was when we walked out to inspect the pitch. The entire stadium was full of Everton fans, despite the fact that the club had only been allocated a few thousand tickets. They were in all four corners of the ground, in every stand with their flags and colours. Jimmy Comer, our masseur and a lifelong Everton fan, was busy trying to convince us he had something in his eye, such was the emotion of the occasion.

How can you quantify the size of a club? Fan base? Trophies? Money in the bank? History? It is all a matter of opinion at the end of the day. All I can say is I doubt any club in England could have produced support like that on that balmy evening in Spain.

Everton played well, especially in the second half. Then, as is often the case in football, a referee's decision – the simple ruling out of what looked like a superb goal from Big Dunc by the world-renowned Pierluigi Collina – denied Everton the tie, the chance to go to the group stages, and who knows what else?

We lost 2-1. It was a real sickener and a missed opportunity. I could see David was gutted after the game. He knew. He knew how close we had come to being in a position to turn Everton's fortunes around. But to his – and our – credit, we kept our collective chins up, got on with the job in hand and continued to try to rebuild the club.

Those foreign matches were amazing. Who gets to go to Kharkov, Minsk, Bergen, Bucharest and Olomouc? We played at Benfica's Stadium of Light and the Olympic Stadium in Athens. The atmosphere at these games was amazing, even better than the Premier League (sorry, but it's true). Thank you Everton. There is something truly special, almost surreal, about stepping out of your hotel in the middle of Belarus and being surrounded by dozens of scousers in Everton shirts.

Following our Champions League disappointment, the subsequent period of five years, up to my departure in May 2010, in which I had the honour to be the head of the medical department at that fantastic football club, proved very successful. It was painstakingly slow – two steps forward and then one back, but the overall momentum and direction was forward with regular top-six finishes.

We enjoyed slow, steady progress on and off the pitch. The older stalwarts like Dave Weir, Alan Stubbs, Lee Carsley, Kevin Kilbane and Gary Naysmith – all good servants – were gradually replaced by younger players. From 2005 onwards David, on a shoestring budget, performed miracles in the transfer market by signing the likes of Mikel Arteta, Tim Cahill, Steven Pienaar, Leighton Baines, Joleon Lescott and Phil Jagielka. All for the kind of fees that now seem almost laughable.

Those years were great for me. I felt well respected and wanted, just as I had at Preston. Some of the fans would even chant my name sometimes, and one occasion in particular stands out. We were playing at St James' Park and it was about one hour before the kick-off. My daughter Lucy, who was studying at Newcastle University, came to watch the match and I arranged to meet her outside. She arrived with her boyfriend and I went out to the main entrance to give them their tickets. I introduced myself to her boyfriend, then made a lame joke about having to go back to the dressing room before I got mobbed by the Everton fans. I had barely finished that statement when a large gang of Everton fans (presumably pissed) spotted me and started chanting my name. It was very embarrassing but, by God, I fucking well loved it.

How ironic that, of the two top-flight clubs I worked for, one lot of fans chanted my name, while the other lot booed me. I do know, however, that if the Everton fans had seen me play back in the 1970s, they would also have booed.

Much as I enjoyed that incident, even greater acclaim was to come. One day, David was being interviewed on Sky Sports and was asked about Nigel Martyn. The reporter put it to David that Nigel (who we had signed for next to nothing) must surely be his best-ever signing.

I a flash, David said, "Actually no, Mick Rathbone, my physio, is my best-ever signing."

Fuck me, I didn't expect that. Good job I was on my own in my office at the time, otherwise I would also have been using the 'there is something in my eye' routine!

David and I had formed a special relationship which started on that warm afternoon in Avenham Park on my first day at Preston. Sometimes I would shrug my shoulders and say, "I am just a physio, David", and he would reply, "You are more than that and you know it." That meant everything to me.

Phil Neville used to wind me up by saying, "Come on, Baz, admit it, you are running the show really." I wasn't but I hope my role did extend beyond that of the medical guy.

With the greatest respect to all the additional staff who have come into the game over the last decade, it was the interface between David and myself, on a daily basis, that was crucial. Once when we were in Salt Lake City, Seamus Coleman had a badly infected foot and I was changing his dressing early one morning. David phoned me to say I was late for the staff meeting and everybody was waiting to start. I apologised but explained how crucial it was to change the dressing and check the wound, and that I would be there in five minutes, so he should start without me.

When I got there, of course, the meeting hadn't started. It couldn't start because despite the best intentions of everybody sat there, laptops at the ready, all the essential dialogue regarding who was training, who had what injury and when they would feature was, by definition, between the boss and the head of the medical department.

Regardless of my involvement, David took the club by the scruff of the neck and, with very little money but lots of grit and determination, dragged them back up to the top end of the table, finishing in the top six most years. Unless you were there during that period, you could never truly appreciate what that man has done for the club – to the point that, by the time I left, he had built a squad of young, very talented, super-fit, highly motivated players who were ready to push on to the next level and knock on the door of another top-four finish and the Holy Grail of the Champions League.

Everton are now based at one of the finest training grounds in Europe (the club moved to Finch Farm in 2007), and all the structures in the other vital areas, such as youth development and scouting, are in place to ensure the steady progress under David can be maintained.

It is also right to mention the contribution made to the club by the chairman, Bill Kenwright. The chairman of any football club is an easy target for criticism and I know Mr Kenwright has had more than his fair share. I also know from my dealings with him, and the way the boss spoke about him, just how committed he is to the club and its wellbeing. I am sure, in the whole of the

Football League, you would not find any chairman who loves his club as much as this man (although Derek Shaw at Preston would run him close).

I will give you an example of how passionate he is. A few years ago, we were going through a bad patch and results were poor. We were at the wrong end of the table and our next away game was against one of the London clubs (a lot of ex-footballers will testify it gets harder and harder to remember exact results and the opposition as the years go by). We were at our hotel in London the night before the game when the boss informed us that the chairman wanted to speak to everybody. That put the shits up a few people and we all thought it was going to be a bollocking of some sort. He dined with us in the private dining room set aside for us.

It was tense, to say the least. Then he got up and addressed us. We were waiting for the flak to fly. We could not have been more wrong. Mr Kenwright spoke of his affection for the club, how he had first started following Everton as a young boy and how it had shaped and enriched his life. He spoke of his admiration for the current set of players, how he wouldn't swap any of them and if we all stuck together, everything would be OK.

It was an amazing and moving speech, and it meant a great deal to everybody involved to be reassured they had such a supportive chairman. In terms of oratory skills, the speech reminded me a little of Abraham Lincoln's Gettysburg Address but, as we'd just eaten our pasta, I preferred to call it the Spaghettisburg Address. The next day we drew and then went on a good run to move up the table.

When you are responsible for the rehabilitation of players with serious long-term injuries, it is very difficult not to get emotionally involved – well, it was difficult for me anyway.

After all, it was me who carted them off the pitch, diagnosed the injury in the dressing room, broke the bad news, comforted and consoled them. It was me who arranged and watched the subsequent surgery, who was at their bedside in those nervous moments before the anaesthetic took effect. It was my face they saw first when they opened their eyes post-operatively (poor bastards), me who spent every day with them, side by side, through the long recovery period.

Mostly, with all the advances in surgery, we got good results and the player returned to action as good as new. Sometimes, however, things didn't work out too well and it caused great personal heartache.

Unfortunately, in my last year at Everton, we had too many serious injuries which caused a huge emotional drain on the medical staff. It really was the perfect storm of injuries. One after another. It was unbelievable, but not unbearable (I can bear anything now, can't I?). I felt personally responsible for not being able to give David a strong team every week, which I had always previously managed to do. David didn't blame me, but those walks up the stairs and the subsequent breaking of more bad news started to make my 51-year-old legs feel their age.

During the prolonged rehabilitation periods, you do get very close to the player and their pain becomes your pain (as if I hadn't already had enough pain in football). One of the guys I got closest to at Everton was Yakubu, as a result of the Achilles tendon he ruptured at White Hart Lane at the end of November 2008. It was a horrific injury and, when I watched the brilliant surgeon, James Calder, repair it, I feared the worst for 'The Yak', especially given the power and size of the man. He was facing nine months out with no guarantees he would recover. He had to spend the first three months wearing a special boot and could not do any training at all. The bookmakers had stopped taking bets on The Yak becoming the first 100kg footballer.

The rehabilitation process was painful and painstaking, and we became good mates. He was the perfect professional and actually *lost* weight. We had a great bond and a great working relationship – even though I nearly drowned him one day. We were about to start the swimming pool phase of The Yak's rehabilitation and, despite his protestations that "black men can't swim", I coaxed him into the pool. He was wearing a lifejacket, a special buoyancy suit and some ankle floats. Just like the Titanic, I thought this man was unsinkable. Nevertheless, once he was in the water he was clutching the side and hanging on for dear life. I explained he could not possibly sink, so he should let go and start paddling his arms and feet.

Eventually, after I had prised his fingers off the safety bar, he reluctantly let go and, fuck me, sank straight to the bottom of the pool. He couldn't have sunk any quicker if he had been wearing a suit of armour. All I could see, way down at the bottom of the pool, was the top of his head and a stream of bubbles was exiting his lungs at an alarming rate.

Luckily, all the other players were around the edge of the pool doing a cooldown, and the ones who weren't helpless with laughter gave me a hand to fish The Yak out. I am sorry, Yak, but that is right up there with the funniest things I have ever seen in football.

All the hard work and dedication, on both our parts, paid off and The Yak returned to the first team at Hull in September 2009. He scored a goal after just 11 minutes and ran 50 yards to embrace and thank me. It was a fantastic moment for me and I have a picture of it on my wall at home. You may not think it means much, but anybody who knows The Yak will testify he doesn't like to waste energy running needlessly. Thanks Yak.

I really enjoyed the challenge of working with the so-called 'injury-prone' players. I had great success with Big Dunc and enjoyed similar results in the two years in which I had the pleasure of working with the charming, highly intelligent and brilliant Louis Saha.

We were excited to work with Louis despite his injury-prone reputation. In his first season at the club, we were extremely careful with him, in terms of not pushing him too hard, and quickly gained his trust because he had intimated that at all his previous clubs he felt this had not necessarily been the case.

By his second season we had developed a relationship that allowed us to push him harder. In those two seasons, Louis played nearly 70 games and scored more than 20 goals for Everton, despite being injured and out for six weeks when he first came to us from Manchester United.

When Louis signed his new contract in February 2010, Bill Ellaby, the player liaison officer, handed me an envelope. He explained it was a thank you from Louis. I was touched he had taken the trouble to thank me in writing. I opened the envelope thinking, "Fuck me, this is a thick letter." But it wasn't a letter; it was an envelope stuffed with £50 notes.

That is the type of gratitude I prefer. After all, let's face it, talk is cheap. Apparently, he rewarded every member of the medical staff in the same way. I think he respected us for the care and time we gave him. It was a magnificent gesture from a great guy. Sometimes, though, things don't work out quite as well, and occasionally a player never fully recovers from an injury. That happened to Li Tie, and it caused me great personal sadness.

Li Tie – the 'Chinese David Beckham' – was the nicest, humblest guy I ever met. He had a great first season at Everton in 2002/03 and the fans loved him. They used to sing, "One Li Tie, there's only one Li Tie." I used to sit in the dugout and think there must be fucking millions of Li Ties back in China!

Sadly, he broke his leg in early 2004 while playing for China and, even though it was a simple fracture, it just refused to mend. We tried everything to make it heal, every type of bone stimulator, but it was a torturously slow process. Eventually, and understandably, I started to get pressure from the boss. Basically, he wanted to know when Li Tie was going to be fit. I told him he would be fit for the start of the New Year.

In the first week of January, I was called to David's office, where the coaching staff were assembled, and again asked the question: "When is Li Tie going to be fit?"

"As I said before, the start of the New Year."

"Baz, it's January now."

"Yes, I know, but don't forget he's Chinese; his New Year is in February."

I consider that to have been one of my finest-ever jokes but, do you know what? Not one person in the room even smiled.

Of course, it wasn't funny. It wasn't funny at all. Li Tie never fully recovered from that injury and left Everton in May 2006, and I felt great sadness and personal responsibility.

While experiences such as those with Li Tie inevitably put a strain on me professionally, the good memories certainly outweighed the bad in my time at Everton.

I have so many fantastic memories from my time at Everton – from running up Bondi Beach with Tim Cahill, to crossing balls for Tim Howard in Soldier Field in Chicago when I went to watch him play for the USA.

I have been to the USA eight times, the Far East twice, Australia twice and virtually every country in Europe. Thanks to Everton, I have been to the top of the Empire State Building, walked over the Sydney Harbour Bridge, visited space control in Houston, drunk a Singapore Sling in the Raffles Hotel in Singapore, seen IndyCar racing in Canada, had a coffee in the first ever Starbucks in Seattle, climbed to the top of the Willis Tower, the highest building in America, taken a trip to an old gold mining place in the Rocky Mountains, watched Shaquille O'Neal play basketball for Miami Heat in Florida and Roger Clemens play baseball for the Houston Astros in Texas, swung myself around on the gym equipment on Venice Beach in Los Angeles, gone to the Blue Mosque in Istanbul, swum in Lake Michigan, stood in the middle of the largest public square in Europe in Ukraine, ridden an elephant in Thailand and witnessed a very unusual game of ping-pong in Bangkok.

A conversation I had with my son a couple of years ago provides an interesting example of just how many places I visited. Ollie came home from school and asked me to help him with his homework about assassinations. There were three he had to learn about.

"Dad, who was the American President who got shot last century?"

"Well, son, that was John F. Kennedy, and he was assassinated in Dallas in the early '60s. In fact, I have stood on the very spot where he was killed."

"OK, and what about that English pop star?"

"Well, son, that was John Lennon. He was murdered outside The Dakota building on the corner of Central Park in New York. In fact, I have stood on the very spot where he was shot."

"And the fashion designer?"

"Well, son, that was Gianni Versace and he was killed outside his mansion on Ocean Drive in Miami. In fact, I have stood on the very spot where it happened."

So many great times, so many wonderful memories, so many famous players I had the honour of working with. And the best one? The best memory?

It has to be going to the FA Cup final in May 2009. Why that one? Possibly because it was the most recent highlight but primarily because, as a child and footballer of a different era, the FA Cup still held an almost mythical, magical place in my heart.

The week before the final, as well as the build-up to it, was a condensation and microcosm of all the hype, all the media interest and all the preparation that surround modern-day football – shoe-horned into that magical but intense period prior to the game.

The regular season had finished on a high with a 2-0 win at Fulham – arguably our best performance of the whole campaign – and a well-deserved fifth-place finish. All the teams breathed a collective sigh of relief that the season was over and went on their holidays – except for the cup finalists, Everton and Chelsea, and Manchester United who were taking on Barcelona in the Champions League final.

The drug testers visited our training ground early in the week. That was the safest bet of the year. I assume they visited Chelsea's too – with only a few teams left in full training, it was predictable. It was always a slight worry when you thought a visit from the drug testers was imminent. Not because you ever suspected any of the players would be guilty of an offence, but because there were lots of thorough and painstaking procedures to be negotiated, just to complete the test within the legal parameters.

All went well, though, so I could relax and start to enjoy the build-up to the FA Cup final. In a funny kind of way, those few days of training prior to the match, with the media attention and heightened importance, were similar to those final few sessions at Halifax before the crucial last game of the season against Hereford United in 1993. A case of just watching the clock and counting down to the kick-off.

It was, of course, the complete polar opposite in the mindset of the personnel involved in either of those situations – Everton's players excited and looking forward to the occasion, Halifax Town's players (and manager) crapping themselves and dreading the game. Maybe the difference in terms of expectations of the outcome was the clearest quantifiable measurement of just how far I had come since then.

We flew down to London on the Thursday by private jet (of course) and stayed in the Grove Hotel near Watford, which is arguably the finest hotel in England. An added bonus of this magnificent place is the fact it has a really good football pitch, so we could train that afternoon and again on Friday morning. Training was fantastic on both occasions and the players were prepared to perfection by the boss.

The weather was gorgeous and, in the afternoon, the staff all sat around the outdoor pool with its lovely little man-made beach and enjoyed each other's company, secure in the knowledge that, whatever the result, Saturday was going to be a day we would all remember for the rest of our lives.

On Friday evening, the boss met the staff in the bar, bought us a couple of beers and thanked us for our work that season. We toasted Everton and retired to our rooms to try our FA Cup final suits on. The outfits were amazing – suits, shirts, ties, shoes, all from one of the finest tailors in London. Rumour had it the whole ensemble cost more than £1,000 per person, with the handmade shoes alone supposedly worth more than £300. A far cry from sharing the beans on toast at the motorway service station.

There wasn't a single cloud in the sky on Saturday morning, literally or metaphorically speaking. I put my suit on and looked at myself in the mirror. I felt intensely proud of what I had achieved, where I had come from. All the hard work had paid off. Ironically, at that moment, it didn't seem like it had been hard work at all – more a question of following the path fate had sent me down.

We got on the coach and left for Wembley. There were TV crews and well-wishers everywhere. All the hotel staff had come out to see us off. We had a police escort for the short journey and the noise of a helicopter buzzing over the top of the coach relayed back those classic cup final pictures that had so excited me as a child – a child who could only ever have dreamed of a moment like this.

And then, just when you thought your senses couldn't absorb any more emotion from the occasion, we turned into Wembley Way and saw – and heard – the Scouse Army. Where were the Chelsea fans? The Toffees had done the impossible and turned the FA Cup final into a home game. Every hair on my body – even the ones that had dropped out long ago – stood up.

I caught the eye of my great friend, Dr Ian Irving, a man who had been with the club for more than 30 years, and I knew in that moment, in that brief eye contact, we were both swallowing hard to stop the tears forming.

I walked into the dressing room – huge, palatial, wood-panelled with a separate medical room complete with ice-making machine and a massive fridge full of drinks. Fortunately, Jimmy Comer – probably the only masseur in the Premier League with the club badge tattooed on his calf – had already put all the gear out so the smell of the wood panelling and 30 pairs of hand-made leather shoes was intermingled with those smells – *the smells of football* – the Vicks, leather of the boots, Deep Heat, shampoo and massage oil.

Close your eyes and inhale the smells, inhale the memories.

Psychologically I felt my journey of discovery was complete; it had gone full circle. I had started at the very top all those years ago at Birmingham and endured one of football's greatest rollercoaster rides. It had been bumpy and there had been highs and lows but I had stayed on it and ridden it from the top division to the bottom division, and all the way back to its final destination – Wembley and the FA Cup final.

EPILOGUE

It would be nice to say we went on to lift the trophy, paraded it around Wembley, returned in glory via an open-top bus to a civic reception on the Liverpool Town Hall steps in front of tens of thousands of delirious Everton fans and all lived happily ever after – The End.

Life's not like that, though (unless you are in an Enid Blyton book), and we lost the FA Cup final 2-1, despite being a goal up after the first minute.

The evening reception at the Grovesnor Hotel in central London was, in spite of everybody's best efforts, a real anti-climax, and the open-top parade remained a pipedream.

I didn't live happily ever after either. Over the next few months, leading into the start of the 2009/2010 season, I began to fall out of love with the whole thing. Even the parts of the job I had always loved started to become less enjoyable.

Undoubtedly, part of the reason for my increasing discontentment was nothing more sinister than me experiencing a degree of 'burnout'. I could readily accept that, at nearly 51 years of age, because of the long hours I had been working for so many years, the job had to take its toll on me eventually. I was tired all the time, even in the morning. Permanently and chronically knackered. I started pulling into Charnock Richard service station again. I didn't go there to stand on the hill and admire my Jag (it was a Merc now anyway) as I had done seven years previously; ironically, I was pulling in for a fucking kip. I would drive to the far side of the car park, recline my seat fully, switch off my phone, pull my cap over my eyes and, just like the rest of the clapped-out sods in my row, drift off for an hour or so.

It was more than that, though. The game was changing, becoming ever more serious. The pressure on clubs to win and secure their places in the Premier League had become all-consuming, to the point that it was a rarity to see anybody smile during a game.

At the same time, the foreign players' personal physios, osteopaths and fitness analysts were appearing on the scene and starting to get involved with the management of the injuries. I don't blame them or the players for that. If I had been playing in Spain or France and got an injury, I would have been keen to be looked after by English medical people I knew and trusted. While I understood it and accepted it, I didn't really like it and felt undermined and dispensable (as you know, I do not like being dispensable).

One particular day when I walked into the medical room proved to be a seminal moment. Tim Cahill was having some soft tissue work from his Aussie physio, Mikel Arteta was getting a deep massage from his Spanish physio, and Johnny Heitinga was chatting on the telephone to his Dutch osteopath.

Now, once again, let me make things clear. These guys were doing good work on the players and giving them the individual attention our medical staff couldn't. I know the players felt much better prepared for the games with this additional therapy, and all three were playing really well at the time.

It just didn't feel right. It didn't feel like my medical room any more. Add to that the fact Sylvain Distin was in Nice at the time getting treatment and I suppose I just felt redundant, and not valued.

Don't get me wrong – those players were all top blokes and I loved working with them, but I realised, at that moment, that the game had moved beyond me. Standing in that doorway, looking into my medical room and realising my ways and methods were becoming anachronistic and obsolete was a chastening experience. I felt like I was the last of the Mohicans, except my hairstyle was more of a reverse Mohican.

A lot of the fun seemed to be going out of the game. I know it is important to win, just as it had been back in the '70s and '80s. But now the financial ramifications for losing were so colossal. They were putting so much pressure on everybody to win that it felt stifling at times. This pressure permeated its way from the manager through to the players and right down to the rest of the staff.

The all-consuming seriousness was evident on the field. At times, the pressure naturally filtered through to the supporters and gave the whole proceedings an even more threatening atmosphere. Sometimes I looked at the spectators, shouting and screaming and swearing, their eyes filled with hatred, and wondered just what would become of me if I stepped in among them. At times, such was the force of invective directed towards me I believe I would have been torn limb from limb and the bits chucked back on to the side of the pitch. And I wasn't even the manager.

When I first started out as a physio, I could have a bit of banter with the punters. They might shout, "Hey mate, give us a drink," and I would throw them a drink and share a joke with them, but not any more – those days have gone. The football arena is the modern-day Colosseum. Unfortunately, you will have worked out by now that I'm not fucking Maximus.

In that 2009/10 season with Everton, at one of the London games, I was walking around the far side of the pitch after attending to one of our players when somebody shouted, "Hey mate." I turned to the direction of the voice only to see a fan with tattoos and earrings glaring at me. (I have got nothing against people with tattoos and earrings – my daughter has both.) He then yelled, "You fucking scouse paedophile," much to the amusement of the surrounding fans who all laughed and started with the usual routine of vulgar hand gestures that would have made Helen Keller turn in her grave. A couple of kids, in a fantastic display of manual dexterity reminiscent of the late, great Ted Rogers of TV show *3-2-1* fame back in the '80s, were giving me the V-sign, the wanker sign and the single finger. I must admit I was deeply, deeply upset and offended. What an absolutely terrible thing to call somebody – a scouser (only joking).

Meanwhile, off the field there was an ever-increasing influx of support staff, such as fitness coaches, sports scientists, statisticians, match analysts and performance directors. It just seemed to me that the game was moving away from the training pitch on to the laptop computer, and we seemed to be spending nearly as much time in meetings as we were actually kicking a ball about.

Perhaps that is more a criticism of me, rather than them, for not adapting to the times. The guys who came to Everton were only trying to do the same as me and earn a living for their families. They were all really good at their jobs and good people too. But I didn't enjoy this new modern environment half as much. I am old-fashioned, I have old-fashioned ways and old-fashioned beliefs. I didn't really like to work in a big team where I wasn't in complete control. I missed the days when Baz was the fitness coach, the masseur and the chiropodist. That golden age when Baz did all the jobs, that magic moment back in 2002 when David Moyes, Colin Hendry and I laughed at how an ex-player could be a 'jack of all trades', had finally gone. It had given me that air of indispensability that my personality and low self-esteem, required. I needed to be needed.

By the end of the 2010 season, my built-in clock was telling me that my football journey was over and it was time to do something different (maybe write a book). I parted company with Everton in May 2010, amicably and with a handshake (and a few hugs), and that was it. Thirty-five years of working in professional football had come to an end.

On the way out of Everton's training ground on my final day – May 14, 2010 – I stepped into the dressing room for the last time, for one last whiff of nostalgia. Ironically, because the lads were off until the end of June, the rooms had been thoroughly cleaned with disinfectant and so, for the first time in so many years, when I closed my eyes and inhaled, the smells that had accompanied me on my journey and played such a big part in my life were no longer there.

Now that is fate.

POSTSCRIPT

Final Thoughts

JIM SMITH
Manager at Birmingham City

"Baz was a very honest young man and a very good player with great potential. He had the ability, but he was also a very sensitive lad and he struggled with the mental side of the game. I think the fact that he was a local lad playing for the local team made things much tougher for him, the pressure of playing in front of your family and all your old schoolmates on top of everything else.

"I know he was in awe of Trevor Francis, but to be honest we all were – when you've got a player of that calibre then everyone is living in his shadow to a certain extent. He was a superstar, and as a Brummie lad Mick knew exactly how much of a hero he was to the whole city.

"I remember Baz's debut for Birmingham City – we lost 4-0 to Norwich and the next week we were playing Liverpool. He knocked on the door of my office in the week and said, 'I can't play against Liverpool.' His nerves were shredded. I told him, 'You've got to play!'.

"He just didn't believe in himself, which was a great shame because he had the talent. I remember very well that day when he put his hand up after I'd said if anyone doesn't want to play for the club let me know. I knew he'd been through a tough time so all I could do was put my arm round him and, for the best interests of the player and the club, find him somewhere where he would be happy. He went to a good club and did very well.

"And, thinking about it, I am not surprised that he went on to have such success as a physio. Baz was always a very bright and caring lad – in fact that was probably his problem.

"People say he is a very funny man. Well, yes, he was very funny indeed in his time at Birmingham... mainly when he was on the football pitch!"

HOWARD KENDALL
Team-mate at Birmingham City and player-manager at Blackburn Rovers

"Baz was a little bit different from other footballers. At Birmingham, I remember he would come in on Sunday mornings for treatment even though he wasn't injured. And he used to call himself all sorts of different names. I've no idea why...

"In my first game as Blackburn Rovers' player-manager, Baz got sent off – for swearing at a linesman, I think. I wasn't impressed. I had to make an impact so I tore into him in the dressing room in front of the other players, told him he was suspended for a month. A few days later, I realised I needed my full back back, so I asked the players if they thought he'd served long enough. Luckily for me, they said yes!

"I'd never have imagined Baz would get into the medical side of the game – full credit to him. I thought he was more likely to get locked up!"

DEREK FAZACKERLEY
Team-mate at Blackburn Rovers

"When he arrived from Birmingham City as a young lad who'd played a few games in the First Division he settled in very well and was a real asset both on and off the pitch. He was a very good player and a remarkable athlete.

"One thing I'll always remember about Baz is that he always

used to bring his dog, Max, a big German shepherd, to training. The gaffer did, too – he had a little highland terrier or something called Skippy. We just trained in a public park in those days so they'd literally just drive up, let the dogs out and they'd run around when we trained. Sometimes they'd join in the training matches if we were short of players. One time, in the middle of training, there was a great big yelping and we saw that Skippy had been attacked by a greyhound. Baz went flying over there as fast as he could and booted the greyhound in the bollocks. The greyhound dropped Skippy and ran off, but that was the end of training because the Gaffer had to take him to the vet. Can you imagine this sort of thing going on in the modern world of football?

"Everything Baz did he did with his whole heart and soul. But I remember that as well as being very funny, with the joke more often than not on himself, he could also be very down at times – especially if we lost. It was like everything was to the extreme with him, the highs were really high and the lows really low. One minute he would be down, the next he'd be laughing and joking away. He definitely had an issue with confidence and sometimes questioned his playing ability – perhaps we all did, which is why we were playing at that level and not the First Division – which is why I admire him so much for what he has achieved, particularly after he stopped playing. I think the measure of the man is that he has always been prepared to tackle his demons head-on, throwing himself into the deep end when the easier option would have been not to. He is very highly respected in football for what he achieved as a physio at Preston and Everton, and in writing this book and standing up in front of people giving talks and lectures he continues to challenge himself and push himself to the limit."

BOB SAXTON
Manager at Blackburn Rovers
"Ah yes, I remember that day when Baz rescued Skippy... and it was two greyhounds not one. I don't blame the greyhounds, that's

how they're brought up, but as soon as he saw was what was happening Baz took off. He must have covered those 150 yards in record time and he absolutely leathered those greyhounds. What a great man.

"I can honestly say that in 50 years of football he is in the top three fittest players I ever came across. He was an incredible athlete, a fitness fanatic and had great ability on the ball for a full back. He was a great pro and he and Noel [Brotherston] on the left were as good a partnership as you'd ever get at that level. They were great years and we probably over-achieved as a team because of the spirit in the team. Baz was always at the heart of it, of course, laughing and joking, acting the goat.

"I can't say that I could have predicted that he'd go on to great things, but he must have put everything into his career as a physio that he put into his career as a player, because you don't get to work at a club like Everton for as long as he did without being the very, very best. I once heard that the lads at Everton were terrified of getting injured because it meant they'd have to go running with Baz, which was not only hard work but the chances were he'd show them up by being fitter than them."

LES CHAPMAN
Team-mate/assistant manager at Preston North End
"When Baz arrived at Preston he was always honest, super-fit and a real team player – you could always rely on him to give everything for his team-mates and the team – but most of all I just remember how funny he was. He was always laughing and joking and he had a great way with the English language.

"Of course, we played together under Big John McGrath, and one of the funniest moments I can remember from Baz's career at Preston was during an away game somewhere down south, I can't remember the game exactly. Baz was sub, and I was on the bench with him with Big John. Baz was such a fitness fanatic and so keen and dedicated that he spent virtually the entire match warming up, jogging up and down the touchline so he was ready if and when he was called upon. After about 50 minutes, during which he'd been literally warming up the whole time, I looked down the touchline and saw a kid ask him for an autograph, so he stopped to sign the lad's programme. At exactly this moment Big John decided to make a change, looked away from the action, and there's Baz signing this kid's autograph.

"'Look at him!' exclaimed Big John, 'He's just fucking stood there!'

PETER WRAGG
Joint-manager at Halifax Town

"Until Baz wrote it in this book, I had absolutely no idea that I was appointed as joint-manager at Halifax above his head. What happened was that I knew Paul Kendall who worked at Halifax from my days as boss at Macclesfield. After they got relegated to the Vauxhall Conference, I was getting nightly phone calls from Paul and others at the club asking for advice on how to prepare for non-league football. They desperately wanted to bounce straight back into the league. The calls were sometimes lasting two, three hours and in the end, they said, 'This is ridiculous – why don't you come in for a chat.'

"I'd been managing clubs part-time for 25 years, and they said, 'You've never been full-time. Why don't you have a go?' If I'd known that Baz wasn't happy about sharing managerial duties that would have been a real problem for me. It's to his great credit that once I was given the job, Baz never made any issue of that and was nothing but supportive.

"Taking the job was the worst decision of my life. The whole thing was a nightmare. We didn't have a secretary, couldn't use the facilities at The Shay because they were rented out and, when I arrived, they only had about three players left, and they were all youngsters. Despite that we beat Bradford and Grimsby to win a summer tournament, but then a week before the start of the season, they sold our goalkeeper and number nine to Bury. A lot of the promises made to myself and Baz were broken.

"I badly needed Baz. I was always worrying, but he was so exuberant and enthusiastic, he kept me going. He played a few games for me, even though he didn't really want to. He was such a great athlete – like Geronimo, much fitter than the other lads. And such was his fitness and enthusiasm, the first 20 minutes of every game he was so busy following the ball he seemed to forget what I'd asked him to do!

"We did manage to beat West Brom 2-1 in the FA Cup that year, live on Sky, but a month later the chairman called me in and that was that. We'd drawn too many games in the league – I always tell Baz it was the games he played in! It was a nightmare at the time, but we've had a lot of laughs since."

BRIAN HICKSON
Kit man at Preston North End

"I was kit man at Preston when Baz came back as physio. That was it, we were the backroom staff – just me and him and 16 players piling onto a minibus for reserve matches or a coach if we were with the first team.

"We had such a laugh, with Baz testing out his after-dinner speeches of the future on me, telling me all his stories. He was a top, top bloke and I just remember laughing and laughing with him, on the coach, at games. One time we played Birmingham in a play-off semi-final at Deepdale and we saw Jasper Carrot going into their changing room with a load of Cristal champagne. We told him we thought that was jumping the gun a bit but he said, 'It's in the bag, it's in the bag'. Anyway we won, and after the game we saw Jasper and we were saying, 'We'll take that Cristal off your hands, mate, tenner a case?' and just laughing and laughing.

"But at the same time he was the ultimate pro. You could tell he would go on to bigger and better things. He was so good with the players, not just as a physio but putting an arm round them if they were a bit low, keeping morale up... everybody loved him.

"He was the fittest man in the world, too, and the players always used to say, 'Don't get injured, Baz will run you into the ground.' We used to call him Forrest Gump because he just never stopped running.

"I always knew he'd go on to bigger and better things. He was such a committed man, he put everything he had into everything he did, and I remember him telling me that he went to Everton because he wanted to challenge himself at the very top. He did that, but he never changed as a person, he never lost touch with his old mates and when you see him he's always asking how you're doing. He's just a great bloke."

CHRIS LUCKETTI
Captain at Halifax

"When Baz came to Halifax I just recall that he was a very likeable guy who won all the players over straightaway – although we all felt that he liked it when players were injured because it meant he could take them running and keep himself fit. But seriously, that side of things was incredible, and players appreciated that here was a physio who wouldn't just say, 'Go and do a 30-minute run', he'd do it with you and more than likely beat you.

"And I have to say that despite the fact that we were fighting at the bottom of the table to keep Halifax in the league, when he took over as manager it was the most enjoyable period of my career. Training was fantastic, he was so positive and the club became a happy place and he had a great knack of lifting people.

"His team talks were legendary; he was so upbeat. 'Listen lads, I've had this team watched three times and we are definitely, definitely going to beat them.' Then straight after we'd lost, 'Forget about that lads, I've had next week's opposition watched and we are definitely, definitely going to beat these!'.

"He just made us all aware how lucky we were to be footballers, he took all the pressure off us. We didn't get the results that Baz deserved and ultimately we were relegated, but really it wasn't his fault and he's always telling me that he could have been one of the all-time great managers!"

COLIN MURDOCK
Captain at Preston North End

"Working with Baz at Preston was like a breath of fresh air. Football can be an arduous and tough life at times, but Baz had a wonderful human touch and this fantastic way of building players up and making everyone feel special.

"We laughed a lot about his fear of Trevor Francis, but a lot of players suffer from these anxieties in football. It's not really talked about, there is a stigma attached. You're not allowed to show any fear or admit nerves. So by joking and laughing at himself he was actually providing great support to many, many players.

"And of course he was such a funny guy, almost like a medieval jongleur, constantly entertaining. This made him much admired and very much loved by all the players, so much so that the entire club used to gravitate to the physio room much to the chagrin of the manager.

"He was so much more than a physio, but when it came down to that side of things he was incredibly conscientious. This was not a guy who would preach about getting fit, he actually went out and trained with the players and did it with them. You cannot underestimate the respect he gained for that.

"I remember one season when David Moyes was manager we went on a mid-season trip to the Lake District. It was the middle of winter and about minus 15, and we were divided into two groups to go mountain biking – one in the morning and one in the afternoon. But Baz being Baz, he decided to go out with both groups, morning and afternoon, in just shorts and a T-shirt. Each session was about three hours long, and I remember him coming back from the second one covered head to toe in mud, he looked like he was going to die of hypothermia. He went to bed for the rest of the evening.

"I always felt that he would go on to achieve great things and he did that with David at Everton. But I am just pleased to say that I know him and am proud to call him a friend."

STEVE WATSON
Player at Everton
"I was at Everton when Baz came to the club, and I remember when David Moyes told us he was bringing in a new physio. He said, 'And he's fitter than any of you lot'. We all thought he was joking but then Baz turned up and he soon showed us it was true.

"He was nothing like any physio I'd ever had before. The thing about injuries is there are of course certain medical procedures that you need to go through, but the key is keeping players motivated, to stimulate them and help them to keep believing. Baz was brilliant at that. He was just such a positive guy, his all-round personality meant you could never stay down for too long. He'd lift you up and you'd inevitably come back fitter than you had been before you got injured.

"He was just brilliant with everyone. I remember one game against West Brom at the Hawthorns, I got a cut on the head which eventually needed six stitches. So Baz is walking me off and Moyes being Moyes he starts screaming, 'What are you doing, why are you going off?' I said, 'Well the ref's told me to,' and Moyes has gone crazy, 'Fuck the ref, fuck the ref.' A lot of people wouldn't have known how to handle it, but Baz just cracked up because he knew how Moyes was, that he was just so wrapped up in the situation, and we went off to get the stitches in."

DUNCAN FERGUSON
Player at Everton
"I remember the day he first turned up at the training ground – he was dressed like a bag of shite. He was top to toe in denim, and I said to him, "Oi pal, this is Everton Football Club, not a building site.""

"With his bald head and grey sideburns he was also the oldest looking 40-year-old I had ever seen, but he was a great physio and a top bloke. I had a lot of injuries at my time at Everton, but he was always so positive. He kept my spirits up through the long, hard days when it seemed like I would never get fit.

"When he arrived at Everton I was having a lot of problems with my sciatic nerve, but Baz found a specialist and found a cure and that probably extended my career by a couple of years. He wasn't just a great character, he knew what he was doing and all the boys appreciated the job he did.

"He was also the fittest physio I had ever come across, but most of all he was just a good fellow and so hard working (well, he had to work hard with me there didn't he?) and I can't ever remember him having a day off.

"Because we worked together so much Baz became a good friend of me and my family. We invited him to several family functions and that tells you all you need to know; we don't invite just anyone, you know – it's a very select crowd!

"The only problem was that in all those years at Everton he never sorted out his dress sense – it was still denim jackets and ripped jeans. What a nightmare."